*Caliban's Freedom*

# Caliban's Freedom

## The Early Political Thought of C.L.R. James

*Anthony Bogues*

Pluto Press

LONDON · CHICAGO

First published 1997 by Pluto Press
345 Archway Road, London N6 5AA
and 1436 West Randolph, Chicago, Illinois 60607, USA

British Library Cataloguing in Publication Data
A catalogue record for this book is available from the British Library

Library of Congress Cataloging-in-Publication Data
Bogues, Anthony.
    Caliban's freedom: the early political thought of C.L.R. James/
    Anthony Bogues.
        p.   cm.
    Based on original research done for author's doctoral thesis.
    Includes bibliographical references and index.
    ISBN 0–7453–0613–6
    1. James, C. L. R. (Cyril Lionel Robert), 1901–1989.
    2. Marxism—Trinidad—Biography. 3. Socialists—Trinidad—
    Biography. 4. Black Radicals/Caribbean—Biography. I. Title.
    HX175.7.A8J3626   1997
    818—dc20
    [B]                                                96–34395
                                                            CIP

ISBN 0 7453 0613 6 hbk

Designed and produced for Pluto Press by
Chase Production Services, Chadlington OX7 3LN
Typeset from disk by Stanford DTP Services, Milton Keynes
Printed in the EC by J.W. Arrowsmith Ltd, Bristol

# Contents

For Grandpa Frank who never lost his vision,
his daughter Jackie who made many things possible
and our son Machel who always seems to understand.

# Acknowledgements

This book is based on original research done for my doctoral dissertation. As such it bears some influences of the many people who worked closely with me on that project. Therefore, I wish to thank Dr Rupert Lewis and Professor Rex Nettleford both of the University of West Indies, who read earlier drafts and made significant and insightful comments. In the early stages of my doctoral work, Professor Roy Augier's seminars on political theory stimulated me to further explorations of political thought and he encouraged me to work on C.L.R. James. Professor Martin Glaberman, a member of the Johnson–Forest Tendency, spent Boxing Day 1990 with me discussing James, commented on some chapters and was kind enough to make accessible his extensive files on James. Special thanks to Jim Murray of the C.L.R. James Institute who sent me the then unpublished version of *Notes on American Civilisation*. To David Abdullah and the Oilfield Workers Trade Union who made available rare James material from the union library, many thanks. Robert Hill, literary executor of the James estate, kindly allowed the use of this material. To Darcus Howe and the Race Today Collective, London, who spent hours discussing James with me, much appreciation. The Ford Foundation gave me a grant in summer 1992, which allowed me to examine James's letters at the Schomburg Center for Research of Black Culture, New York. Numerous people, including George Dalley, Karen Perry-Lloyd, Jean Benedict, Pearl Cunningham, Jacky Prendergast and Norma McNeil, either sent material from abroad or typed and retyped many drafts. To them much thanks. To Joye Foderingam, many thanks for early editing. Many, many thanks to Taitu A. Heron who did the final editing. Thanks to Judith Wedderburn who did the the final reading. Much appreciation and love to Gen for reading the proofs. To Richard Small, one love for introducing me to James's work years ago, and to my publisher Roger Van Zwanenburg, much appreciation for faith in the project. As usual I take responsibility for all errors of judgement.

# Preface

As a student and political activist in the 1970s, I participated in all-night debates about the nature and character of socialism. In the course of these debates, I became aware of the work and writings of C.L.R. James, in particular, *Facing Reality*, his work inspired by the Hungarian Revolution of 1956. James's vision of the possibilities of a new society based on the creative capacities of the working class and ordinary people stood in sharp contrast to the dogmatic and doctrinaire espousal of Marxism-Leninism favoured by many of the young radical students at the University of the West Indies, Mona Campus. My political instincts were awakened by a Jamesian vision of the future. It was the beginning of a twenty-year journey with left politics.

It was therefore not surprising that when I returned to academic pursuits after many years in journalism and political activity, I would complete a doctoral dissertation on the political thought of James. However, my experiences in left politics in England and the Caribbean would inform my approach to the subject. For although James was a multi-faceted individual, he was essentially a political personality and this meant that any engagement with his work could not overlook this explicit dimension. My study of James, and my examination of political theory in general, led me to a process of re-evaluating radical political thought.

Pursuing this project, I became convinced that the history and narrative of twentieth-century political thought cannot be reviewed adequately without identifying the contributions of Caribbean personalities. From Henry Sylvester Williams, who established the first Pan-African Congress in 1900, to the work of James himself, there is a tradition of Caribbean thinkers and political activists about whom a lacuna exists in Western political thought. This led me to a second proposition: James, along with Marcus Garvey, W.E.B. DuBois, George Padmore, Frantz Fanon, Malcolm X and the plethora of black thinkers who have vigorously pursued freedom for hundreds of years in the Americas, represented a black radical tradition, a counterpoint to the European Enlightenment and the political theories which emerged from this framework. The obvious conclusion from this was that any reconstruction of radical political thought in the present should take into consideration the works of the black radical tradition.

I believe that the theory and actions of the individuals in this tradition raise fundamental issues in political theory. What is the nature of equality when examined from this tradition? What becomes of the content of freedom if a large section of humanity is excluded from the ground floor on which the notion is built? Radical and traditional political theory have largely ignored these issues. As a consequence, the work of the thinkers from within the black radical tradition is viewed as specific to the tradition, and has no impact or influence on what is considered to be the mainstream. Indeed, when these questions are studied this is done from the perspective of the influences which the mainstream, whether traditional or radical, has on the current of black radicalism.

This work is an attempt to rethink our perspectives on political thought with reference to the experiences of the black struggle for freedom. It argues that, while James was a Marxist whose work can be located within a stream of Marxism, it was the black radical tradition which was the source of his radicalism.

C.L.R. James's political theory had a central impulse, a focus on the creative capacities of the working class and ordinary people, an impulse rooted in his Caribbean experiences as well as in his understanding of the historical logic of capital.

This work is the first of two volumes which examine James's political thought. This first volume examines his early years and ends with his deportation from the United States in the early 1950s. Volume 2 will study his political thought and activity in the Caribbean, Africa, England and the United States between 1953 and 1989.

In the end, only concrete life answers major philosophical and political questions. To escape its present cul-de-sac, radical political theory needs to focus on a logic of emancipation. This can be discerned in all peoples, but it is perhaps important to study the freedom struggles of those whose trajectory undermines the intellectual foundation which has enslaved humanity for centuries. In this project, all aspects of human endeavour are critical. It means we should break through the discourse of narrow boxes with their fixed co-ordinates and frameworks. I would suggest that James's attempts to reconstruct a Marxism for his time is one such source of inspiration for those who think that human emancipation is a possibility, no matter how dim its prospects seem today.

Anthony Bogues
Cambridge, MA
June 1996

# CHAPTER 1

# Issues in James's Political Thought

> To establish his own identity Caliban, after three centuries, must
> himself pioneer into regions Caesar never knew.
>
> (C.L.R. James)

In an interview in 1981, responding to the question of what he
considered his greatest contribution to political theory to be, C.L.R.
James stated: 'My contributions have been, number one, to clarify
and extend the heritage work of Marx and Lenin, and number two,
to explain and expand the idea of what constitutes the new society.'[1]

Against this backdrop, any study of James's political thought
should begin with an examination of this claim. However, given
the range of his accomplishments, such a study finds itself in a maze
of possibilities. Should James's thought be studied thematically?
Does his political thought lend itself to periodisation? Does one
study James as author, political activist and theorist, as historian
or cricket commentator, or is there an essential James? If so, what
elements of his political thought can be legitimately called a Jamesian
political theory?

James's literary output was prodigious. He wrote several major
books, hundreds of articles and produced numerous pamphlets while
participating in the international revolutionary Marxist movement.
As is common in the life of many revolutionaries, particularly those
attached to small groups, significant works remain unpublished.
In James's case, these include many lectures, articles and essays in
which he attempted to develop within the Marxist tradition an
integrated social and political theory of human society and
civilisation. His revolutionary vision was broad and drew its strength
from the concrete global activities of the proletariat. In this effort
he followed the current in Marxism which placed at the centre of
revolutionary praxis the life of the proletariat and mass of ordinary
people, their activities and consciousness.

In 1940, having recognised the limitations of the Trotskyist
movement, James attempted the massive project of reconstructing
Marxism for the immediate post-World War II period. Here, his
aim was similar in some respects to that of the Italian Marxist thinker
Antonio Gramsci. Within the classical Marxist revolutionary
tradition, the major political thinkers and activists of the early
twentieth century, Lenin, Rosa Luxemburg and Leon Trotsky, had

1

operated from the foundation of the success of the Russian
Revolution and its immediate aftermath. Gramsci, on the other hand,
wrote his major essays during the 1920s and 1930s, when the
revolutionary temper, particularly in Europe, had begun to subside,
and within the framework of emerging new tendencies which were
restructuring capital. Gramsci's central objective was the survival
of the 'philosophy of praxis' (his phrase for Marxism) and the core
of his work – *the role of consciousness* and the development of the
notion of hegemony – was an attempt to explain the failure of the
proletarian revolution in Europe. By focusing on consciousness,
he was battling against mechanical determinist currents which had
by then affected the character of Marxism.

When Gramsci died in 1937, James was already a member of a
Marxist group. While Gramsci's subtext was the Old World
(Europe), James's was primarily the New World (the United States
and the Caribbean). His focus was the social and political
consequences of rapid developments in the productive forces which
were having a profound impact on society. In the early 1950s, facing
deportation from the United States and after producing *Notes on
Dialectics* (1948) which established the new categories of his political
thought, James drafted a writing programme which noted that 'the
subject matter is the United States, the ideas are general, a view
of modern society as a whole, the totality of the present crisis, its
antecedents and the perspectives that arise from it'.[2] Included in
this plan was a biography of the West Indian personality L.C.
Constantine, a study of modern politics and revolutionary
movements, and the publication of a series of lectures on some of
the critical literary figures in Western literature and thought:
Aeschylus, Shakespeare, Rousseau, Melville and Dostoevsky.

James's immediate purpose at that time was to destroy 'the great
illusion that exists in Europe about the United States, that the
working people are so well off that they consider themselves
essentially a constituent part of the American Way'.[3] The plan also
proposed an examination of the 'revolution in popular art', in
particular what James called the greatest artistic achievements of
the twentieth century, the films of Charlie Chaplin and D.W.
Griffith. From this perspective, James's political discourse extended
a tradition in Marxism which focused on *consciousness*. The
uniqueness of his work, moved beyond the traditional conceptions
of political ideas to single, discrete and thereby exclusive entities,
to include cultural norms and the everyday notions of the mass of
ordinary people. Ultimately, the aim of the Jamesian project was
to identify ways in which the agents of contemporary social change,
the proletariat, had from a Marxist perspective developed their own
self-activities and perceptions of themselves as subjects of historical
processes. Such a perspective was predicated on the central Marxist

notion that both an emancipatory logic and a logic of domination coexisted within the structures of capitalist society.

However, while it is necessary to note the fundamental importance of Marxism to James's political thought, this study would be inadequate if it did not acknowledge that James's political activities and work were linked to the radical and progressive political currents other than Marxism which have been influential in the twentieth century – Black Power, Pan-Africanism and West Indian nationalism. As such James's political thought is a rich stream in which tributaries criss-cross and intersect with each other, providing clues and insights into twentieth-century global political process and radical political theory. In particular, it allows us to discern a dimension which has been invisible in classical Western radical political thought – 'the black radical tradition'.[4]

## The Black and Anti-colonial Tradition

Western political thought in its homogenising universality has not yet recognised a black radical intellectual tradition. Traditional Western radical discourses and schools of thought do not consider the work of Black radicals to be part of a radical tradition of political thought which is either critical of Western civilisation or has made any significant contribution to political theory. The political theory and activities of Marcus Garvey, George Padmore, W.E.B. DuBois and Aimé Cesaire, for example, are typically viewed as specific trajectories within a black tradition, rather than as a current which is integral to a radical critique of Western society and capitalism.

Cedric Robinson, in his book *Black Marxism*, examines the thought of James, Richard Wright and DuBois and concludes that the black radical tradition developed within the context of 'conflicts extant between Western radicalism and the struggle for black liberation'. As such, the historical record of twentieth-century Marxism is replete with individuals leaving the socialist and communist movements because of these movements' deficient analysis of the role of race, white racism and the character of black nationalism. However, no radical, whether black or white, can ignore the independent black nationalist tradition of which the Garvey movement remains the most spectacular example. Garvey's success was rooted in the soil of the nationalism of an oppressed race and indicated both the strength of black nationalism and the simplicity of one-dimensional socialist and radical theories of racial oppression.

This lacuna in radical Western political discourse is the result of the racial nature of modern capitalism, the character of European Enlightenment and the general failure of radical theory in its

Marxist-Leninist guise to recognise the emergence of new social forces. The black radical tradition in Western society spans anti-slavery and anti-colonial struggles, labour struggles, socialist movements, and democratic and civil rights campaigns. Its discourses, texts and forms have been varied, but at each stage, particularly in American society, its impact has been significant, influencing other social groups. DuBois, for example, in both his historical works (e.g. *Black Reconstruction*) and in his political activity, had noted that the alienation of the African-American community was not a negative but a positive impulse, and that the examination of American society would demonstrate how this impulse became a revolutionary sentiment in the activities of blacks. He demonstrated as well that radical political and social activity on the part of blacks tended to equalise the American society.

Four major themes span the various struggles within the black radical tradition. First, race and white racism and their character-istics in Western society. Here the questions posed are not only about the nature of social and economic relations but are also ontological. White racism dehumanises the black population. For blacks to recover their authentic humanity, acts of political or social resistance are necessary as well as a redefinition of the self, both collectively and individually. From this fundamental perspective, as well as from a philosophical standpoint, the object struggles to be the subject, and thereby defines the self. If society and social life are a complex totality, then each moment of the struggle for this definition creates new forms, which then manifest themselves in new cultural rep-resentations and images, particularly in the public sphere. In the black radical tradition this process has been critical; and while historians have described these forms, social and political theorists have yet to uncover their meaning. In other words, the struggle against racism, because it seeks to establish *humanness,* is a contestation in all spheres of human endeavour and therefore is a totality and a critique of the dominant mainstrain conceptions.

The second characteristic of the struggles within the black tradition is a consequence of the first. Since the terrain for analysis and struggle is Western civilisation and its critique, then the construction of a new historical framework which seeks to define the activities of blacks as significant and contributing to social progress is imperative. Imperative as well are the new ideas and interpretations of the old that emerge from this new framework.

For the anti-colonial stream of the tradition, the central landmarks that redefine a colonial people are the reclamation of history and the establishment of sovereignty. In the main, Marxist political praxis excluded these struggles from its analysis, although within the classical tradition Lenin's work on self-determination and the nationalism of oppressed people attempted to include the struggles of the colonial peoples from the margins of the socialist movement. It is also true that various communist movements have periodically analysed the race question, both in its colonial context and in the United States. However, no major recognised Marxist theorist within the classical tradition has explored these matters as a fundamental of social revolution.

The third point about the black radical tradition is the 'triangle of liberation'. Here I refer to the fact that black liberation struggles historically have had a diasporic quality. In the Western world, anti-colonial and black freedom was perceived through the lens of Pan-Africanism, whether it was the activities of Marcus Garvey in the early twentieth century or Rastafari in the 1950s. This connection to Africa was a fundamental feature of radical Caribbean political activity both in pre-slavery and post-slavery societies as well as in the United States. In the 1930s, it expressed itself in its Caribbean segment when the Trinidadians James and Padmore joined forces to establish the journal *International African Opinion*. In the United States, the political and intellectual activities of DuBois within the different Pan-African Congresses held in the first half of the century demonstrates this tendency.

The fourth critical element of the black tradition has been its humanist approach. This element became an essential ingredient in James's political theory, with a particular emphasis on the issues of agency and historical transformation in society.

The radical activities of the black populations in both Africa and the African diaspora have challenged the intellectual basis of Western civilisation, its notions of happiness, concepts of individualism and individuality, and expanded notions of freedom and equality. These issues have been raised in the arts and popular culture as well as in political theses and mass political activities. The tradition therefore constitutes a specific anti-capitalist discourse, and while the present work is limited in how it interfaces with and relates to other radical critiques of Western civilisation, no study of James's political thought would be complete without reference to its impact on his intellectual evolution. For, while James absorbed the intellectual traditions of Western society, his insights into the human condition were gleaned from contact with and the study of the black Trinidadian working class, who by the 1920s had come of age, stamping their influence on the contours of that society. The perspective he gained while growing up in colonial Trinidad stayed with him all his life and became the basis for his revolutionary optimism. The black radical tradition, which remained vigorous and dynamic even in periods of retreat for the proletariat in European society, allowed individuals like James to transcend the confines of traditional Marxist analysis and radical theories.

James's major political and social theme – the *self-activity of the oppressed* and their *self-actualisation* – was rooted in his fascination with the capacity of ordinary people to transform their lives and society. He had gleaned this insight at an early age from both his reading of European literature and his observation of Trinidadian colonial life. In a fragment of his unpublished ad hoc biography he writes:

> I had been reading from early Aeschylus, Sophocles, Thackeray, Dickens and later Dostoevsky, Tolstoy and a whole list of writers. I got a conception of human character and the interesting aspects of human personality and the plain fact of the matter is the middle class people, to whom I belonged and among whom I lived, were busy trying to shape their lives according to the British idea of behaviour and principles. They were not very interesting but the people who had passion, human energy, anger, violence and generosity were the common people who I saw around me. They shaped my political outlook and from that time to this day, those are the people I have been most concerned with. I didn't learn everything from Marxism ... Even in my days of fiction I had the instinct which enabled me to grasp the fundamentals of Marxism so easily and then to work at Marxism having the basic elements of a Marxist view – my concern with the common people.[5]

Although steeped in the Western intellectual tradition – as he himself comments in *Beyond a Boundary*, 'I was a British intellectual at 10' – James grew to adulthood in a colony in which black nationalism was a strong political current. He read the papers of the Garvey movement and watched even if he did not participate in the development of the Trinidadian labour movement. When he arrived in England and became active in Marxist politics, he fused this black anti-colonial tradition and Marxism with a novelist's sensibility. All these elements combined to make him one of the most outstanding revolutionary Marxist theorists of the twentieth century.

## Classical Marxism

The final element necessary to establish the intellectual tradition in which James operated is classical Marxism. John Molyneux notes in *What is the Real Marxist Tradition?* that:

> this tradition runs from Marx and Engels, through the revolutionary left wing of the Second International ... reaches its height with the Russian Revolution and the early years of the Comintern and is continued, in the most difficult circumstances

possible, by the Left opposition and the Trotskyist movement in the 1930s.[6]

He further lists the elements of this tradition as:

theory of the party (Lenin), the mass strike (Luxemburg), permanent revolution (Trotsky), imperialism and the world (Luxemburg, Bukharin, Lenin and Trotsky), the counter-revolutionary role of Stalinism (Trotsky), fascism (Trotsky) and the restoration of the activist, dialectical element in Marxist philosophy (Lenin, Gramsci, and Lukács).[7]

From this writer's perspective the other features of this classical tradition are:

- its concrete participation in activities and in revolutionary action;
- its consequent emphasis on the unity of theory and practice; and
- its ability to comprehend new realities with the establishment of new social and political categories.

By the late 1930s this classical tradition was isolated and marginalised as Marxism became dominated by Stalinism. A decade later, the Trotskyist movement which had its origins as an oppositionist current to Stalin's politics, was itself in a process of codification, unable to grasp the new shifts in global capitalism. The result was that its *Transitional Programme,* which proclaimed that conditions were ripe for a socialist revolution in the post-World War II era, lacked mass appeal.

When James joined the Marxist movement, it was entering an era of theoretical crisis. Although different currents and tendencies were successful in recruiting major intellectuals, the nature of the Soviet Union increasingly raised questions about the validity of Marxism. At the same time the acrimonious debates within the Trotskyist movement seemed so abstract that many were disenchanted with revolutionary politics. However, the rise of fascism and the Spanish Civil War served as points of regeneration for many. After World War II there emerged within Western political thought a concern about the exhaustion of progressive ideas; at the same time there was an emerging view about the convergence of the Soviet Union and the Western capitalist world. Theorists such as Karl Mannheim argued for a return to the traditional values of Western civilisation, which he stated 'will differ from the relativist laissez-faire of the previous age, as it will have the courage to agree on some basic values which are acceptable to everybody who shares the tradition of Western civilisation'.[8]

From the left, the discrediting of the Soviet Union created a crisis in Marxist political thought. How was one to distinguish the politics of the Soviet Union and its allies from those of classical Marxism? Were there tendencies in classical Marxism that facilitated the development of Stalinism? From all sides the political and intellectual landscape for a radical critique of capitalism seemed bleak. In the early 1940s, James, with typical Caribbean audacity, recognised this landscape and set out with a group later called the Johnson–Forest Tendency to create an independent Marxism of their own.

One more fundamental question needs to be asked in any discussion of the classical Marxist tradition. What are the criteria for arguing and identifying a particular tradition as classical? With respect to Marxism, one approach is to undertake an exegetical reading of Marx's major texts and then relate the work of various theorists to what Marx wrote and meant. Three problems are inherent in this approach. First, it assumes that there is absolute consistency in what Marx wrote and that there was no evolution in his thought. Secondly, it fails to distinguish what was methodological and theoretical in Marx from what was of immediate political and ideological value. Thirdly, it treats Marx's work as dogmatic doctrine with the imprint of absolute scientific truth. An alternative approach would be to isolate Marx's methodology and his theory of social change, seek to locate the questions they attempt to answer and then ask whether or not a particular theorist belongs to that tradition. This study locates C.L.R. James within the classical Marxist tradition because he asked similar questions to those Marx asked, used a similar methodology and posited answers which attempted to lay the framework for the socialist revolution in his age.

But his work should also be seen as a critical part of the black radical tradition. Here the central issues are whether or not James's political insights were rooted in this tradition and whether Marxism provided an explanation and theoretical framework for them. There are as yet no definitive answers to these questions, but for the moment James's Marxism can safely be called a 'black Marxism', a term which would indicate the relationship of the two traditions.

Marxism as a political theory developed within the trajectory of Western political thought. While liberalism was the doctrine of revolt against the absolutist order in Europe, Marxism influenced by Enlightenment became the subversive doctrine of capitalism. Its dynamic and subversive character attracted thinkers and political activists who were oppressed by European colonialism. In the dialectic of history, as capitalism colonised many parts of the globe, those who were colonised developed a trajectory of struggle of their own, influenced by external political ideas but rooted in the specificity of their colonial oppression. Some individuals moved on to the world stage and made significant contributions to modern radical political theory. C.L.R. James was one such individual. His sojourn on the terrain of Marxist and radical political theory was like that of William Shakespeare's character Caliban, mapping the contours of the new and negating the old, while creating new global political categories. It is to this saga that we now turn.

CHAPTER 2

# The Making of a Marxist

C.L.R. James was born on 4 January 1901 in Tunapuna, Trinidad. It was a transitional time for Caribbean society. Although a Crown colony, Trinidad was increasingly coming under the influence of a growing nationalist consciousness and the stirrings of working-class organisations. Importantly, by the end of the nineteenth century, a native intellectual tradition had emerged. All these factors would have their impact on James, and so it is to a description of these that we now turn.

## The Societal Context

At the end of the nineteenth century, Trinidad and Tobago were dominated by the sugar plantations. The social structure of Trinidadian society revolved around the white owners of the sugar estates, the British colonial officials, the black ex-slaves and Indian indentured workers.[1] However, while sugar plantations dominated the country's economic landscape, a parallel class of small landowners had emerged who farmed other crops, particularly cocoa.[2] From these whom an independent group of blacks had emerged who over time became the source from which the native intelligentsia would spring. The political structure of nineteenth-century Trinidad was typical of a British Caribbean colony. Like many other British colonies, all the members of its Legislative Council were appointed by the Crown. Although an amendment to the legislation in 1862 allowed for 'unofficial' members appointed by the Colonial Governor, these unofficials could not provide effective opposition to the Colonial Governor, as their privileges were dependent on his favour.

By the end of the nineteenth century, with growing opposition to the colonial government, a number of politically moderate, black middle-class reform movements began to form. The dispute about the financial independence of the Port-of-Spain Borough Council, which led to its closure in 1898, signalled the end of a phase of constitutional/political struggle led by a section of the black middle class whose political vision was limited to political representation. In the next period, the black working class became the major force of protest. Its principle organisation was the Trinidadian Working Men's Association (TWA). Formed in 1887,

10

the TWA explicitly appealed to working-class supporters and focused on both traditional trade union matters and broad political issues, including self-government.[3]

Another important political organisation at that time was the Pan-African Association. Inspired by a visit from the Trinidadian Pan-Africanist, H. Sylvester Williams, groups were formed in 1901. Although the Association never became a mass movement, its influence was extensive. In 1903, the social and political ferment in Trinidad culminated in the 'Water Riot', during which the Legislative Chamber was destroyed. The central organisation at this time was the Rate Payers Association, whose leadership of 'coloured' businessmen were disputing the new water meter charges of the colonial government. But the riot marked a turning point in Trinidad's social and political history: for the participation of black working-class activists indicated political stirrings by wider social forces.

Nineteenth-century nationalism in Trinidad – as in the rest of the Caribbean – was a significant prelude to twentieth-century political and social developments. The contours of that nationalism were shaped by slavery and colonialism and, as a consequence, Caribbean nationalism was complicated by the factor of race.

The nature of Caribbean society and its social and colour hierarchy gave rise to two distinct streams of nationalism in many of the islands. One stream was a black nationalism expressed primarily by the black population, and the other, a Creole nationalism of the mulatto community. In the early twentieth century, black nationalism evolved into Pan-African consciousness and the Garvey movement, while Creole nationalism became, in many instances, the ideological framework for the constitutional decolonisation in the territories. While black nationalism would flourish in the early twentieth century in mass movements, during the nineteenth century it was a Trinidadian schoolmaster, J.J. Thomas, who had developed a sustained critique of the confrontation between the colonial master and the native on the matter of race. The English historian J.A. Froude had visited the Caribbean in the 1880s, following which he published *The English in the West Indies: or the Bow of Ulysses*, in which he assumed the innate superiority of whites and argued that the notion of self-government for the Caribbean was ridiculous. Thomas's response to Froude came in his book *Froudacity* (1889), in which

> Thomas takes Froude's book to pieces, analyses it paragraph by paragraph and refutes prejudice after prejudice, with that comprehensive irony and controlled rage which has become one of the characteristic features of black protest.[4]

The Caribbean political thinker Rupert Lewis summarises Thomas's place in Caribbean history as that of 'a Caribbean intellectual who reflects in his writings the striving of the early Trinidad nationality for self-expression'.[5]

James was born into a black lower middle-class family at a time when a native intellectual tradition was being established. Given the character of colonial Trinidad, James's family status was defined by their skin colour. However, both his parents strove to make his life comfortable, and 'Between both of them I had everything that a black person could reach for in Trinidad.'[6] James's earliest memories were of his mother, books and cricket. In a letter written in July 1944 to his second wife, Constance Webb, an actress, writer and political activist, James notes:

> My chief memory is of my mother sitting reading and I lying on the floor near her reading ... As she read a book and put it down I picked it up ... my life until I was nine centered around books and games ... when I was about seven I sat up late one night and wrote a poem ... Then came the Sunday cricket ... We played every day and Saturday.[7]

This fascination for books was not limited to his mother's house. James continues in the same letter:

> Books, books, books. There was a rainy season and a dry season and in the rainy season we got fever. So we were sent to Tunapuna to my grandmother's every rainy season for some months. There I used to climb to the top of the wardrobe by way of the window-sill and take down the books. I remember *The Throne of the House of David*. I read it to pieces! ... Long before that I had appropriated my mother's Shakespeare.[8]

The exclusion of the black middle class from economic power and property drew them into the professions, especially teaching. One consequence of this was that they developed a vigorous intellectual life centred on teachers and literary magazines. So it is no surprise that a black lower middle-class family home would be filled with books and for reading to be encouraged.

It is important at this point to appreciate the essential elements of the native intellectual tradition which was emerging at the time. First, its framework was Western philosophy, language and thought. Thomas, for example, was fluent in French, Spanish, Latin and Greek and was a member of the British Philological Society. Second, that the engagement with this tradition was conducted by individuals who were oppressed by the tradition. As a consequence, engagement was often both mastery and critique. Third, the character of the synthesis which emerged from this engagement constituted an intellectual tradition which, while nurtured in the Caribbean, blossomed outside of it. This can easily be validated by a review of some of the major literary and political figures of the early and mid-twentieth century in the West. Individuals like Aimé Cesaire the Martinique poet and political personality; George Padmore the Trinidadian political activist and thinker who became known as one of the fathers of African Independence; Claude McKay, the Jamaican poet; Marcus Garvey and James himself are among the central figures in the political and intellectual tradition of the twentieth century. The framework of this intellectual tradition, as James noted in 1969, was Western:

> I want to make it clear that the origins of my work and my thoughts are to be found in Western European literature, Western European history and Western European thought. I did not learn literature from the mango tree. I set out to master the literature, philosophy and ideas of Western civilisation.[9]

However, we should observe that in the mastery of the requirements of this civilisation, these figures then developed theories and engaged in political activity and literary work which critiqued the major elements of Western civilisation. All this was the result of the tension engendered by being a part of, yet an outsider to, the tradition – that *double consciousness* of which DuBois often spoke.

The fourth element of this intellectual tradition was its social basis, a fact validated by James's observations about his father:

> My father's experience illustrates what circumstances were like in the West Indies. In a West Indian island in those days ... if you wanted to know what was happening in the British Parliament or if you wanted to know about the revolution in Turkey ... or who had written this or that book, or what books Dickens had written ... you came to the teacher to find out.[10]

A precocious student from an early age, James won an exhibition scholarship to Queen's Royal College where he received a classical education: Western classical, literary and colonial. In his book *Beyond a Boundary* (1963) he outlines the curriculum: 'I studied Latin with Virgil, Caesar and Horace, and wrote Latin verses. I studied Greek with Euripides and Thucydides. I did elementary and applied mathematics, French and French literature, English and English literature, English history, ancient and modern European history.'[11]

As education was essential to success and race and colour were determining factors in class and social relations, it was crucial for the black middle class to distance themselves from the black working and peasant classes. They did this in two ways: first, through the construction of 'respectability', and second, by the career path plotted for the educated members of the class. Commenting on respectability James writes:

> My grandfather went to church every Sunday morning at eleven o'clock wearing in the boiling sun a frock-coat, striped trousers and top-hat, with his walking stick in hand ... respectability was not an ideal, it was an armour ... the family fortunes declined and the children grew up in unending struggle not to sink below the level of the Sunday morning top hat and frock coat.[12]

On the nature of his career path, James comments: 'Exhibition, scholarship, profession, wealth, Legislative Council and the title "honourable" ... that was the course marked out for me.'[13]

Born in a social and class context in which he was expected to be a 'black Victorian', James followed the tradition and immersed himself in British and European culture, but as he grew older, he began to rebel against aspects of the traditional trajectory of the educated black middle class – a rebellion that was sustained in the main by cricket and literature.

Fascinated by cricket from an early age (his father gave him his first bat when he was four years old), James spent hours at his grandmother's house watching cricket being played from a window. Not only did he develop a lifetime attachment to the game, but his social conceptions were profoundly influenced by it. In particular, two personalities – both lower-class blacks, Matthew Bondman and Arthur Jones – impressed him:

> [Bondman's] eyes were fierce, his language violent and his voice was loud ... my grandmother and my aunts detested him ... but that is not why I remember Matthew. For a 'ne'er-do-well', in fact vicious character, as he was, Matthew had one saving grace – Matthew could bat.[14]

It was cricket, then, that drew James in the direction of the black masses in Trinidad. A contemporary of James, Olga Winifred Comma-Maynard remembers that as a teenager, James was popular with his schoolmates. He would take the tram to Queen's Royal College and jump off at times to play truant. She also recollects that he lost interest in the school curriculum and chose instead to spend all day in the public library reading literature.[15] From this we can see that the seeds of rebellion were germinating in this precocious student. The question was, how would it express itself and would James would travel the road of politics?

## Working-Class Rebellion

By the time James was 18, global revolutionary events had made their mark on Trinidadian society. The Russian Revolution of

1917 offered an alternative to capitalism and in the United States for the black world the Garvey movement had become an international mass movement which was shaking the foundations of white colonial and racial oppression. By the late 1920s there were thirty branches of the Universal Negro Improvement Association (UNIA) in Trinidad.[16] So influential was Garveyism that by 1919 the British Colonial Office had banned the Movement's newspaper the *Negro World* in many islands. Both the Russian Revolution and Garveyism stimulated Trinidad's black population, influencing their rebellious activities, particularly the waterfront workers' strike of November 1919.

During World War I, West Indian soldiers volunteered to fight in the British Regiment. Although admitted to the Regiment, they were not allowed to act as regular soldiers or see active combat, but were given menial tasks or used as ammunition carriers. Disgruntled by this, West Indian soldiers stationed in Italy formed a Caribbean League in December 1918. The objective of the League was to foster 'close union among the West Indian islands and the demand that the black man should govern himself and that force should be used if necessary in the objective of attaining self-governing status'.[17]

On their return to Trinidad, the soldiers found abysmal social conditions, described by the historian Kelvin Singh as:

- two city asylums overcrowded;
- bands of destitutes especially prostitution of East Indians;
- high infant mortality; and
- the situation where the number of applications granted for pauper or poverty certificates rose from 25,212 to 300,000 (excluding the boroughs of Port of Spain, San Fernando and Arima), with one third of the applicants being school children.[18]

Rising prices exacerbated these conditions – prices doubled in some districts.[19] However, the immediate triggers for the waterfront workers' strike in Port-of-Spain were wages and overtime working. The strike, led by the TWA, had in its leadership former soldiers who had come under the influence of Garveyism. Although strike action began on the waterfront, it expanded into a general strike, which lasted for nearly three weeks and marked a new stage in the island's political evolution. From this foment of anti-colonial and working-class activity Captain Cipriani emerged.

Cipriani had won a reputation as a fighter for black soldiers' rights, and for this reason was offered the leadership of the TWA in 1920, which he accepted:

> Cipriani accepted the leadership of the organisation which had already laid a base in the society. Because of its background,

the people's movement started off the 1920s by clamouring for a greater franchise, and representative Government based on Borough Councils made up of leaders from various counties.[20]

Under Cipriani the TWA participated in local elections and won the council on the following platform:

- an eight-hour working day;
- abolition of the Habitual Idlers Ordinance;
- the old age pension;
- better working conditions; and
- removal of minimum rent restrictions for city council voting.

Absent from this platform, however, was the demand for self-government. In 1925 Cipriani was elected to the Legislative Council on a limited franchise and he immediately introduced a Compensation Bill for an eight-hour working day. But again, there was no mention of self-government. Although the 1920s was a period of mass activity for the Trinidadian black working class, there were no significant political victories. As Reinhard Sander notes, 'the TWA achieved a number of important reforms during the 1920s ... but the Trinidadian working class began to by-pass the organisation in their fight for better conditions. In fact, Cipriani became more and more identified with the status quo.'[21]

As a consequence, by the late 1920s and early 1930s, other organisations, including the National Unemployment Movement and the Negro Welfare Association, began to challenge the TWA and Cipriani's leadership. Alongside this burst of working-class activity, native intellectuals began to undertake research into the cultural and social forms of Trinidad. This activity was represented by the formation of the League of Literary and Cultural Clubs in the Arima and Tunapuna districts in 1925. These clubs not only had literary objectives but also focused on the need to prepare 'individuals for intellectual self-improvement and for training in the conduct of public affairs'.[22] In this project, as was the case in many other colonial territories, ambivalence became a feature of the native intelligentsia.

Where was James in all this? Unlike many revolutionaries who by their late teens and early twenties are involved in radical politics, James, in spite of his rebellious nature, was concentrating his energies on being a schoolmaster at his old college, playing cricket and deepening his understanding of Western literature. Although swimming against the traditional current by opting out of the plotted career path which would take him abroad to qualify as a professional, then take a seat in the council, he had not yet broken free of black Victorian middle-class respectability. It would take fiction writing to do this, laying the groundwork for the rapid development of his political thought once he left the West Indies.

## Literature, the Other Link

In *Beyond a Boundary* (1963), James reveals that he was attracted by two things – cricket and literature, especially Thackeray's novel *Vanity Fair*: 'My mother had an old copy with a red cover. I had read it when I was about eight … It became my Homer and Bible.'[23] As a black middle-class intellectual, James had little regular direct contact with working-class blacks, except through cricket. Education had created a distance between himself and the black masses. This was a tension he had to overcome.

Early in his life, James had decided that he wanted to be a writer. English composition came easily and his hobby of collecting magazines helped him at the age of 15, win an essay competition on the topic, 'The Novel as an Instrument of Reform', perhaps indicating that while he was immersed in European thought, James was already thinking about how changes were effected in society. In 1919, James became secretary of the Maverick Club, a literary group which published lectures and whose members wrote essays on English literature. Paul Buhle comments that this group sought to find their way as non-whites in a white literary world. 'They read carefully the British and French political and cultural magazines and set out to master the literature, philosophy and ideas of Western civilisation.'[24]

At the age of 21, James directed an opera.[25] So far his intellectual developement was traditional for a native intellectual grappling with the literary ideas and philosophy of the colonising civilisation. These he would master and by the time he moved to London in 1932, he could have been described as a native intellectual with a literary bent. James's literary efforts bore fruit in 1927 when the British *Saturday Review of Literature* published his short story 'La Divina Pastora'. Its publication was a boost to the group of young intellectuals who launched their own magazine *Trinidad*, in 1929 with Alfred Mendes as editor, to provide an outlet for their work. The magazine appeared twice, at Christmas 1929 and in early 1930.

Two of James's short stories, 'Triumph' and 'Turner's Prosperity', appeared in the Christmas 1929 edition. These were written in the Trinidadian dialect and reflected James's attempt to examine at close quarters the lifestyle and values of the Trinidadian lower classes, thus marking a break from his middle-class background. There was, however, a tension in James's intellectual thought that was typical of the ambivalence of the native intellectual in the colonial context. Although the native intellectual masters the canons of the colonial tradition, nationalism and self-determination require a degree of legitimisation and validation of at least some aspects of the native culture. Thus for James the pull of literature on the one hand and his growing preoccupation with the life of the Trinidadian masses on the other became a testing ground in his intellectual formation. James's literary orientation would begin to challenge some of his Victorian assumptions and would ultimately impact significantly on his political thought.

## Literature, Politics and James's Early Thought

In the main, much of Marxist literary criticism has centred on the problematic of form and aesthetic, and their relation to a base/superstructure paradigm. However, there is another current which views literature as material practice related to ideology. From this perspective the author, vis-a-vis society, is also a social individual and operates within a specific space and time. This is further reinforced once the author begins to operate within a particular language. The material so produced by the author is called 'aesthetic ideology'.[26] This ideology comprises a set of values and beliefs, and an examination of a body of work would reveal clues to the author's perspectives. An examination of James's short stories reveals early elements of his political and social thought.

Edward Said has observed that in the 'long struggle to achieve decolonisation ... literature has played a crucial role in the re-establishment of a national cultural heritage, in the re-instatement of native idioms, in the re-imagining and re-figuring of local histories, geographies and communities'.[27] From this perspective, James's political thought should naturally include an imaginative dimension. Indeed years later, in 1948, his conceptual apparatus would continue to be influenced by 'certain mass impulses, instinctive actions, spontaneous movements, the emergence of personalities, the incalculable activities which constitute a society'[28] – all qualities which defy analysis from a strict positivist tradition which increasingly became the dominant current within Marxism.

James's short story 'Triumph' is regarded as the most successful of his early writings. Written in the style of an eighteenth-century novelist with the ironic distance of the author, the story is about three women in a barrack yard in Port-of-Spain. It focuses on the women's relationship with men, their values and humanity. Mamitz, one of the chief protagonists, has lost her man and hence her livelihood. Her friend Celestine, of quick temper, believes that Mamitz's misfortune is the result of the work of a jealous neighbour. She persuades her to 'get a bath', introduces her to a new man and eventually things begin to improve. Mamitz's eventual triumph is celebrated with the other women in the yard, and the last scene describes her jealous rival being so enraged that she breaks a good china dish. The story is evocative, with detailed descriptions of the social conditions of Trinidadian barrack yard life. It is written in the style of a reporter/observer piecing together discrete scenes. Mamitz and Celestine emerge as strong women, though dependent on men for their upkeep.

'Turner's Prosperity', is about a clerk who is a chronic debtor. Promised assistance by his employer, he and his wife decide to ask for more than they need. In the end he loses both his job and the offer of help.

'La Divina Pastora' is the recounting of a folk-tale and indicates James's ability to listen keenly and reproduce the stories of ordinary people. In its sympathetic portrayal of the lives of the 'ne'er-do-wells', James's literary work was a progressive anti-colonial development, as one of the bases of colonial hegemonic ideology is the supposed 'natural inferiority' of the colonised. A work which is sympathetic to the native represents a break with one part of the colonial tradition as well as a partial break with black middle-class respectability.

In March 1931, the first edition of *The Beacon* published by Albert Gomes appeared. Over the next three years, the magazine became the focal point of the group which had gathered around the *Trinidad*, though unlike the *Trinidad*, *The Beacon* was multi-racial. In his autobiography, *Through a Maze of Colour* (1974) Gomes comments that the group was 'a movement of enlightenment'.[29]

*The Beacon* published articles on the nature of Caribbean identity, on Africa and India and on capitalism and colonialism. In his study on literature in early twentieth-century Trinidadian society Reinhard W. Sander notes:

> The Trinidad establishment was even more disturbed by the articles and editorials in the *Beacon* that expressed anti-Catholic views. The Catholic Church frequently brought pressure to bear on small businessmen who advertised in the paper ... Gomes has admitted that the magazine would hardly have survived beyond the first four issues had it not been for his mother.[30]

James became a contributor to *The Beacon*, writing fiction, reviewing articles and submitting critical commentaries. He is listed in one edition as: 'C.L.R. James, Negro. Born 1901. Teacher and freelance journalist. Writes fiction and has had some success, but is tired of hearing them said over and over again. So will not mention them. Married – nothing else of importance.'[31]

James's first *Beacon* article was a 'Problem of Knowledge' in which he demonstrates his familiarity with Western thought and is critical

of a work on the historical development of civilisation which accords
Northern European success to its climate: 'Assyria and Babylon
had laid the foundations of civilisation as we know it; the Greeks
had laid down for all time the roads that art and philosophy were
to travel.'[32] His analysis of the relation of Greek thought to Western
intellectual tradition would remain with him throughout his life.

In another article, 'Revolution', James writes of an interview with
a Venezuelan on the state of Venezuelan politics. The end of the
story is perhaps significant, giving a glimpse of James's future
methods. After recording the interview, he writes:

> Since then I have read of the most able and trustworthy of local
> journalists writing of the many benefits that the Gomez
> government has conferred on Venezuela ... All sorts of rumours
> are afloat. But I don't pay much attention to them ... But I am
> not really concerned with Gomez and his rebels. What I want
> is to manage another interview with my Venezuelan friend.[33]

James's interest here is the text of an ordinary person's discourses,
not learned opinions. Later, grappling with the impulses, thoughts
and activities of ordinary people would become a critical component
of his analysis. Five more articles were written for *The Beacon*: 'The
Star that would not Shine', 'Books and Writers', 'The Intelligence
of the Negro: A Few Words with Dr Harland'; a column on 'Books
and Writers' which included a review of Gandhi, and an analysis
of the work of Michael Maxwell Phillip. Two of the columns
demonstrate James's literary bent. 'The Star that would not Shine'
is in the mould of 'Revolution' and recounts the story of a young
man who refuses to become a movie star. 'Books and Writers' is
an assessment of Arnold Bennett in which he comments: 'when
Arnold Bennett died he was the first among living English
novelists'.[34] James also reviewed books. In his reviews, there is
nothing striking about what he has to say, but how he says it
demonstrates a distinctively engaging style which was to become
his literary hallmark. In 'The Intelligence of the Negro', James refutes
an earlier article by Dr Harland on the 'inferiority' of blacks. As
part of this refutation, James traces the *Encyclopedia Britannica*'s
discussion of Africans through successive editions, from supposed
inferiority being attributable to the size of the cranial structures.
He compares the *Encyclopedia* of 1884 to the 1929 edition and
observes: 'there seems to be no marked difference in ... intellectual
power. The differences are rather differences in disposition and
temperament.'[35] James agrees with this latter view by listing the
success of educated Trinidadians in mastering Western civilisation.
He notes: 'Yet since the War, from Trinidad alone we have seen
Negro students defeating all comers at English law examinations,

we have seen them winning gold medals at competitions of the Royal
Academy of Music.'[36]

There are, perhaps, two aspects of this article which indicate
James's early directions. James typically begins with the historical
background and then proceeds to use the example of the
revolutionary Toussaint L'Ouverture as representative of the
potential and capacities of people of African descent. This shows
James's early appreciation of Toussaint L'Ouverture and the
Haitian Revolution. Quoting a historian on Toussaint, he writes:
'no one before him had succeeded in uniting both the Spanish and
French settlements.'[37] James would return to the example of
Toussaint in 1938 when he published *The Black Jacobins*. Second,
the example indicates the passages and connections between James's
thought prior to his moving to London: it shows continuities.

The other important aspect of this piece was James's view on
the race question. He writes in the Conclusion:

> which brings me to my second reason for writing. This strangely
> enough has nothing to do with the race question at all. I am
> not 'touchous' on the race question. If at times I feel some
> bitterness at the disabilities and disadvantages to which my
> being a Negro has subjected me it is soon wasted away …
> Looking back at my life. I see that on the whole white people
> have befriended me far more than Negroes have … Now as I
> think over the Doctor's article I find my chief reaction to it is
> not racial but educational.[38]

This was the typical response of a native intellectual who had
mastered the constituent parts of Western civilisation and its
intellectual traditions. Part of the response was an ambivalence which
did not admit to hostile racial feelings. Black intellectuals immersed
in the colonisers' tradition sometimes tended to reduce racial
matters to ignorance or education. The statement also points to a
recurrent feature in James's life. Here was a young, gifted intellectual
immersed in Western thought from the perspective of the Other;
rebelling against black Victorian respectability; having social
relations with whites; a member of the Maple cricket club, rather
than The Shannon, the club of the lower-class blacks; and writing
fiction about the barrack yard life of Port-of-Spain. James's literary
work is an attempt to resolve this contradiction. He writes in the
ad hoc fragments of his autobiography:

> I was reading Shakespeare, Euripides, Aeschylus … I had the
> clash of passion and lust and revenge and friendship and all that,
> that I could see around me among the ordinary people. That
> is where *Minty Alley* and my story 'Triumph' … come from.
> That did not come from the middle class at all. That's how I

grew up. I was trained in one and saw the other ... and that's
the way I began to write.[39]

James's other column was an appreciation of the former Solicitor
General of Trinidad and Tobago, Michael Maxwell Phillips. Here
James describes Phillips 'as a man of varied power and breath of
culture'[40] and warns against political extremism, asserting that
'radicalism unchecked degenerates into chaos'.[41] Importantly, in
this essay James continues his theme that the educated West Indian
is equal to any educated white European. He comments on the
islands' Colonial Governor Sir William Robinson, and observes that
the former Solicitor-General 'Sir Phillip was a man of whom
Trinidad might well be proud. He was not only a remarkable man
in Trinidad, but was a remarkable man in the West Indies and would
have been a remarkable man anywhere.'[42]

Implicit in James's approval of the Colonial Governor's assessment
was that Sir Phillip, the highly educated man in the Western
tradition, a man who after dinner would give his daughters lessons
in Italian,[43] represented the capacity of the native intellectual. In
his final article, a book review on Gandhi, we observe James
grappling with the fundamental issues of historical analysis:

> the second is the solution of a historical problem which has in
> the past caused me some difficulty – whether great men make
> history or are but the crests of inevitable waves of social evolution.
> I am now more than ever inclined to believe that they shape the
> environment more than the environment shapes them.[44]

Here we find an early sign of a problematic which would dominate
James's historical writings: the role of personality and the issues of
agency and social structure. In this article James affirms the
supremacy of agency; later, he would attempt to develop a flexible
approach to this question within a Marxist paradigm. Of James's
three major short stories, two deal with women and their relationship
to men, and all deal with the 'immense vitality' of ordinary people
and 'the way they meet their problems'. It is clear then that James's
literary imagination had seized upon the 'ne'er-do-wells' of
Trinidadian society. Mamitz and Celestine in 'Triumph' were the
descendants of Matthew Bondman and Arthur Jones.

Although concentrating on literature at this time, James
nevertheless interviewed Marcus Garvey when he visited Trinidad
and so must have been aware of the social and political ferment in
the country. He also wrote for Cipriani's paper and before leaving
for England had written Cipriani's political biography, *The Life of
Captain Cipriani*. Published in England in 1932, it became James's
first sustained piece of political and historical writing.

## James as Anti-Colonial Writer

James was fascinated by Cipriani and viewed him as the embodiment of the Trinidadian people's ability to rule themselves. Writing of Cipriani's efforts to resuscitate the TWA, he states: 'If there is anything which can prove the fitness of the people of Trinidad for self-government it is the progress of this resuscitated Association.'[45] Besides demonstrating how Cipriani's activities and life motivated the ordinary Trinidadian, James analyses Caribbean colonial society and the abilities of the Caribbean black population. He asserts that the Caribbean people are

> the descendants of those African slaves who were brought almost continuously to the West Indies ... Cut off from all contact with Africa for a century and a quarter, they present today the extraordinary spectacle of a people who in language and social customs, religion, education and outlook are essentially Western, and indeed, far more advanced in Western culture than many a European community.[46]

This is an early enunciation of the view which James was to express in the 1960s – that Caribbeans are a unique people. James's pamphlet draws attention to the racial and class definitions in Caribbean society and the nature of the political institutions, in particular, the Legislative Council. He then addresses himself to the central anti-colonial issue, that of self-government. However, his notion of self-government does not lead to radical social transformation, but is based on the concept of the equality of the native and colonised:

> For a community where although there is race prejudice, there is no race antagonism, where the people have reached their present level in wealth, education, and general culture, the Crown Colony system of government has no place. It was useful in its day, but the day is now over. It is a fraud because it is based on assumptions of superiority which have no foundation in fact.[47]

James's anti-colonialism, therefore, is based on his view that 'a people like ours should be free to make its own failures and successes'.[48] The pamphlet was written in the tradition of nineteenth-century anti-colonial thought in Trinidad and the Caribbean, with its principal focus on the capacity of Trinidadians to be self-governing. It should be observed that in spite of James's immersion in the life of Afro-Trinidadians as expressed in his fiction, he still considered the Caribbean people a Western people and regarded Africans as primitive. He notes that the English have difficulty dealing with the Caribbeans because many colonial administrators have a 'wide

experience in dealing with primitive peoples in Africa'.[49] For James
what made the West Indian distinctive was the pervasive influence
of Western culture. James's thought echoes the sentiments of many
educated black anti-colonialists and expresses an ambivalence
which is characteristic of many nationalist movements. This is
exemplified in an acceptance of the values, norms, institutions
and manners of the colonial power, combined with a fierce desire
for self-government. For many intellectuals, Western culture was
the yardstick by which all 'civilised' culture was measured. James's
view would change, but politically on the eve of his departure to
London, he was still operating within the framework of Western
thought with its racial hierarchy which posited Africans as non-
historic people.

An interesting criticism of James's biography of Cipriani came
from Albert Gomes and Ralph Mentor, two fellow contributors to
*The Beacon*. They attacked the book for what they called James's
'senseless worship' of Cipriani. James's interest in dominant
personalities would be a constant feature of his intellectual and
political thought. He would always attempt to examine the individual
personality, social structure and the making of history. Indeed, a
superficial reading of some of James's writings and lectures can give
the impression that his work is a series of commentaries on great
men in history. But such a superficial reading would lose an
essential part of James's methodology which integrates and links
the novelist's preoccupation with individual characters to the keen
eye of the historian for the details of social structure and the nature
of events. Although *Captain Cipriani* was not a revolutionary
pamphlet, it established one part of the pattern which would
characterise James's intellectual and political thought.

Before his departure for London, James also completed his only
full-length novel, *Minty Alley*. He claims that in this work he was
practising how to write. Based on James's personal experiences the
book was written in the realist tradition: 'I was about 27 or 28 at
the time when I went to live in that household described in the novel
... the people fascinated me, and I wrote about them from the point
of view of an educated youthful member of the black middle class.'[50]

The novel's narrator is Haynes, who wishes to break from the
black middle-class career path mapped out for him. He therefore
moves into a lower-class dwelling yard as part of his rebellion. A
critical element of the novel is his relationship with Maisie, a
working-class girl. Not only does the relationship develop from
friendship to a sexual liaison but it is Maisie who helps Haynes
become a self-confident human being: 'little by little she was
making a human creature out of him'. This was the total reverse
of the civilising mission of the educated middle class. Many years

later, in 1971, James noted that the central theme of the novel was 'the fundamental antagonism in West Indian society between the educated black and the mass of plebians'.[51]

James claims he was already engaged to be married when he wrote the novel and that he went to live in the household of which he writes. It is speculation, but if we consider the contradictions in James's life at that time, then Haynes can be seen as James's attempt to break out from the mould of black middle-class respectability. He was not aware of the political implications of this, but it represented the core of the contradiction of the educated elite and the masses in many British colonial countries. James himself maintains that many of the events in the novel actually occurred,[52] although 'I never slept with Maisie but I imagine at 20 I would have found it very exciting to sleep with Maisie. I was about 27 or 28 when this was going on, but I made Haynes in the novel 20 years.'[53]

The literary critic Sander suggests that the pioneering achievement of James's novel was in its presentation of the lower class.[54] This would soon be transposed to the political realm.

## James's Early Political Thought

In John La Guerre's opinion, by 1932 'James was a nationalist without a political theory'.[55] He further contends that 'when James arrived in England, he was at best a liberal'.[56] But this is a superficial analysis of James's political evolution and misses its complexity as well as ignoring his fictional works.

What is clear is that while James was breaking with the traditional patterns of the Trinidadian black middle class he had not yet fully grasped the political implications of his focus on the popular classes. Still viewing himself as a promising young writer, he left Trinidad as many others had done before him to find a publisher and make a mark in the metropole. His training, particularly in literature, and his passion for cricket created the basis for his perception of the world. Unlike many political theorists within the Marxist tradition, James's sensibility as a writer and his understanding of cricket – and therefore sports generally in human society – laid the basis for an integrative approach to politics and to Marxism as a radical critique.

Although deeply influenced and shaped by the training of the educated black middle class in the values of Western civilisation, it was the sensibility which he developed as a writer that became his dominant political theme and rescued him from the well-trodden path of other scholarship winners of his class. James's nineteenth-century Western intellectualism was juxtaposed to the realities of Trinidadian working-class life. So while it is true to say that he left Trinidad without a formal political theory, to characterise James as a 'liberal' is simplistic since in his fiction he showed different concerns which would quickly propel him on to the path of revolutionary political theory. In other words, James's rapid transition to Marxism can only be understood in the light of his experiences in the Caribbean and his focus on the lives of ordinary people as expressed in his fiction. In his autobiographical notes James writes that 'even [in] my days of fiction I had the instinct which enabled me to grasp the fundamentals of Marxism so easily'.[57]

To what extent was literature a substitute for direct political activity in James's early life? The speed with which fiction writing drained out of him to be replaced by revolutionary politics hints at a relation between the two and a possible substitution. James himself, in response to questions about his early life and politics, notes that 'Before I left Trinidad I wanted to take part in politics. I hadn't been able to because I was working with the Government Service and I would have been fired or something.'[58] This may have been said with the benefit of hindsight, but what is clear is that it was the principal element of his 'aesthetic ideology' which led him to Marxism.

## Conclusion

James came to Marxist politics as an anti-colonial intellectual. He was aware of the race question, but had not yet developed a radical perspective on it. Colonial Trinidad produced an individual steeped in the traditions of Western civilisation, but who recognised that elements of this tradition were in contradiction with the 'ne'er-do-wells' like Matthew Bondman. The developing Caribbean intellectual tradition of which James was a part prepared him for his sojourn on the world stage, just as it had prepared George Padmore and Marcus Garvey before him. James's contributions to political theory, therefore, should be viewed as part of the intellectual tendency from within the Caribbean which in the early twentieth century realised itself outside the Caribbean. The participants in this tradition were prepared by their Caribbean experience – an experience which had at its core the self-affirmation of the black Caribbean individual.

The journey from Trinidad to London where James became a Marxist was a long one. In England, Marxism provided for James, the intellectual/political framework for a full exploration of human society and revolutionary politics. However, the signposts on this journey were James's training in the Caribbean, the honing of his literary imagination, and the development of a methodology which was empirical and rooted in the fine-grained observations of the real lives of the lower class. The backdrop for all this was the mass activity of the Trinidadian black working class in the early 1920s and the developing Caribbean black intellectual tradition.

Writing after his political theory had evolved, James observed in *Beyond a Boundary* (1963) that:

> It is only within very recent years that Matthew Bondman and the cutting of Arthur Jones ceased to be merely isolated memories and fell into place as starting points. In reality, they were the end, the last stones put into place of a pyramid whose base constantly widened, until it embraced those aspects of social revolution politics and art laid bare when the veil of the temple has been rent.[59]

James's political theory began symbolically with Matthew Bondman and his efforts at self-realisation. His theoretical discourse would be shaped by the interventions of the masses in history, and political categories marked by their creative ability to discover new social and political forms. Caliban had begun his journey.

# CHAPTER 3

# James's Early Marxism

## The Transition

In March 1932, James set sail for England. He was then 31 years old and his colonial education had prepared him for the political and literary world of pre-war Europe. In his own words, 'The British intellectual was going to Britain.'[1] What were the motivating factors that sent James to London? First, he had decided to become a writer. Colonial Trinidad did not have a large reading public and had not yet developed a publishing tradition. His sojourn in London was in this sense typical of many colonial intellectuals who went to the metropole to hone their talents. Secondly, James was not an active participant in the labour and nationalist movements of the period. There was therefore no compelling reason for him to remain at home. On arrival, James went to live in Nelson, Lancashire at the home of the West Indian personality and cricketer, Learie Constantine. There he mixed with members of the British Labour Party, acquainting himself with socialist ideas. The contact with British working people made a profound impact, jolting James out of his nineteenth-century intellectualism. 'My labour and socialist ideas had been got from books and were rather abstract. These cynical working men were a revelation and brought me down to earth.'[2]

As might be expected, James soon involved himself in anti-colonial agitation and became a popular speaker. He joined the British Labour Party and became increasingly drawn to political activism. At the same time, he continued to pursue his interest in cricket and became a correspondent for the *Manchester Guardian*. His colonial agitation led to the publication of *The Case for West Indian Self-Government* and to a study of revolutionary Marxist ideas.

James moved to London in April 1933 and within a few months had become a Trotskyist. This was predictable since he himself notes that although he was a 'Labour Party man ... I found myself to the left of the Labour Party in Nelson, militant as that was'.[3] Within a short period, revolutionary politics had replaced fictional/literary writing. By now James was absorbed in the study of Marxist theory. His first serious study importantly was not a classical work of Marx or Engels but Trotsky's *History of the Russian Revolution*, hailed by many commentators as a masterpiece of historical writing. James was therefore drawn to the Russian Revolution and to Marxism by history. However, it is important to observe the centrality of his Caribbean preparation for entrance into European revolutionary politics:

> Something happened which I found among the Marxists whom I got to know. They read the Marxist documents and then read some of the classics of European literature, fitting them into Marx's historical scheme. Not me. As I read Trotsky's book I was already familiar with all the references to history and literature that he was making. I was able automatically and without difficulty to absorb his argument and the logical line that he presented.[4]

James claims that he learnt Marxism in the Trotskyist movement and that 'fiction writing drained out of me and was replaced by politics. I became a Marxist, a Trotskyist.'[5] James's commitment to left-wing politics was typical of the mood of many English intellectuals of the period. Stuart Samuels, in his essay *English Intellectuals and Politics in the 1930s*, notes that:

> [the] most outstanding characteristic of English intellectual life in the thirties was the development of political consciousness; then the most agonizing dilemma for the young, sensitive intellectual, was not so much the problem of choosing between the appeals of left-wing communism and right-wing fascism, as it was whether to become politically active at all.[6]

Sensitive to currents around him and with the experience of observing lower-class Trinidadian life, James was easily drawn into revolutionary politics.

## James as a Trotskyite

By 1934 Europe was in ferment. The rise to power of the Nazis in Germany in 1933 was catastrophic for left-wing politics, and in the Soviet Union Stalin's purges had destroyed the inspiration and hope of the Russian Revolution. In Britain socialism and left-wing politics had been dominated by the Labour Party since its formation in 1900. The party had its origins in the struggles of the British proletariat but, as David Coates observes, the party 'grew out of a non-revolutionary tradition'.[7] Labourism was therefore a political praxis which accepted the possibility of social change 'within the existing framework of British society'.[8] The historical tradition of parliamentarianism in British politics was, in general, a political weight considered by all radical political currents. One consequence was that throughout its history, the Labour Party has been an organisation with divergent political tendencies which continuously attempt to influence party policy. In the 1930s these attempts culminated in a shift in Labour Party policy with sections of the 1935 conference explicitly calling for working-class power.

James's membership of the British Labour Party occurred at time when the party was being profoundly influenced by currents which were attempting to push it to the left. One of these was the Independent Labour Party (ILP).

Traditionally to the left of the Labour Party, the ILP members were amongst the most militant activists in the labour movement. In 1932, the ILP broke from the Labour Party when its Members of Parliament were expected to vote for legislation which would introduce cuts in unemployment benefits. Torn between being a parliamentary group and being a revolutionary Marxist current, by 1934 the revolutionary tendency within the ILP had established itself as 'the Marxist Group' and had attracted some one hundred people, including James himself. The political objectives of the Marxist group were to work for a united front with the ILP and to win the mainstream of militant workers by united front activity in support of Trotskyism and the banner of the Fourth International.

Another factor which influenced left politics in Britain was the international debate in which the Marxist movement was engaged at the time. The communist movement was split between Stalinism and Trotskyism, and Marxist theoretical discourse was primarily focused on the nature of the Soviet state and its defence. For Marxist revolutionaries, the Russian Revolution was viewed as the start of a new historical phase in human society. To them, the works of Lenin and Trotsky contained lessons for revolutionary political praxis and seemed to provide answers for the creation of a new social order. Lenin, as the leading Marxist revolutionary in the early twentieth century, had established a body of thought and a corpus of activities known as Leninism. These included notions of the vanguard party, imperialism, national self-determination and the nature of the state in socialist society. For many, Leninism became the Marxism of the day, since it had contributed to a Marxist theory of politics and added concrete organisational focus to Marxism as a revolutionary political theory capable of organising people and seizing state power. At that time, in radical political discourse, the legacies of Lenin were important. Central to the conflict between Stalinism and Trotskyism, was who was the authentic claimant of Lenin's legacy.

In the main, groups and currents which represented Trotskyism were small and marginal to revolutionary politics and in many instances their internal political life was dominated by polemics. Because Stalinism represented Marxism as a monolithic political theory subordinated to the political practice of the Soviet Union, the Trotskyist current, in spite of its organisational limitations, attracted many talented intellectuals. A mind like James's, concerned with the sensitivity and nature of human personality, was repulsed by the machinations and brutality of Stalinist ideology.

## The Features of Trotskyism

By the mid-1920s the Russian Communist Party had become a bureaucratic organisation and the degeneration of the Soviet state had begun. Lenin had recognised this fact and in an important party debate on the role of trade unions had declared: 'It is natural for us to write about a workers' state in 1917; but it is now a patent error ... The whole point is that it is not quite a workers' state.'[9] Later, he would describe it as a 'workers' state with bureaucratic distortions'.[10] Developing this position, in 1923 the 'Left Opposition' led by Leon Trotsky pressed for policies which would democratise the party and for economic programmes which would revive the Soviet working class who had been ground down by civil war and strife.

By the late 1920s the Left Opposition had been defeated and Trotsky had gone into exile. Central to Trotsky's political programme was the nature of the Soviet Union. From this analysis all else flowed – strategy, tactics and the character of revolutionary politics. Critical to this analysis of the Soviet Union was the nature of leadership. As a consequence Trotskyist groups focused their energy and polemics on the nature of revolutionary leadership. In the end, because as a tendency it never moved beyond opposition to Stalinism, all the major political questions were eventually reduced to the betrayal or actions of leadership. Within the Trotskyist perspective the working class was not only objectively but also subjectively revolutionary and all that was required was correct political leadership. The major political task was therefore to build an alternative revolutionary leadership.[11]

On joining the Marxist Group, James quickly became a major contributor to its theoretical discussions. His first such analysis was a paper on the social and economic situation in the Soviet Union. John Archer, a former colleague, describes the article and its importance as 'an original analysis of the social and economic inequalities in the Soviet Union. C.L.R.'s paper was important if only because it tried to explain Stalin's regime in terms of the struggle of classes and not of human wickedness.'[12]

James soon emerged as one of the leaders in the Marxist Group and one of its leading spokespersons and theorists. As his reputation grew throughout Europe, he was called on to speak on the nature of Stalinism, particularly in late 1935 and 1937 in response to the Moscow trials. In 1936, he edited the revolutionary Marxist paper *Fight*. B.L. Gupta remembers him at this time:

I had rarely come across a finer political polemicist than C.L.R. James. His attacks on Stalinism were absolutely devastating. He was then thinking in terms of building an independent Trotskyist party. I joined him readily. Our main task was to bring out the *Fight* and to make an open propaganda in street corner meetings. We built a portable platform and the three of us, James, a tall West Indian; Stanton, very Jewish-looking chap from the East End and myself an Indian, taking the portable platform to the shopping centres all over London, regarding ourselves as the vanguard of the British proletariat.[13]

James rose to become a national figure in the ILP. By 1935 he was engaged in an internal political battle on the issue of anti-imperialism motivated specifically by Italy's invasion of Abyssinia. This engagement led to his establishing relationships with such people as Fenner Brockway. However, by 1936 the ILP, needing to maintain its links with the Labour Party, began to move away from the revolutionary anti-imperialist position which James had established. At its Easter conference that year, one observer noted: 'CLR delivered such an oration as no one who heard it was to forget. He spoke as a statesman on the world stage, for millions and millions of black people throughout the world.'[14]

But the difficulties within the ILP were profound, given its link to the Labour Party and the demands of supporting a non-revolutionary parliamentary party. These difficulties were compounded because of the Trotskyist political conception of 'entryism', which questions when and on what basis Marxist revolutionaries enter and exit from mass organisations. The basis of this tactic was a political analysis which asserted that revolutionary upheavals were imminent and that the task of revolutionaries was to go to where the masses were (betrayed by reformist or Stalinist leadership) and prise them loose by consistently revolutionary propaganda. Increasingly, the Trotskyists became disenchanted with the ILP and by April 1938, the Marxist group, along with other small Trotskyist groupings, merged to form the Revolutionary Socialist League. It was the beginning of James's long association with small revolutionary Marxist groups.

Factional disputes were always at the centre of the Trotskyist movement and by the 1940s James and his political ideas were central to these disputes. Emerging from this pattern, James became preoccupied with the role of the small Marxist group and in the 1950s and 1960s his political organisational focus would be the relationship of the small Marxist group to revolution, to new social forces and to how the new society could be born.

However, James's political activities were not confined to sectarian Marxist politics as he continued to agitate around the anti-colonial question, broadening his focus from the Caribbean to embrace

Africa. Along with Amy Ashwood (Marcus Garvey's first wife) James started the journal *International African Opinion*: 'As I remember it, there was nobody concerned about the colonial movement in Western politics. Nevertheless, something was happening. Mussolini attacked Ethiopia and Mrs Garvey and I said that we were openly opposed to that.'[15] James's political activity in the mid-1930s, then, was of a dual nature. At the same time that he was developing an international reputation as a Trotskyist he continued anti-colonial agitation, particularly around Africa. This blend of political activity would result in the writing of his most famous work to date on the Haitian Revolution, *The Black Jacobins*.

The 1930s was a watershed in world politics. The economic depression shook traditional conceptions of capitalism. Mass workers' activity in Europe and the USA and clashes between the state and the proletariat in many countries suggested to some that the world was on the verge of a revolutionary wave similar to that of the early part of the twentieth century. However, unlike the early twentieth century, there was a different political response to the crisis – fascism. One writer of the period notes that 'fascism and the traditional reactionary forces multiplied their activities with unrestrained violence and demagogy, and found response among the millions of desperate members of the middle classes who had been severely affected by the crisis, and even among the proletariat'.[16]

Although in 1936 the Spanish Civil War broke out and the French proletariat staged huge battles the crisis did not lead to a revolutionary wave. Throughout this period the communist movement shifted its policies from that of sectarianism to the development of a popular front. But the basis for these changes and shifts was Soviet foreign policy, not proletarian internationalism. The zigzags of policy and the continued bureaucratic deformations in the Soviet Union were by then even more apparent and it became increasingly important for the Trotskyist movement to explain this phenomenon. James took up this challenge and the result was his first major Marxist work, *World Revolution 1917–1936*.

## World Revolution *and its Contradictions*

One commentator described *World Revolution* as James's 'least original work'.[17] While a justified criticism, it ignores two issues: first, that James wrote the book as a Trotskyist within the confines of the Trotskyist movement; and secondly, that a close examination of the work gives clear indications that James was already developing political ideas which would eventually lead him to break with Trotskyism.

In the Preface to the first edition James states that 'the book is an introduction to a survey of the revolutionary socialist movement since the war – antecedents, foundation and development of the Third International – its collapse as a revolutionary force'.[18] The book's methodology was based on the fundamental ideas of Marxism as elaborated by Trotsky. In the first chapter, James outlines what he considers to be the tenets of Marxism. The chapter begins with a phrase which would become the major political theme for the rest of his life. 'Socialism', he states, 'and its attainment is neither pious hope nor moral aspiration but a new form of society which will arise for one reason and one only, the unavoidable decay of the old.'[19]

For James, the essence of Marxism was revolutionary politics, class struggle and the inevitable breakdown of capitalism. Basing his analysis on the Marxist prognosis of periodic commerical crises in the capitalist system, he states:

> The economic disorder would be translated as always into political struggles and be resolved by the revolutionary victory of a new class. For this revolution to occur a social class was necessary which would be driven to seize state power and create the political conditions for the new capitalist regime. This class Marx and Engels found in the proletariat.[20]

So far, James had said nothing new or startling, but had only repeated the standard version of Marxist political analysis. However, in discussing economics, he states – almost prophetically – that 'for Marx and Engels, collective ownership did not mean socialism'.[21] Although in the same chapter he reaffirms the necessity of collective ownership for a socialist society, the statement was an early indication of a different reading of Marx from the then norm in all Marxist political currents. For Trotsky and the Fourth International, collective ownership equalled state ownership and a workers' state in the Soviet Union. It was a consequence of the October Revolution and therefore was the basis of a workers' state, whether deformed or degenerate. From this perspective, the resolution of contradictions in the Soviet Union required a political, not a social, revolution to overthrow the bureaucracy, since property and production relations were socialist. Trotsky elaborated this clearly in 1938:

> The political prognosis has an alternative character: either the bureaucracy, becoming ever more the organ of the world bourgeoisie within the workers' state, will overthrow the new forms of property and plunge the country back to capitalism; or the working class will crush the bureaucracy and open the way to socialism.[22]

By contrast, James, although following this standard position, focused his attention not on *property relations,* but on the *nature of production itself* and the *relationships thereof.* It was this feature which gave *World Revolution* a new political and analytical flavour and made it 'the bible' of the Trotskyist movement in the period.

The other major feature of James's exposition in *World Revolution* was the role of individuals within the revolutionary process. Warning that 'revolution was not to be played with',[23] and citing Marx that it was a 'calculus with very indefinite magnitudes the values of which may change every day',[24] James paraphrased Marx's notion about the quality of individual genius. Informed by his literary leaning, James was preoccupied with the human personality and the quality of genius. This led him, in his later works, to examine individuals like Shakespeare and Lenin and to suggest insights into the fundamental features of their personalities. Critically, it allowed him to write history from a standpoint where the *actions* of people determined their fate, and where structures were both limiting and enabling.

## The Role of Individuals

James's preoccupation with the role of individuals finds its expression in this book with a discussion on Lenin. For James, Lenin was a model intellectual; without him there would have been no Bolshevism:

> Marxists believe in the predominant role of the objective forces of history, and for that very reason are best able to appreciate the progressive or retarding influence of human personality. For the moment it is sufficient to state our belief that without Lenin there would have been no October revolution and another Tsar would have sat in the Kremlin.[25]

The observation raises critical issues of agency and structure and James's view that 'without Lenin there would have been no October revolution' demonstrates a conception of the role of individuals that places the emphasis on agency. This view would consistently influence his conceptions of socialism and validate his revolutionary optimism. James describes Lenin as a personality deeply rooted in the intellectual tradition of Russian society. Besides his deep knowledge of Marxism and his tactical ability, James notes that he had qualities which made him superior to the other talents in the revolutionary struggles of the period. 'Lenin's superiority, the breadth of his spirit, knowledge of men, his tolerance, enabled him to use them all.'[26] James suggests that these qualities, despite the difficulties of the early stages of the Russian Revolution, allowed

Lenin to keep the revolution within the framework of classical socialist theory.

The other feature of Lenin's political personality which attracted James was his ability to discern the mood and aspirations of the masses. James recounts how when Lenin was in hiding a working woman put on his coat, telling him as she did that if he were Lenin she would help murder him. James's comment: 'He pondered long and deeply over this manifestation of working class feeling.'[27] In other incidents, James notes that 'near the end of April some of the Bolshevists raised the slogan "Down with the provisional government". Lenin checked them sternly. The masses were not ready yet to take action on such a slogan.'[28]

How can we explain James's attraction to this quality in Lenin? Bearing in mind James's political evolution and his preoccupation with the lives of ordinary people, it was easy for him to be intrigued with a political personality whose major strength was such an ability. From this perspective, James would also claim that the workers were naturally revolutionary, and that it was the intellectuals who found it difficult to understand this spontaneous revolutionary temper. Early in James's political thought, therefore, we can discern the notion of revolutionary masses and the dichotomy between them and intellectuals. It was the theme of *Minty Alley* transposed to politics, the alienation of the educated social group unable to grasp the humanising social force of the working class. This thematic became a constant feature in James's Marxist politics. Later, adopting Marx's phrase 'invading socialist society', James would develop notions of how the concrete revolutionary practice of the masses challenged capitalist hegemony. As a consequence the independent Marxist tendency which he founded would have as one of its political strengths the concrete exploration of the social and cultural life of ordinary workers. However, in 1937 James did no more than pose this question of the apparent contradiction between intellectuals and the masses, and left the issue unresolved, because in *World Revolution* he was arguing for the Leninist vanguard party. This notion, developed by Lenin and expounded in his pamphlet *What is to be done?*, argued for a centralised organisation of revolutionaries, noting that workers, unless they were revolutionary, would attain no more than trade union consciousness. From this basis, the logic of the revolutionary party was to be the conscious force of the proletariat. James, on the other hand, while holding to this notion in 1937, does so tentatively and is clearly more intrigued with the natural instinct of revolutionary workers. This is articulated in *World Revolution,* where he warns: 'No party can succeed without a strong centralised discipline, and an international without centralism is no international at all. But centralism is a dangerous tool for a party which aims at socialism, and can ruin as well as build.'[29]

According to James, Lenin was able to overcome the dilemma of centralisation because 'Lenin was a man big enough to forge this weapon fearlessly, use it to the utmost limit ... he was a dialectician and knew that democratic centralism was very near to democracy at one time and equally near to pure centralism at another.'[30]

James clearly is walking a tightrope here, and there is tension in his early Marxism between his evolving view on the revolutionary instincts of the proletariat and the demands of a Leninist party formation.

As a Trotskyist and one who was committed to the reconstruction of the revolutionary party along Leninist lines, James argued for a centralised revolutionary party. However, we should note here that at the general level of Marxist political discourse, the issue of the relationship between consciousness, organisation and revolutionary praxis has been problematic for many revolutionaries.

History has not yet demonstrated a successful universal revolutionary model of organisation, and the revolutionary praxis of the twentieth century has demonstrated different revolutionary models ranging from guerrilla movements to mass political organisations. James's early Marxism recognises this, but shies away from possible answers:

> There is no specific answer for this problem. It will have to be fought out – in each party as every emergency presents itself. But that can best be done only when there is a clear understanding of the issues involved. It is perhaps the greatest of the many bows that the revolutionary Ulysses will have to bend.[31]

He then proceeds critically to assess Stalin's policies (both national and international) from 1924 to 1937 and argues that:

> After nearly twenty years of unparalleled effort, turmoil and suffering, the workers' state presents a spectacle which is a caricature of socialism ... The Soviet Union remains a backward country.[32]

This would force James to develop a definition of socialism that would distinguish his political theory from other left tendencies. In conclusion, three critical areas of James's political thought are raised in *World Revolution 1917–1936:* the role of the individuals in history, the vanguard party, and the nature of the Soviet Union. Although none of them is resolved, they were indicative of the areas which he would attempt to resolve later and of some of the theoretical dilemmas which faced the Marxist movement.

*World Revolution* propelled James into international political leadership within the Trotskyist movement. He became a member of the British delegation to the Geneva Conference which formed the Fourth International and was recognised as a 'brilliant propagandist of ideas'.[33] John Archer, in a critical comment, reveals that in the 1930s James had two significant disagreements with Trotsky: 'The first was his belief that ever since 1923 Stalin had been engaged in some sort of conspiracy to betray the Russian revolution and to help Hitler to win ... Then again the question of supporting labour in elections.'[34] Archer notes that these disagreements were summed up in a meeting between Trotsky and James in April 1939 when Trotsky warned James, 'what is much more dangerous than regarding the Communist party as an agency of Stalin's foreign policy is the sectarian approach to the Labour Party'.[35]

It is significant that the areas of disagreement were tactical and not philosophical. It is obvious that the British Trotskyist movement, impressed as it was with James, did not recognise the early elements of his political notions, which eventually would lead him to break away from the Fourth International. At the same time many in the Trotskyist movement would not have been happy with James's dual political praxis. It is to this dimension we now turn.

## The Black Tradition

Black colonial intellectuals are a distinct social group in the 'mother country'. Equipped with the intellectual tools learnt from the colonial power, and although having absorbed the language, norms and values of the colonial power, they remain outsiders. A key factor here is race. It would have been unusual for James not to have been aware of this, and indeed his first sustained piece of political writing was anti-colonial and his first practical political activity in England was as a popular anti-colonial speaker where he would have had to confront the question of race. The problem of synthesising different political currents would arise as he moved to embrace Marxism. But as a West Indian intellectual, James was particularly well suited to this task.

In the British Marxist movement, James consistently raised the issue of anti-colonialism. In September 1935, he sought to pass a resolution at the ILP conference in support of the anti-colonial struggles. The resolution read in part:

It is necessary to support the anti-imperialist mass movements arising among 'coloured' peoples in all countries in connection with the Abyssinian crisis, and to create a firm alliance between the international working class movement and suppressed peoples.[36]

It also called for an 'international working-class boycott of imperialist Italy and its allies and the prevention of transport of troops to Africa'.[37] One observer at the meeting noted that James appealed as a black worker for help for the population of Abyssinia.[38]

The anti-colonial question with specific reference to Abyssinia was a crucial one for the Left in general as the cause of Abyssinia became a rallying cause for blacks internationally. Indeed, when it was discovered that the Soviet Union was selling arms to Italy which were being used to attack Abyssinia, many blacks left the communist movement in revulsion, particularly in the United States. In England, the ILP executive did not support James's resolution. And Trotsky himself, commenting on that particular ILP conference, observed, 'the cause of the ILP seems to me to be hopeless'.[39]

By this time James was well aware that the traditional Marxist movement whatever its guise did not fully grasp the race and anti-colonial question. He himself would continue to be engaged in both currents and so it comes as no surprise that after *World Revolution* he wrote *The Black Jacobins* and subsequently *A History of Negro Revolt*. James, however, not only wrote in support of African anti-colonialism but volunteered to fight too:

> My reasons for this were quite simple. International socialists in Britain fight British Imperialism because obviously it is more convenient to do so than to fight, for instance, German Imperialism. But Italian Capitalism is the same enemy, only a little further removed. My hope was to get into the army. It would have given me an opportunity to make contact, not only with the masses of the Abyssinians and other Africans ... I believed also that I would have been useful in helping to organise the anti-Fascist propaganda among Italian troops ... I did not intend to spend the rest of my life in Abyssinia, but, all things considered ... *given the fact that I am a negro and am especially interested in the African Revolution, it was well worth the attempt.*[40] (emphasis added)

Two critical elements emerge from this. First, James's concept that his Marxist commitment meant fighting imperialism internationally, and secondly, his interest in Africa and the positive affirmation of race.

In the mid-1930s, the resolution of the Seventh World Congress of the Comintern put a brake on anti-colonial activity. This caused some consternation among many black radicals, and consequently

many left the communist movement. One of these was George
Padmore, the one-time leading black communist international
official of Trinidadian origins. A fundamental contradiction of the
Comintern's policy was that while they were stepping down anti-
imperialist agitation, the period was also characterised by the
growth of anti-colonial nationalism in the colonies.

The Italian invasion of Abyssinia galvanised black anti-colonial
intellectuals and activists in England in the International African
Friends of Abyssinia, thereby continuing a trend in Pan-Africanism.
However, by 1936, the organisation had split between those who
sought a more radical approach and the moderates. Working with
Padmore and Amy Ashwood Garvey, James and another group of
black activists, which included Ras Makonnen, a Caribbean
personality, and Jomo Kenyatta, formed the International African
Service Bureau (IASB) in 1936. The IASB was a non-party
organisation which represented the democratic demands of Africans.
It was 'an organisation which supported democratic rights and
liberties and self-determination'.[41]

*International African Opinion* became the organisation's paper.
They agitated and published anti-colonial material, all of which
served as one of the bases for the modern black anti-colonial
movement. In addition to James's *The Black Jacobins* and *History
of Negro Revolt*, Padmore published *How Britain Rules Africa* and
*Africa and World Peace*. The group also published Eric Williams's
*The Negro in the Caribbean*, a pamphlet titled *The Native Problem
in South Africa* and Jomo Kenyatta's study of the Kikuyu tribe, *Facing
Mount Kenya*. James sums up the work of the group in this way:

> Padmore was tireless. He had wide connections while he had
> been an official of the Comintern ... From Africa, the Caribbean
> and elsewhere, they came to see him and his organisation in a
> ceaseless stream. But what I think was even more important,
> was that we allowed no opportunity of our case to pass us by.
> We had a lot of assistance from the Independent Labour Party,
> but whenever there was a meeting held by the Labour Party,
> or a conference organised by the Communist Party or some trade
> union group, or a meeting of liberals who were interested in the
> 'Colonial Question', we were always there.[42]

James notes that the work of the group was significant and that
as far as 'political organisations in England were concerned, the
black intellectuals had not only arrived, but were significant
arrivals'.[43] It is against this background that we now examine
James's *The Black Jacobins*.

## The Black Jacobins

In *Beyond a Boundary*, James notes that soon after arriving in Nelson, he began to import from France the books necessary to write a biography of Toussaint L'Ouverture. *The Black Jacobins* was published in 1938. Twenty-four years later James observed:

> In England I had been studying Marxism and had written a history of the Communist International which involved a fairly close study of the Russian Revolution. In France, I read … masters like Jean Jaurès, Mathieu and above all Michelet. I was therefore specially prepared to write *The Black Jacobins* … at the same time I was working closely with George Padmore and his black organisation which was centered in London … *The book was written not with the Caribbean but with Africa in mind.*[44] (emphasis added)

While *World Revolution* was polemical and demonstrated the nature of Stalinism, its focus was on the degeneration of a revolution. *The Black Jacobins*, on the contrary, was about a successful slave revolt and gave more scope to James's creative and political talents. Fundamentally, the story was about the energies and capacities of people, once slaves, who transformed themselves through revolution. As such its canvass was richer and allowed James, breaking from the strictures of factional Trotskyist polemics, to hone his political ideas and elaborate a political theory of revolutionary struggle, national oppression and resistance of the colonial people in Africa and the West Indies.

*The Black Jacobins* was a remarkable achievement, both as a work of literature and as a political theory. James's skill as a narrator is evident. At one level, the book can be read as a story of slave revolts and a leader, Toussaint L'Ouverture. The narrative is assured and swift and the description of personalities and events evocative. Here is an account of Toussaint's early military tactics:

> Toussaint alone among the Black leaders, with freedom for all in his mind … organising out of the thousands of ignorant and untrained blacks an army capable of fighting European troops … They did not rush forward in mass formation like fanatics … they carried out their preliminary manoeuvres in dead silence, while their priests (the black ones) chanted the wanga, and the women and children sang and danced in a frenzy.[45]

The great literary achievement of the work was that it transformed a factual historical event into a narrative of 'gripping adventure and high drama'.[46] At the level of political theory four distinctive issues emerge from this work:

- the nature of Caribbean society;
- the role of slavery in the development of the modern world;

- the relationship between a dominant personality and society; and
- a theory of social change.

Archie Singham in his essay *C.L.R. James on The Black Jacobins – Revolution in San Domingo* states that *The Black Jacobins* 'represented not only a major contribution to the study of Marxist revolutionary theory, but marked the beginning of Caribbean social theory'.[47] The foundation of this theory was the nature of Caribbean plantation society and its evolution.

Describing San Domingo society, James traces the slave trade, racial divisions and the role of slavery and writes: 'The slave trade and slavery were the economic basis of the French Revolution. The features created at Bordeaux, at Nantes, by the slave trade, gave to the bourgeoisie that pride which ruled liberty and contributed to human emancipation.'[48] This was a 'sad irony of human history'.[49]

James's notion of the role of the slaves in the West differs from the traditional Marxist conception:

> The slaves worked on the land, and, like revolutionary peasants everywhere, they aimed at the extermination of their oppressors. But working and living together in gangs of hundreds on the huge factories which covered the North Plain, *they were closer to a modern proletariat than any group of workers in existence* and the rising was, therefore, a thoroughly prepared and organised mass movement.[50] (emphasis added)

James's description of Caribbean slaves as 'closer to the modern proletariat than any other group of workers in existence'[51] is a central tenet of his political analysis of capitalism, slavery and Caribbean society. For James the nature of modern slavery was based on an economic model – capitalism – a method of capital accumulation and slavery – a model for the exploitation of labour. This fusion created a peculiar phenomenon of an 'advanced' mode of production grafted on to a 'backward' mode of labour. The articulation and relationship of these two modes laid the basis for the conception of the Caribbean slave as sharing social similarities with the proletariat. This in turn was one of the bases for James's notion that the Caribbean population was a unique and modern one. The idea was fundamentally Jamesian and would remain unchanged throughout his political career.

It is in the narrative and discussion about Toussaint, the black slaves, leadership and the revolutionary process that James is most perceptive and creative. Stating of Toussaint that the 'revolution had made him',[52] James comments, 'it is impossible to say where the social forces end and the impress of personality begins'.[53] Here he is echoing the problem of history to which he drew attention as early as 1931 in *The Beacon*. Toussaint, James notes, in spite of his revolutionary dedication, had a leadership flaw:

> His error was his neglect of his own people. They did not understand what he was doing or where he was going. He took no trouble to explain. It was dangerous to explain, but still more dangerous not to explain … It is no accident that Dessalines and not Toussaint finally led the island to independence. Toussaint, shut up within himself, immersed in diplomacy, went his tortuous way, over-confident that he had only to speak and the masses would follow.[54]

James then suggests that this, together with Toussaint's belief that the French ruling class would not restore slavery, alienated him from the black ex-slaves. The former slaves found Toussaint's policy of reconciliation with local whites incomprehensible. 'The black labourers had their eyes fixed on local whites and resented Toussaint's policy … the blacks could see in the eyes of their former owners the regret for the old days and the hatred.'[55]

The question of race, so central to Caribbean society, was crucial to Toussaint's downfall. Whilst acting with restraint towards the whites, he imposed a harsh discipline on the blacks, some of whom were his closest comrades. James notes, 'while he broke the morale of the black masses, he laboured to reassure the whites'.[56]

The other issue posed by James is the character of revolutionary leadership in the transition of the old society to the new. Comparing Lenin's leadership to that of Toussaint's, James writes:

> But whereas Lenin kept the party and the masses thoroughly aware of every step, and explained carefully the exact position of the bourgeois servants of the Workers' State, Toussaint explained nothing and allowed the masses to think that their old enemies were being favoured at their expense. In allowing himself to be looked upon as taking the side of the whites against the blacks, Toussaint committed the unpardonable crime in the eyes of a community where the whites stood for so much evil. That they should get their property was bad enough … to shoot Moise, the black, for the sake of the white was more than an error, it was a *crime*. It was almost as if Lenin had Trotsky shot for taking the side of the proletariat against the bourgeoisie.[57]

The leadership issue was made even more complicated by the question of race, of which James astutely writes:

> The question is subsidiary to the class question in politics and to think of imperialism in terms of race is disastrous. But to

neglect the racial factor *as merely incidental is an error only less grave than to make it fundamental.*[58] (emphasis added)

This is a forerunner to James's position on the black struggle in the United States and is informed by a Leninist analysis of the national question and James's practical political involvement with the Pan-Africanist movement. The central thematic of *The Black Jacobins* is the capacity of slaves to transform themselves, and the presentation of this paradigm of social change is outstanding. James notes that 'The transformation of slaves, trembling in hundreds before a single white man, into a people able to organise themselves and defeat the most powerful European nations of the day, is one of the great epics of revolutionary struggle and achievement.'[59]

In the context of racial domination, this insight was a powerful force and the affirmation of the historical role of blacks a necessary process for establishing human authenticity. At the political level, the success of the revolution and the creation of an independent black state was a social and political achievement, which demonstrated that African people were capable of self-government. It is critical to note here that in a comparative study of *The Life of Captain Cipriani*, James's first major anti-colonial text, and *The Black Jacobins*, certain themes – self-government, dominant political personality – are present in the latter, but they are discussed from an explicitly Marxist revolutionary position.

As such, James's paradigm for social change and his notion of freedom were influenced by Marxism: revolution was the 'volcanic eruption' of centuries of oppression. Critical in this were the activities of the oppressed – in the case of the Haitian Revolution, the slaves. However, because these activities are shaped by social factors, there was a crucial relationship between external and internal factors which became central to James's notion of social change.

James argued that the activities of the French masses were a major factor in the success of the Haitian Revolution. As he observes:

The workers and peasants of France could not have been expected to take any interest in the colonial question in normal times ... but now they were roused. They were striking at royalty, tyranny, reaction and oppression of all types, and with these they included slavery. On August 11th, the day after the Tuileries fell, Page, a notorious agent of the colonists in France, wrote ... 'One spirit alone reigns here, it is horror of slavery, and enthusiasm for Liberty' ... Henceforth the Paris masses were for abolition, and their black brothers in San Domingo, for the first time had passionate allies in France.[60]

James's understanding of the external influences on the Haitian Revolution was shaped by his reading of French history:

> It is impossible to understand the San Domingo Revolution unless it is studied in close relationship with the revolution in France. Fortunately the French historical school of the French Revolution is one of the greatest historical schools of Western civilisation, combines scholarship with the national spirit ... and with that respect for the Revolution without which the history of revolution cannot be written.[61]

The dialectic of the writing of *The Black Jacobins*, therefore, is the reinforcement of one strand of Marxism – French political history. This serves as a factor in a Caribbean slave revolution, which is then written by a West Indian Marxist for the purpose of preparing for the African anti-colonial revolution. It is the conjunction of all these political currents which gives the work power.

In the foreword to the 1980 edition of *The Black Jacobins*, James tells the story of how he met a political activist in Ghana in 1957 who explained that he had read the book, copied sections of it and circulated it. He comments, 'I could not help thinking that revolution moves in a mysterious way its wonders to perform.'[62] There was no such fate for *World Revolution* – not because the national liberation struggles dominated the world immediately after 1945 giving potency to *The Black Jacobins*, rather it was that freed from polemical and narrow sectarian restraints, James explored the fundamental issues facing revolutionary praxis in the twentieth century: race, the transitional society, the relationship of the leadership to mass movements and the creative capacities of the working class. That these questions were examined within the context of Caribbean society and the thrust for African independence indicates that in the coming period these contentious issues would be alive in the ex-colonial world.

James's other major published writing in this period was *A History of Negro Revolt*. In it he chronicles the key revolts of blacks across the diaspora. His major political purpose was to debunk the myth of blacks having no record of struggle against colonialism. Published as a series of articles, the work is descriptive, but there are two aspects of it which we should note.

First is James's hostility to the Garvey movement, which is tempered only by his recognition of the movement's significance:

> One thing Garvey did do. He made the American negro conscious of his African origin and created for the first time a feeling of international solidarity among Africans and people of African descent. In so far as this is directed against oppression it is a

progressive step. But this movement was in many respects absurd and in others thoroughly dishonest.[63]

Here James repeats a view held by other individuals such as Dr W.E.B. DuBois. However James's observation ignores one fundamental point – that Garvey's work was an important requirement in the process of black self-determination. James's views ignore the essence of racial oppression: the negation of the humanity of the racially oppressed. As a result of his negation, nationalism and national consciousness were the framework for self-identity and a prior condition which opened passages to radical political and cultural activity. James's comments on Garvey in this regard are in line with traditional Marxist and communist movements. The second aspect is James's continued insistence on and his usage and understanding of 'primitive', a feature already noted in his early work on Captain Cipriani. James describes the revolts in East and Central Africa thus: 'In Eastern and Central Africa, more primitive territories, we have had during the last thirty years a series of risings of an entirely different type.'[64] Obviously here the conception of 'primitive' is a Western one. While there is a recognition of the nature of colonialism and racial oppression, James continues to view these issues from the perspective of Western thought and tradition. This framework extended not only to notions of 'primitive' and 'civilised', but also to conceptions of beauty and physical characteristics. On James's meeting with the African-American Paul Robeson, who played the leading role in James's play *Toussaint L'Ouverture* (staged in March 1936 at the Westminster theatre) Robert Hill notes that:

> Robeson broke the mould in which the West Indian conception of physical personality in James had been formed. That was a time when black West Indians grew up with an unconscious prototype of the white Englishman and white English woman as their absolute standards of physical perfection and development.[65]

It is here that the intricate connections between a philosophical framework grounded in one tradition and a critique of that tradition burdened by many assumptions of the dominant discourse are strikingly revealed. For even Marxism as a radical social and political critique of colonialism and imperialism encoded assumptions about personhood that were rooted in the European Enlightenment. Therefore when James became a Marxist his conceptions of personhood were inherited from this tradition – one in which the distinction between 'primitive' and 'civilised' persons had already been embedded. James had a long way to go to come to terms with the distinctive African contributions to human civilisation.

## Conclusion: The Marxist Tradition and James's Early Marxism

James's work in the IASB and in the Marxist Group prepared him for a political career in small revolutionary groups. For the rest of his active political life James worked by drawing a few associates together and then concentrating on publication and the clarification of critical ideas. In the end it would mean that his work would be restricted to a few people only. However, its significance would outlast its immediate value and purpose. In the case of the IASB it created the political foundations for African independence and, in relation to Marxism, it would become a signpost for many new left activists who, in the 1970s, were searching for a revolutionary theory.

James's early political thought was well within the Marxist tradition. However his anti-colonial agitation would eventually lead him to a fundamental reconsideration of race. *The Black Jacobins* had raised issues in radical political theory which would resonate years later in the Caribbean and African colonial revolution. Perhaps a keen observer would have noted that James the political personality moved easily between cricket, literature and politics. If they noted this, they might have forecast that this Caribbean intellectual would bring something new to the radical tradition. How do we summarize this period of James's political thought?

By the mid-1930s capitalism was reorganising itself. The fall in export prices and declining capital inflows created difficulties for many advanced capitalist countries. In 1930 debt was a major problem and by 1931 the Great Depression had begun. In 1932, 32 countries suspended their gold payments and the international trade and finance system collapsed.[66] Many Marxists thought that the collapse of capitalism was not only inevitable but imminent. It needed only revolutionary leadership. But the revolution did not happen and World War II broke out. When James left England for the United States in 1938, a phase in Marxist political theory had come to an end. The consolidation of Stalinist authority in Marxist politics, theory, philosophy and economics was complete. The Russian Revolution had been successfully isolated and throughout Europe the twentieth-century legacy of the Enlightment and the modern idols of reason, science and progress would soon be forsaken. At the same time, European colonial dominance was coming to an end and another civilisation was emerging to dominate the world.[67]

In this context, James was Caliban in search of history and purpose. His dual political praxis saved him from sectarian politics and allowed him the space and canvas for political creativity. Within the Marxist tradition, James would shift the co-ordinates of the Marxist political project, developing an independent Marxism, but increasingly he would accomplish this from the perspective of the Other.

Both liberalism and socialism – as central doctrines of Western political thought – posit notions of equality, democracy, justice and the character of human society. Fundamental to these notions and their development is the relationship between the state and civil society. In Europe, the defeat of the proletariat and the consolidation of Stalinism stifled the creative exploration of these issues as a branch of Western political thought. The classical socialist tradition developed as a critique of Western bourgeois society; consequently, various tendencies were largely preoccupied with the European socialist revolution. Thus, it is not surprising that any review of major Marxist theorists up to 1938 would not include any African or black political theorist, in spite of the international diffusion of Marxist theory and politics during this period. After World War II, the divorce of Marxism from political praxis continued. While one of the causes was the defeat of the European proletariat and the emergence of totalitarianism, across the Atlantic, in the United States and the Caribbean, as well as in Africa, India and China, new social forces and movements were beginning to stir which would impact on the architecture of Marxism, creating the basis for innovations in Marxist political theory. In the late 1930s and early 1940s, the United States became the epitome of capitalist development unencumbered by feudalism, thus opening new possibilities for politics and working-class activities. Although James had contacts in Europe, particularly France, who would work with him later, after he broke with Trotskyism all the new questions he would attempt to answer were present in the United States.

According to Hegel, the new never appears suddenly but is formed within the old. James's move to the United States, after he had internalised the nationalist ferment of the Trinidadian working class, the Pan-Africanist Movement in England and the traditions of European revolutionary political praxis, would now provide the opportunity for the development of a modern, independent Marxism. Caliban was ready to chart a new course.

# CHAPTER 4

# The American Years

## *The Context*

When James sailed to the United States in 1938, the major Western powers were on the brink of war and in the midst of an economic crisis which had begun with the Great Depression. In the United States the impact of the economic crisis was acutely shaping the political agenda of Franklin D. Roosevelt. Roosevelt's expansionist economic package (the New Deal) lifted GNP to a higher level than it had been in 1929 and by 1938 he had embarked upon a second New Deal, thereby winning increasing political support. However, the economic and narrowing political factors were not the only critical features at that time. Central to any analysis of America in the 1930s was the growing social significance of the labour movement. One writer of the period commented:

> In the last half of the 1930s, working people made America a more democratic nation. By organising, protesting, sitting in and voting as a progressive bloc, they forced the federal government to begin acting as a guarantor of workers' rights to organise, bargain collectively and earn a decent wage, as well as of citizens' rights to liveable housing and a secure retirement.[1]

The activities of the American proletariat would have a profound impact on James's political thought. The other aspect which formed the context in which James would pursue his political project in the United States was the decline of Europe and the sense which pervaded many European intellectuals – that the entire edifice of Western society and civilisation was collapsing. The English historian Arnold Toynbee had earlier observed in 1931, that at that time 'men and women all over the world were seriously contemplating and frankly discussing the possibility that the Western system of society might break down and cease to work'.[2] However, this pessimism never infected James for two reasons. First, his early years in the Caribbean during the period of working-class nationalist stirrings gave him a vision of human possibilities and optimism. And second, the United States did not become burdened by this sense of collapse, as it emerged from the war as the world's most powerful economy.

49

The context of James's sojourn in the United States was thus radically different from his journey to London. In moving to the United States James was returning to the New World and to a situation where fundamentally new political issues would be raised. He was well prepared by a unique blend of nineteenth-century Caribbean Creole intellectualism and European Marxist theoretical training.

In 1938 the American working class went on the defensive. The Congress of Industrial Organisations (CIO), formed in the early 1930s as a result of labour upsurge in the Depression, reported only marginal increases in membership. Strike activity had declined and by 1939 was only half that in 1937. This was in contrast to the early 1930s when a series of strikes in the rubber industry had introduced a new technique of labour activity – 'the sitdown' strike. The labour historian Daniel Guérin describes the method and its implications:

> The upsurge was a closely knit combination of spontaneity and planning; the elemental thrust of the masses complemented perfectly the experienced leadership of a minority of trade union organisers. The movement was at one and the same time centralised and democratic. The strike committees had considerable powers. They were sometimes compelled by circumstances to take certain decisions in secret. But, apart from the exceptional cases, their decisions were subject to daily review by general assemblies of strikers.[3]

The obviously democratic nature of the 'sitdown' movement was an indication that although the American proletariat lacked the mass socialist traditions of the European working class, they nevertheless contained revolutionary impulses. Guérin again:

> The two factors characteristic of all revolutionary action – spontaneity and consciousness – had come together. Though they were less co-ordinated than the French factory occupation, the American labour movement which had been categorised in Europe as 'backward', thus offered a model for the proletariat of the whole world to follow.[4]

In the mainstream political domain, the election of President Roosevelt in 1932 opened a liberal phase in traditional US politics. Roosevelt's New Deal established major, job-creating public works programmes. Section 7a of the National Recovery Act (NRA), as a policy statement, encouraged union activity without company or government interference. This proved a fillip to union organisers and facilitated the revival of working-class militancy, so much so that by 1934 the unions had gained strength, and strikes became more frequent.

Increased worker militancy left many employers disenchanted with the Roosevelt administration, and by 1935 the administration had been forced into a new coalition which included labour. The following year, Roosevelt won the Presidential election with significant support from labour. However, by the late 1930s many in the labour movement too were disillusioned with the administration. But by this time Roosevelt had succeeded in recruiting sections of the labour leadership to his political cause. Thus he had to contend with the legacies of mass worker militancy in the 1930s which were still present amongst the rank and file of the American proletariat. The impulses of this legacy would result in bitter struggles between rank-and-file workers and a developing trade union bureaucratic leadership.

The 1930s had also been the era of 'mass society' in which cars, radio and money had transformed popular culture in America. This was a critical development as one writer put it: 'Mass culture was a vast Americanisation programme, but one that was redefining national values. Many of the celebrities of the 1930s were popular precisely because they spurned middle class ways.'[5] The creation of 'mass culture' and 'mass society' would have a decisive impact on James's political thought as he sought to develop an interpretative theory and radical critique of the nature of modern society.

## Arrival in America

By the late 1930s, Trotsky had come to the conclusion that the race question was crucial for the American Trotskyist movement. James, who had been active in the anti-colonial struggle and had written *The Black Jacobins*, was the most attractive candidate for the job of developing a revolutionary programme on the race issue. After discussions between Cannon (then leader of the Trotskyist party – the Socialist Workers' Party) and Trotsky, James was invited to undertake a six-month lecture tour in the United States. The tour never ended and for nearly 15 years, before his expulsion in 1953, James lived under various pseudonyms, battled with the immigration authority, divorced his first wife whom he had left in Trinidad, remarried, founded an independent Marxist tendency and embarked on one of the single most important political/intellectual projects of the twentieth century within the Marxist tradition.

A member of the Trotskyist movement recounts James's first public appearance on the SWP platform:

> At his first appearance he shared the platform with Shachtman and Cannon in the Irving Plaza meeting hall ... Shachtman was the first speaker and was not brief. James came on next and even though his talk was longer than Shachtman's, he completely

captivated the audience and received a big ovation. Cannon was the last speaker ... he put aside his notes and congratulated James on his speaking ability and welcomed him to the Socialist Workers' Party.[6]

James immediately got to work and began drafting articles and resolutions on the race question. He lived in New York and as was his custom spent a great deal of time watching and listening to the subjects of his study. He attended black churches, clubs and community events, visited the Apollo theatre in Harlem and observed the black population's enormous energy. This he commented on in his ad hoc autobiographical notes:

> I noticed the extraordinary power that came from them. I have never seen and never was to see or hear an audience anywhere ... that was giving out so much in response to a public performance ... all the power is hidden in them ... and the day when it comes out and it takes a political form, it is going to shake this nation as nothing before has shaken it.[7]

Importantly, it was at one of these political meetings in 1939 that he met his second wife, Constance Webb. Webb would become not only his closest confidante and lover in the 1940s, but would reawaken his artistic sensibilities, which had been subordinated to the rigours of revolutionary politics. In one of his 150 letters to Webb we gain a sense of James's early political focus and his working methods in the United States:

> I have now four speeches working at, one to whites on the Negro Question and one to Negroes on the same, one on the war which may come at any minute and one specifically to Negroes on war. One gets ideas and works on them and jots them down and bit by bit they take shape.[8]

In order to give expression to this project, James asked Shachtman if he could have a 'Negro' column in the SWP's paper, *Socialist Appeal*. However, he wrote to Constance Webb:

> the attitude of the SWP to the Negro question has been most disquieting and unless the Party can find a way to the Negroes, i.e., to the most oppressed, it will degenerate. The Negroes as the *most* oppressed *must* [triple underscore] become the very vanguard of the revolution.[9] (emphasis in the original)

James's first two years in the United States were, then, a period in which he educated himself about American society, travelled to Mexico to meet Trotsky to discuss the race question, attempted to influence the SWP on this issue by resolutions, fell in love and completed his Marxist education in political economy. He summed up his studies on political economy in a letter to Constance Webb:

> And now for *Das Kapital*. My dear young woman, I have some news for you. One C.L.R. James, reported Marxist having thought over his past life and future prospects, decided that what he needed was a severe and laborious study of? guess! The Bible? Wrong. Ferdinand the Bull? Wrong again. Not *Das Kapital*? Right. I shall do these three volumes and nothing will stop me but a revolution.[10]

He was not fully involved in SWP's organisational life but was more a public figure, as Martin Glaberman observes.[11] However, international events were fast approaching which would be divisive for the Trotskyist movement and change the course of James's political and personal fortunes.

## The Left and James's Arrival

In 1938, the American Marxist movement was small and fragmented, its development influenced by both the Russian Revolution and the internecine nature of immigrant politics. The origins of the movement lay in the left wing of the Socialist Party, a confederation of different nationalities, which had split in 1919. In the aftermath, the delegation of the Russian Federation called itself the Communist Party. In October 1928, the Party expelled three of its members, James Cannon, Max Shachtman and Martin Abern, who had aligned themselves to Trotskyist political positions. The group attracted new members and although small in number – not more than 200 by 1933 – they made vigorous attempts to influence the American labour movement,[12] playing a vital role in the Minneapolis teamsters' strike of 1934. In 1938, the Socialist Workers' Party (SWP) was formed, with James Cannon as its leader. Its formation coincided with the Fourth International and it became one of the largest groups affiliated to it. When James arrived in the United States to join them, SWP membership was about 1200. They were playing a minor role in the labour movement, but were not influential in the main progressive labour organisation, which at that time was the Congress of Industrial Organisations (CIO). This was in contrast to the Communist Party which Guérin estimates had sympathisers in about 40 per cent of the CIO.[13]

If in the United States the Trotskyist movement ignored the labour upsurge and was hopelessly out of depth about Black Liberation, it was attempting to make a contribution to a Marxist understanding of Soviet society, an issue that would soon become the fundamental factor in defining the politics of the movement. In September 1938, James wrote to Constance Webb, outlining the debate that was beginning to take place in the organisation on the nature of Soviet society. His letter suggests that he had the genesis of an alternative position to traditional Trotskyism: 'The Political Committee of the Trotskyist Party meets tomorrow – we shall tackle *The Russian Question*. Is "R" a workers' state? Some of us will argue "no".'[14] By 1940 the debates on the nature of the Soviet Union would split the SWP and the Fourth International, and James would leave the party with a faction led by Max Shachtman.

## The State Capitalism Debate

Coalescing as an opposition tendency to the Stalinist leadership of the Soviet Union, the central question in the Trotskyist movement was always the nature of the Soviet Union. At the core of Trotsky's orginal analysis was the notion that the Soviet Union was a contradictory society, half-way between capitalism and socialism.[15]

As World War II progressed and Germany attacked Poland, Stalin's foreign policy objective switched and the Non-Aggression Pact with Hitler was signed. Its implications were enormous. The Communist parties changed their position to one of non-support for war, while the Trotskyist movement, given its analysis of German fascism, found that its slogan the 'unconditional defence of the USSR' was a two-edged political sword.

Within the SWP, Shachtman and James Burnham began to raise the Russian question. For nearly a year, the SWP debated the issue. Burnham, who was viewed as the ideologue in the debate, began to argue along with Shachtman that the Soviet Union was a new form of class society and therefore should not be defended by the Marxist movement. Cannon's response was that the signing of the Pact did not indicate any fundamental changes in the character of the Soviet economy.[16] By the time of the April 1940 convention, the two groups were at loggerheads over the Russian Question. Trotsky supported Cannon and earlier in September 1939 confirmed that the nature of the coming revolution in the Soviet Union was 'political' and against the bureaucracy, but that it would leave in tact 'state property and a planned economy';[17] and furthermore that the 'defence of the USSR coincided for us with the preparation of World Revolution'.[18] At the party conference, Cannon and his group, with the moral authority of Trotsky, prevailed, labelling the Shachtman–Burnham faction petty bourgeois. The convention then suspended Shachtman and Burnham as leaders of the party, leaving the door open for other faction members to return to the fold.

In May 1940, the Fourth International supported the SWP's convention decision which would, by September 1940, be characterising the dissident group thus:

> [the] Burnham–Shachtman–Abern group has undergone a political evolution which has widened the chasm between them and the Fourth International. Burnham has drawn the final conclusion … has openly deserted to the class enemy. Shachtman and Abern lead a petty bourgeois semi-fascist sect.[19]

The resolution then recommended the group's expulsion along with all its faction supporters.

Where was James in this debate? He had not intended to remain long in the United States (he was on a six-month visa), however increasingly he was being drawn into the party debates. Obviously his abilities as a writer, speaker and theorist were skills which any revolutionary organisation would welcome. From his base in New York and on his speaking tours, James had made contacts, particularly with Raya Dunayevskaya who would later become the co-founder of the Johnson–Forest Tendency. Operating under the pseudonym of J.R. Johnson, James was feeling his way intellectually and politically to a new Marxist project.

James sided with Max Shachtman in the 1940 SWP split and immediately assumed a leadership position in the new party, the Workers' Party, becoming a major theoretical contributor to the party's magazine, *New International*. But now he faced a major personal and political dilemma: how was he to stay in the United States in the leadership of a tiny sect, without the moral authority of Leon Trotsky? To challenge Trotsky on the fundamental issue of global revolutionary politics – the Russian Question – was a significant step. But what was to become of the Caribbean intellectual nine years after shaking the colonial dust of Trinidad and Tobago from his feet? James handled the situation with the methodology which would become his political hallmark – he isolated the issues, identified the central principle and then built around this. He describes this in another fragment of his ad hoc autobiography:

> The question was where should I work? After all I had a good job in England that gave me a lot of time and also allowed me a lot of movement. I was already established in the literary world with three books that had made quite an impression and I was known as a speaker. Furthermore I had close connections with a highly educated body of Marxists in France. The question was should I go back to England and begin that work there or should I stay in the United States? After a while I was very uncertain. The decisive role in this matter was played by a member of the Trotsky party called Freddie Forrest [sic] known today as Raya Dunayevskaya.[20]

The decision made by James and the Tendency began what was to become one of the most significant political and intellectual projects of the twentieth century within the Marxist tradition. James was now 40 years old. While his intellectual training in both the Caribbean and Europe had equipped him for the task, it was his Caribbean audacity which gave him the confidence. It was the same audacity which led Garvey to build the UNIA in the USA in the early twentieth century, and George Padmore to become the most important black official of the Communist International. A black Caribbean man and a Russian woman about to embark upon a revolutionary intellectual project in the New World was certainly a historical precedent which would be of enormous significance in defining the revolutionary politics of the Johnson–Forest Tendency.

## The Nature of State Capitalism

James quickly put together the group of three and began to work on developing a position on the nature of the Soviet Union. By 1941 they had produced the 'Resolution on the Russian Question' and had submitted it to the Party Convention. It was the first document of the Tendency to call the Soviet Union a state capitalist society, and the first document within the mainstream of the revolutionary Marxist movement to define the Soviet Union as such. Starting with the traditional Trotskyist as well as the Marxist-Leninist notion that state ownership of the means of production was sufficient to characterise a society as socialist, the 1941 resolution shifted the parameters of the debate, focusing instead on Marx's method:

> In order to achieve the bourgeois democratic Revolution in 1917, the proletariat was compelled to seize power. But this seizure of power was due chiefly to the incapacity of the ruling class and the conjunctural historical circumstances. The working class lacked the maturity in production of a proletariat which was a majority of the population ... The whole society has turned itself slowly over and once more the working class has been pushed back into that submissive role in production which is determined by the low technical level of the productive forces judged on a national scale. The bureaucracy is completely master in the productive process, that is the basis of its 'political power'.[21]

The resolution then charts the development of the Russian economy from 1917 and demonstrates that the classical Marxist categories of the 'law of value', and the contradiction between production for use and exchange value still operated. It further rooted political developments and the consolidation of the Stalinist constitution in 1936 in the economic domain:

... to meet the threat of Japan, compelled industrialisation at a feverish pace ... This economic necessity compelled an enormous increase in the repressive apparatus, the consolidation of the ruling democracy by concrete privileges, honours, authority, and the restriction of persons and ideology connected to the October Revolution.[22]

The climax of this process was *statification*, a process whereby the 'state acts as the entrepreneur and exploits the workers'.[23] Arguing that, for Marx, labour was the main factor of production, the resolution claimed that socialism was only possible when 'labour controls accumulated labour'.[24] At the political level, the Tendency characterised the Russian economy as state capitalist and described the state as 'fascist'.[25] It then noted that:

If the relations of production in Russia are capitalist then the state is fascist. Fascism is a mass petty bourgeois movement, but the fascist state is not a petty bourgeois state. It is the political reflection of the drive towards complete centralisation of production which distinguishes all national economies today.[26]

James and Forest also spelt out in the resolution their conception of socialism as the 'working class control over production on a world scale and the production of use values'.[27] On these grounds, the Soviet Union was state capitalist.

It is important to note that, from the outset, the Tendency extrapolated from their analysis of the Soviet Union global tendencies of capital, which would later provide the basis for their analysis of the world economy and politics. Their position on the Soviet Union had important political conclusions from which James did not shrink. These conclusions were clear and precise:

- No defence of the Soviet Union.
- The Communist Parties were agents of a fascist power.
- Propaganda about socialism was necessary.
- Party cadres should study Marxist economics, particularly the volumes of *Capital*.

The resolution placed them in immediate conflict with the Workers' Party leadership, who had developed a theory of Soviet society as 'bureaucratic collectivist'. In this they were influenced by the work of Bruno Rizzi whose work on bureaucratisation was popular in European and American intellectual circles at the time.[28] He asserted that 'the USSR was a new type of society'[29] and that a global pattern was emerging in the advanced capitalist countries in which 'a new managerial class in the process of formation announces that capital is at the service of the state'.[30] Shachtman, developing his analysis after the 1940 split, declared that the Soviet

Union was a 'bureaucratic collectivist' society, and noted that the 'norm of capitalism is the private ownership of capital'.[31] In relation to state capitalism, Trotsky had declared in *The Revolution Betrayed*:

> state capitalism has oftenest been understood to mean a system of state interference and regulation ... There are undoubtedly points of contact between state capitalism and 'statism' but taken as systems they are opposite rather than identical. State capitalism means the substitution of state property for private property ... The first concentration of the means of production in the hands of the state to occur in history was achieved by the proletariat with the method of social revolution and not by capitalists with the method of state trustification [sic].[32]

James and Forest's analysis of state capitalism ran counter to Trotsky's. Indeed, Shachtman's analysis was closer to Trotsky's and carried his political conclusions to their logical end. By insisting on the political character of statification during the Russian Revolution, Trotsky concluded that a political revolution was necessary to restore full socialism to the Soviet Union. Basing his arguments on the economic analysis Shachtman asserted: 'on the contrary, the proletariat's relations to property, to the new collectivist property ... the political expropriation of the proletariat ... is nothing more or less than the destruction of class rule of the workers, the end of the workers' state'.[33]

For James, the cardinal principle was that statification of production did not mean socialism, but represented a new stage of capital in the 1930s and 1940s. As a consequence, the 1917 Russian Revolution was not betrayed by Stalinism, but was overthrown, and the emergence of the Soviet Union from the 1930s onwards marked a new stage in world politics. To consolidate this analysis, James had to critique Trotsky's work.

## The Assessment of Trotsky

James's essay on Trotsky was published in September 1940. It is not only a political analysis. James's skills as a literary critic and his mastery of the Western intellectual tradition are fully displayed in an essay that allows us to glimpse some of the reasons which drew James to Trotskyism. Recall that Trotsky's *History of the Russian Revolution* had been critical to James's early Marxist training, and that James placed Trotsky as second to Lenin amongst world leaders of the time. His justification was based on: Trotsky's theory of Permanent Revolution, his leadership in the Russian Revolution, his writings on fascism, and his defence of the legacy of the Russian Revolution. Yet, James would write of Trotsky: 'this superbly gifted theoretician, executive and leader of men on the grand scale, who achieved so much in the realm of politics, was a very defective politician'.[34] James observes that Trotsky did not build organisations and that although he was popular with the masses, he was 'pushed out of power as if he were a fourth-rate bureaucrat'.[35] For James, Trotsky's greatest strength was as an intellectual and writer: 'Trotsky, man of action, was therefore above all an intellectual, a man of theory'.[36] It is here that James's analysis is at its finest as he attempts to create a portrait of the Russian revolutionary and assess his contribution to revolutionary politics. Again his eye for detail is apparent: 'Lenin, it is known, loved conventions, conflicts over resolutions, the wear and tear and hurly burly of political strife. Trotsky, it is clear, hated them. He would have preferred to be elsewhere at his desk. His political work was a duty.'[37] James, clearly sympathetic to a further feature of Trotsky's character, writes:

> Another was his attitude to the masses. He had a passionate faith in them and no great work for socialism, theoretical or practical, can be done without it ... it is often characteristic of the gifted intellectual and particularly of men who are somewhat aloof from their followers. It is the chief ingredient in the complex of psychological traits which make the great mass orator.[38]

Then James gives the key to his historical writing and political theory: 'Men make history and to understand history we must understand men.'[39] Here is the core of one dimension of Jamesian political theory. For James, agency was fundamental to the making of history, hence there would have been no Russian Revolution without Lenin, an observation he made in *World Revolution*. From this, James's focus on history would always be the specific activities of people. In his political praxis this would lead him to concentrate on what the proletariat actually did within the productive process. James's assessment of Trotsky's *History of the Russian Revolution* as was stated before demonstrates his mastery of Western thought but it also gives clues to how he perceived his own work. The first claim he makes in assessing the *History of the Russian Revolution* was that it was 'the climax of two thousand years of European writing and study of history'.[40] James then reviews historical writing from Herodotus to Michelet's work on the French Revolution. He suggests that Trotsky's historical analyses were the widest because he represented new social forces. He then develops a critique of Trotsky which integrates Trotsky's artistic and creative powers with his interpretation of Marxism: 'That history is what it is, is due certainly to Trotsky's power as a writer. There is no substitute for a great artist.'[41] But he further argues:

> Politically, mankind came of the age with the Russian Revolution. Caesar, Cromwell, Marat, Robespierre and other famous men

had worked largely by instinct. For the first time in history a man had foreseen the main lines of a great historical event ... Lenin had to revise his conceptions, not Trotsky. Any writer, any artist would know the extraordinary power and confidence, the certainty of direction ... the interplay of class as a whole and individual artist are fused here as nowhere else that we know in writing ... into the book went all the historical knowledge and understanding which Marx and Engels had started to accumulate ... The artist in him suppressed for 40 years by the needs of revolution, now opened out, and with the same personal force, discipline and will which always distinguished him, he hammered this mountainous mass of facts and ideas around the theme of class struggle into one of the most powerful, compact and beautiful pieces of literature that exists in any language, prose or poetry.[42]

Is it any wonder that James, reading Trotsky's *History of the Russian Revolution*, would have been drawn to him? Certainly the artist/novelist in James would have recognised a kindred spirit. The *History of the Russian Revolution* represents for Marxist history what James's *The Black Jacobins* – an original work, drawing from classical Marxist discourse – represents for the new social forces and the universalisation of the concepts of the 1789 French Revolution: Liberty, Fraternity and Equality. If, in other words, *History of the Russian Revolution*, is 'the first classic of socialist society',[43] *The Black Jacobins* is the first modern classic of the African and Caribbean revolutions and is a marker within the trajectory of an alternative discourse and tradition of radical political theory. It is so since it was the Haitian not the French Revolution which gave full freedom to black slaves.

## New Ground

Forced to consolidate their position, the theoretical work of the Johnson–Forest Tendency required a return to classical Marxism. In this project they were ably assisted by Grace Lee Boggs, a philosophy postgraduate who was recruited in 1941. Commenting on her recruitment she states:

> When I met CLR I had already decided to commit my life to revolutionary struggle ... As soon as CLR discovered that I could read German and had studied Hegel, he had me translating sections of *Das Kapital* and comparing the structure of capital with Hegel's logic.[44]

For the next decade, the Tendency under James's leadership studied Marxist economics, philosophy and politics. During that period they left the Workers' Party (in 1947), rejoined the Socialist Workers' Party (in 1948), left it again (in 1951), and finally established an independent political organisation, Correspondence, in 1952 – all the time clarifying and redefining Marxism as a revolutionary social and political project. Between 1942 and 1944, the Tendency rigorously continued to study the Russian Question and the original works of Marx. Forest wrote extensively on labour and society, basing herself on Marx's early economic and philosophical writings, and in September 1944 in the *American Economic Review*, published a critique of Stalin's revision of Marx's law of value. James meanwhile focused his energies on the national question in Europe and the politics of state capitalism, and continued to tour the United States: 'Late in 1941 I left New York and went into the wilderness for 10 months, a tremendous experience involving thousands upon thousands of workers, black and white.'[45] In earlier letters to Constance Webb, he affirmed that he had not lost his passion for ordinary people, as he revealed to her:

> I can listen for hours and hours ... to all sorts of people, especially strangers. And my greatest weakness? Impatience at party meetings and committees ... I have sat for hours in America listening to people, all sorts of poor working people, telling me all about themselves. It is indispensable for my understanding of anything. It must go side by side with the books.[46]

This ability to listen for hours and absorb the 'stories' of working people, a feature of James's early literary career, was now transposed to the political domain. It marked his political methodology and was the essence of his political imagination and style. In the final analysis this would become the hallmark of the organisational and theoretical work of the Johnson–Forest Tendency and the basis of its independent revolutionary politics and its critique of capitalist society.

## The Politics of State Capitalism

By 1943, James had developed the idea that within the degeneration of capitalism was the germ of 'totalitarianism', which represented the contradiction of modern society carried to its logical extreme. Marx's classic statement that capitalist society would either move to 'socialism or barbarism' was crucial here and a defining contribution to James's political thought. As James noted:

> Socialism is not an abstraction nor an ideal in the distance. It is the concretely developing alternative to a society that can no longer exist without destroying its own achievements and at the

same time creating the social relations which are to replace it.
All Europe is the exemplification of the main theme – socialism
and barbarism. The concentration of the means of production
and the socialization of labour ... the advancing socialist society
compels the capitalist to treat the productive forces as a
social force.[47]

James was developing further the idea, first discussed in *World
Revolution*, that socialism developed in the womb of capitalism.
Critical to such a conception was the fact that the tangible elements
of the alternative to capitalist society were the practical activities
of the working class. The logic of the position, therefore, was that
any revolutionary Marxist group had to base its politics on these
practical activities. And to locate them James turned his attention
to the American proletariat.

By the early 1940s, rank-and-file militancy was the order of the
day amongst important sectors of the American working class.
World War II had created jobs, taking women out of the home and
putting them into the factories and services.

> The AFL and the CIO, including the Communist-led unions
> within the latter, opposed all strikes during the war and often
> showed signs of opposing labour struggle altogether. But
> industrial workers, especially those in the mines and defence
> plants, refused to abandon the strike weapon. While most AFL
> and CIO unions tried to build their unions through Government
> support and take advantage of the labour shortage to encroach
> on certain management prerogatives, they found millions of
> American members insisted on adopting a more militant, direct
> action approach.[48]

During this period rank-and-file labour activity resulted in widescale
spontaneous wildcat strikes:

> During the Second World War, 6.7 million strikers participated
> in 14,471 strikes, far more in each case than there were in the
> CIO's early hey-day from 1936 to 1939 ... Many of these
> implicitly challenged the leaders of the CIO and their pact with
> capital and the state. But while the class struggle continued,
> indeed *accelerated on the shop floors*, on the shipyards and in the
> mines, during the war, it did not become politicised in a socialist
> direction.[49] (emphasis added)

Two major events initiated this militancy and determined its
character: the struggle in the car industry against the 'no strike pledge
clause' proposed by the government and accepted by the United
Auto Workers leadership (UAW), and the miners' strike of 1943.
Spontaneous action during the war years was the context which

informed James's conception of socialism and remained the foundation of the political praxis of the Johnson–Forest Tendency. Working-class activity in America had just as profound an impact on James's political evolution as Trinidadian working-class activity had done in the 1920s.

## History as Necessity

In an essay published in 1943, *The Philosophy of History and Necessity: A Few Words with Professor Hook*, James critiqued Sidney Hook's book *The Hero in History*. The review again demonstrates James's familiarity with the history of Western civilisation and philosophy. But in an effort to demonstrate Hook's theoretical weakness, James failed to distinguish the subtle interplay of social forces and personalities in the historical process, finally adopting a mechanical understanding of historical materialism. 'The interpretation of history is a class question ... It is to Hegel and Marx that are due the modern practice of dividing world history into a sequence which shows some *historical* inevitability or *necessity*' (emphasis added).[50]

Although he had read Marx's *Economic and Philosophic Manuscripts* James retreated to the structuralist primacy of mechanical Marxism in which necessity is a law independent of human agency. His one concession to the notion of agency was the statement that when 'Marx used the Hegelian method to discover the "necessity" he elaborated a philosophy which was a guide to action for the working class'.[51] Working-class action was therefore both historic and purposeful to the end of creating a new society. In this formulation James's historical materialism was based on the absolute primacy of the mode of production and therefore of structure. The critique of Hook's book shows James in a deterministic frame of mind as he insists on necessity and inevitability in social processes.

This aspect of his thought could be identified in particular when he was writing within the Trotskyist framework. In spite of his early break with traditional Trotskyism, James at this time had still not freed his thinking from the narrow strictures of a Trotskyist interpretation of historical materialism. Although the Trotskyist movement differed from the Stalinist tendency in its attitude to the Soviet Union, it still abided by the key notions of Marxism developed by Marxist thinkers in the late nineteenth century, many of whom were profoundly influenced by a mechanical view of science. As James's political project grew, he moved from this view of history to a more flexible appreciation of human agency, as his next major essay, *Dialectical Materialism and the Fate of Humanity* (1947) demonstrated.

During the mid-1940s, many intellectuals and political thinkers in reviewing the characteristics of fascism and Stalinism concluded that the historical process was in reverse. The leadership of the Workers' Party espoused this view. James took up the cudgels on the side of historical materialism and, in late 1945, published 'The Historical Retrogression or Socialist Revolution' in the *New International* in which he once again asserted the progressive nature of historical materialism and posited the view that state capitalism was a theoretical explanation of the nature of the totalitarian state. However, this debate was now secondary to the internal political struggle being waged by the Johnson–Forest Tendency in the Workers' Party about the nature of the revolutionary party and the Americanisation of Bolshevism. James's salvo in this debate was his pamphlet *Education, Propaganda, Agitation: Post-War America and Bolshevism*, his first major revolutionary statement on the character and organisation of the American socialist revolution.

## What is to be done? – *The American Context*

After three years in the Workers' Party, James turned his attention away from theoretical concerns to organisational questions. In analysing this aspect of politics, he focused on the general organisational problem of the Trotskyist movement and observed that 'all analyses so far have been how to build the party ... however none has been built ... the failure of the Trotskyist movement is that great events have come and gone and we have made no impact'.[52]

James begins the analysis by reviewing the history of the Russian Social Democratic Party and the work of Lenin. In relation to Lenin, he makes the point that Bolshevism was Marxism directly applied to Russia. Turning to the American situation, he observes that while the European worker will read the *Communist Manifesto* with his European experience:

> for the average American Worker these books as a beginning are alien ... what they cannot give to him in sufficient measure is that sense of reality of development of his own country ... such historical data, knowledge, general reading, social experience as he has, the structure in which his theoretical experiences must grow, are American. We have to begin now, not to write a few pamphlets, but to build up the American counterparts of the *Communist Manifesto* ... and perhaps even more important, the American counterpart of *What is to be done?*.[53]

James's answer to the problematic of building a Leninist vanguard party in America was to argue that the Workers' Party should focus on the industrial working class, and its journal *Labour Action* carry more articles on socialism. All this however should be done within a framework:

> Every principle and practice of Bolshevism to be translated into American terms. Historical Materialism, the Marxian economic analysis, the role of the party, the relation between democracy and socialism, the relation between trade union and the party, reformists and revolution, the role of social democracy, the theory of the state, the inevitability of socialism (here James was still mechanistic), every single one of these can be taught, developed, demonstrated from the American economic, social and political development.[54]

The Americanisation of Bolshevism, James felt, was the special contribution that the Workers' Party could make to the American labour movement. He therefore argued that the principal task of the party was to publish Marxist studies on the Civil War and the historical signifiance of the CIO, to study Marxist economics and to complete a serious study of the Negro Question.

For James, the issue of the development of the American revolutionary party was part of an overall direction which was necessary for the development of Marxism. The other two dimensions of this development were the statification of production (state capitalism) and internationalism. Again, we should note that despite James's state capitalist analysis he was still operating within the confines of traditional Marxist-Leninist organisational paradigm. So although the Johnson–Forest Tendency was pursuing a study of classical Marxism, they had not yet developed new categories of political organisational forms.

In 1946, James returned to Trotsky's legacy when he published a critique of his major work on the nature of Soviet Society, *The Revolution Betrayed*. In this article, James noted that Trotsky's major preoccupation was in the sphere of consumption and hence the relationship between the wages of the workers and those of the bureaucracy. To this view he counterposed Marx's theory of society: 'Marx's theory of society is a theory of the activity of men ... as active in the process of production ... his labour process ... for Marx, the essence of private property was the alienation of labour and not the fact that property belonged to private individuals.'[55]

Arguing that Trotsky's conception was different, James states: 'Stalinist society, rulers and ruled ... is the ultimate, the most complete expression of class society, a society of alienated labour.'[56] In contrast to this kind of society James asserts that socialist society is one where 'the individual is able to exercise his gifts to the highest capacity and become truly universal'.[57] Paying tribute to Trotsky, James at the same time lays the basis for a break with him: 'For many years Trotsky led a profound and brilliant opposition to the

Stalinist bureaucracy despite his fundamentally false theoretical orientation. But a false theory always takes its toll in the end.'[58]

In effect, James had publicly broken with some of the fundamentals of Trotskyist movement; however, both he and the Tendency continued to operate organisationally within the confines of Trotskyism. It was a contradiction which would only be resolved in 1951.

## The Workers' Party Split

In February 1947, encouraged by the Fourth International, both the Socialist Workers' Party (SWP) and the Workers' Party (WP) agreed to unity talks. However, by July the talks had all but broken down. The Johnson–Forest Tendency, then ardent advocates of unity, began to reassess their political evolution. During the initial split in 1940 on the Russian Question, neither James nor Dunayevskaya had played a pivotal leadership role. All the evidence suggests that they had not yet analysed the political consequences of the split for the small American Trotskyist movement. However, in 1947, faced with the political trajectory of the Workers' Party away from the labour movement, the Tendency began to reassess its position and came to the conclusion that the split was unprincipled. Simultaneously, the Tendency held its first independent national conference on 5 July 1947 and adopted a resolution, written by James and Dunayevskaya, which spoke to the fundamental questions of political praxis for the American revolutionary left. The resolution addressed the following issues: the unity question, the nature of the WP, and the character of the American Revolution and American radicalism. In part it states:

> In the 1940 split and in its subsequent evolution, the WP expressed in concentrated form a basic problem of American Radicalism: hostility to world imperialism but an inability to assimilate the principles of Bolshevism owing to the absence of any conscious revolutionary perspective in the United States. This deficiency is rooted in the whole history of the country.[59]

James and Forest continued to root their analysis of the WP within the framework of Trotsky's analysis outlined in the Fourth International's transitional programme, 'The Death Agony of Capitalism':

> The WP ... is a petty bourgeois tendency functioning in the period of the death agony of capitalism, in the United States where no mass Social Democratic party exists. Hence the WP is torn between the increasing barbarism of bourgeois society and its own ability to find a basis in American society to

concretise and develop the political and organisational principles of Bolshevism.[60]

The need for unity, James and Forest argued, was a result of 'the crisis of humanity which is the crisis of the proletariat leadership'[61] and the fact that the American proletariat over the years had 'given ample warning to the revolutionary movement that it had entered upon the years of decision'.[62] The resolution ended with a political declaration: 'The Johnson–Forest Minority has come to the conclusion that it can do nothing further to influence the WP majority politically. Political differences have been clarified as far as possible; the lines have been drawn.'[63]

In August 1947, the Tendency produced *A Balance Sheet: Trotskyism in the United States, 1940–1947*, a comprehensive critique of the Workers' Party and of the Trotskyist movement in general. It admitted that the Tendency had made an error in 1940 and reflected on Trotsky's role in the split, observing that during this period, Trotsky had struggled against intellectuals in the American Marxist movement who were hostile to the dialectic. He argued that it was no accident that the American radical intellectual accepted Marxism without the dialectic, since 'In no other country has there been such a rejection of class struggle as in the land of unlimited opportunity.'[64]

James and Forest agreed with this position and suggested that the rejection of the philosophical method of Marxism had led American radicals to pragmatism and the theory of 'American Exceptionalism'. Johnson–Forest's *Balance Sheet* was based on the WP's refusal to accept elements of Trotsky's transitional programme and combined this analysis with arguments about the Americanisation of Bolshevism, Marxist economics and the nature of the American proletariat, as argued in 1945 by James. Politically, James was hostile to the notion of the backwardness of the American proletariat:

> nowhere in the world is the doctrine of social equality so much a matter of both theory and practice as among the people of United States ... yet the American people associate changes with individuals. Social movements are rarely looked upon as the outcome of profound trends and deep forces.[65]

Within this framework, James felt that the American working class had made a positive impact on society. As he notes, 'the wide public interest in personalities, the proletariat through the CIO had taken the initial step of breaking with the bourgeois past'.[66] For James, the CIO was the expression of the American proletariat breaking through its passivity. It combined '[t]he tradition of individual leadership with its own creative mass activity in one of the most astonishing proletariat movements of all times'.[67]

It was clear that by 1947 the Johnson–Forest Tendency was deeply influenced by the power of the CIO and working-class activity, but still wedded to the central notions of the Fourth International programme – the decay of capitalism and its inevitable collapse, the Leninist Party and the crisis of leadership. James himself felt that the American working class was on the verge of revolutionary action, requiring only organisational unity for the development of the revolutionary party as the leadership for the revolution.

By the end of 1947, six years after publicly declaring itself a Tendency, the Johnson–Forest group had published a series of important documents within the Trotskyist movement which signalled a radical break with that current. In doing so they had also developed the outlines of an independent Marxism. In August 1947, the group translated into English and published selected essays from Karl Marx's *Economic and Philosophical Manuscripts*, and James wrote a major essay, *Dialectical Materialism and the Fate of Humanity*. In the same year, the group also published its first independent and comprehensive political document, *The Invading Socialist Society*.

From 1941, the Tendency had carefully and systematically begun to work on the development of its independent Marxist project. It had attracted many others and developed as a faction within the WP. James describes the growth of the group and its activities over the years:

> One day some time in 1946 or 1945 one of our friends brought up a young man to me who went by the name of Willie Gorman. I was struck at once by the extraordinary combination of penetration with which his mind functioned. He soon became one of our intimate circle working at the theory. I was to do the British and French revolutions and the Russian revolution also besides keeping my eyes on things in general. Ray as we called Forest was to translate everything that Lenin had ever written from his earliest days to what has been published after his death. She was also to watch the development in Russia according to the Russian documents. Grace [Lee] had hold of books in Philosophy by Kant and Hegel her business which was to study philosophy from Kant to Feurback [sic] and Hegel and also his writings of Marx which was published in original German but not yet in English or French. Gorman read everything that was produced and took part in all discussions. We also had a basis for meeting and for finances. The man in charge of finances was Lyman Paine and closely associated in everything was his wife Freddie. Their house 629 Hudson Street, was at our disposal

in our group meetings and individual meetings. We were members of the workers' party which consisted of about one thousand members many of whom as I shall show had left New York and went to live in Detroit. At the centre of the Detroit group was Martin Glaberman and his wife Jessie and their house was a small but diminutive function of 629 so that is what we were and we got to work immediately.[68]

Grace Lee, commenting on James's leadership style, observes that 'one of CLR's great gifts was that he could detect the special abilities and interests of individuals and encourage them to use these to enrich the revolutionary struggle. That is one of the main reasons why the few dozen of us in the Johnson–Forest Tendency, as we were known, were able to write so much on so many subjects.'[69]

At the same time, the Tendency was operating on two levels. On the one hand, it was critical of the WP for not being Leninist and Trotskyist. On the other, its study of classical Marxism led it in other directions. A reading of the documents and publications produced by the group exposes these two levels and the contradiction between them. There was both the *Balance Sheet* and the introduction to Marx's *Economic and Philosophical Manuscripts* and the influence of the early Marx.

## The Impact of the Original Marx

Organisationally, the Johnson–Forest Tendency operated against the political trajectory of the Workers' Party. James behaved as a faction leader sending instructions to the leading members from his various political tours. As Constance Webb comments, 'When on tour, Nello sent his political reports to me to transcribe, make copies and deliver.'[70] This was at one level. But at another the group's theoretical work laid the basis for the new conceptions which were enunciated in 1948. This can be gleaned from an examination of James and Forest's introductory essay to the translation of Marx's *Economic and Philosophical Manuscripts*. Reviewing Marx's notion of alienated labour, they state that 'the Marxist problem became the analysis of the labour process'.[71] Asserting that for Marx the worker 'was dominated by the objective results of his labour', they noted that the resolution of the contradiction was for use-value to dominate. 'Many Marxists still see the domination of use-value in a mere multitude of use values, for consumption. They are unaware that they are merely repeating the mistake of Ricardo on a higher scale substituting results for activity.'[72] For James and Forest, use-value of labour had to become the dominant form in production. This had profound implications for political thought since James suggested that 'freedom is an economic necessity and proletarian democracy an economic category. This is no longer a theoretical problem.'[73] James and Forest then root the problem of freedom and proletarian democracy in the 'creative forms imbedded in the senses of modern man and implanted there by the productive forces and productive process'.[74]

This force – which Engels referred to as 'latent socialism' – would inform the text of the Johnson–Forest Tendency's further political evolution. To James and Forest the difference between 'the proletarian revolution and all others is that the revolution itself releases the new economic forces, the creative power of the people, the greatest productive force history has known'.[75] Therefore, Marxism was:

> concerned first and foremost with the creative powers of the masses. That is not Marxian politics and sociology and philosophy. It is Marxian economics. The degeneration of the Russian Revolution has obscured this truth. The revolutionary regeneration of the world proletariat will make it the foundation of every aspect of modern life and thought. Without it there is no escape from barbarism.[76]

From an analysis of revolutionary politics, they moved to the question of the industrial personality:

> The problem of the modern personality is the problem of modern capitalist production ... Man's capacity for seeing, touching, hearing, teaching, feeling, exists in the multitude of objects of productive wealth and the achievements of science which surround him. The masses of men must appropriate these or perish ... the greater the needs of social living, inherent in the socialised nature of modern production, the greater the need for individual self-expression, the more it becomes necessary for the masters of society, themselves slaves of capital, to repress this social expression which is no more and no less than complete democracy.[77]

Inspired by Marx's early work, James and Forest located the nature of the totalitarian state in the context of the divorce between intellectual and manual labour. On the nature of the human individual, they wrote:

> the psychological appeal of totalitarianism and of Fascism in particular, is to transcend all social and individual frustration in the nation, the state, the leader. It cannot be done. In one of these essays Marx says that we should especially avoid re-establishing 'society' as an abstraction opposed to the individual. The individual is the social essence.[78]

This essay represented a critical breakthrough in James's political thought and challenged the traditional conceptions of leading Marxist theorists. The issues of economics, politics and society in general were now to be solved from the perspective of the 'creative powers of the masses'. By developing this line of reasoning, James and Forest restored to Marxism the centrality of agency, which had been lost. The next step for James was to answer the question: if Marxism's chief concern is the 'creative powers of the masses', what should the role of the Marxist organisation be? James and Forest, now freed from the strictures of traditional Trotskyism, had opened the door to redefining the entire architecture of twentieth-century Marxism.

While this essay analysed Marx's notion of labour and sought to develop new categories, *Dialectical Materialism and The Fate of Humanity*, published in September 1947, analysed historical and dialectical materialism in the movement of history. Basing himself on Hegel's notion of contradiction, James argues that the dialectic means that 'Marxism is not a closed system'. From within this perspective he then seeks to develop a notion of inevitability, a conception of the purpose of human beings and a view of Bolshevism as the revolutionary politics of the period.

While in 1943 James's notion of inevitability was mechanical, in 1947 he suggests a qualification and argues that inevitability does not necessarily mean socialism but also barbarism. For James then, the conception of the bankruptcy of bourgeois democracy and the universality of the proletariat were two conflicting forces. The resolution would mean either the victory of socialism or the bourgeoisie suppressing the proletariat – hence barbarism. Inevitability is thus rooted in the outcome of the social and class conflict of capitalism and the timescale was historical. It should be noted that James does not define what constitutes barbarism, other than the suppression of the proletariat. The essay is pivotal however, because for the first time James begins explicitly to tackle the major issues of classical Western political theory. For example, in seeking to develop a notion of what constitutes individual happiness and the character of epistemology, he states:

> Hegel and Marx did not arrive at a theory of knowledge which they applied to nature and society. They arrived at a theory of knowledge from their examination of men in society. Their first question was: What is man? What is the truth about him? Where has he come from and where is he going?[79]

Reviewing these issues, James says that both Marx and Hegel believed that human beings were destined for freedom and happiness. To demonstrate this, James traces the history of Western man and the evolution of Western civilisation. Noting that early Christianity attempted to embrace a universality that was 'extremely concrete, commonality of goods and absolute equality',[80] James claims that 'international socialism is the concrete embodiment of the abstract principle of Christianity'.[81] Here he is not speaking about contemporary efforts to link Christianity with social action (known today as liberation theology), but rather is arguing that the purpose of humanity has been to express concrete universality. For James this universality evolved and showed itself in different forms. According to him:

> To Christian man, the conception of heaven was real and necessary, an integral part of his existence in the objective world ... The history of man is his effort to make the abstract universal concrete. He constantly seeks to destroy, to move aside, that is to say, to negate what impedes his movement towards freedom and happiness. Man is the subject of history ... This is the cardinal principle of the dialectic movement.[82]

At each stage when fundamental transformations occur in this movement, James states that mediation occurs and blunts the drive for concrete universality. This mediation 'usually assumes the form of the state power, and the specific ideological combinations of abstract and concrete, to bind the new relations, are developed by the philosophy of the age'.[83] Criticising Hegel, James writes:

> Hegel saw objective history as the successive manifestation of a world spirit. Marx placed the objective movement in the process of production. Hegel had been driven to see the perpetual quest for universality as necessarily confined to the process of knowledge. Marx reversed this and rooted the quest for universality in the need for the free and full development of all the inherent and acquired characteristics of the individual in productive and intellectual labour ... Marx saw future society as headed for ruin except under the rulership of the proletariat and the vanishing distinction between intellectual and manual labour.[84]

Concrete universality, therefore, and the struggle for happiness and freedom – the process of self-actualisation – was only possible with proletarian self-emancipation. The social personality of Matthew Bondman had now found a theory and purpose. For James in 1947, this theory was Bolshevism. He notes that 'for Lenin, reason, order, historical creativeness, lay precisely in the forces which would destroy the old world'.[85] For the intellectuals, James argues, this fact was difficult to grasp. In 1947 James had not yet decided that the age of Bolshevism had passed. However, the major issues raised by the Tendency increasingly ran counter to a key element of Bolshevism – the Leninist vanguard party – and it was only a matter of time before this tenet would be challenged.

## Invading Socialist Society

Written by James, Forest and Grace Lee Boggs and published immediately after leaving the WP, *Invading Socialist Society* was, in James's words, 'the fundamental document of the Johnson–Forest Tendency'.[86] It restates the theory of state capitalism and critiques the work of the leading Trotskyist economist Ernest Mandel on the nature of Soviet society. At the level of political analysis, the document marks a fundamental break with traditional Trotskyist and Leninist analysis, particularly in relation to the party, spontaneity and the mass movement. It also places in sharp definition James's conception of socialism and the relationship between democracy and socialism.

The document characterises the fundamental conflict in the current stage of world history as 'capital labour' antagonism in the context of a world market. In this situation, it argues, 'Russia must fight for world domination or perish. It is subjected to all the laws of the world market. Socialism in a single country is dead even for Stalin.'[87]

All this was not new for the Tendency, but was an elaboration of positions developed between 1941 and 1947. However, *Invading Socialist Society* was pivotal because for the first time the Tendency explicitly raised the critical issue of the party and the masses. This it did at two levels. At the first level it criticised the traditional Trotskyist analysis of Stalinist parties as 'tools of the Kremlin'[88] suggesting instead that they were the 'organic product of the mode of capitalism at this stage'.[89] At the second level the Tendency discussed the role and function of political parties as political instruments and their relation to the mass struggle of the proletariat. Here James revisited traditional arguments in Marxism, with one major difference. While many Marxists had argued about the relationship between consciousness, organisation and spontaneity within the framework of the democratic centralism of the Leninist party, James's focus was the party itself:

> The self-mobilisation of the masses is the dominating social and political feature of our age ... The workers today are aware of the tremendous problems involved in the overthrow of bourgeois society. They seek a philosophy of life, a place, an organisation, a social force which will not only be the direct expression of the proletarian class struggle, but direct force with which to rebuild society ... The genuine mass organisation of the American

proletariat, the socially most advanced social entity the world has ever seen ... this is the invading socialist society of our day.[90]

It is clear that James and the Tendency now viewed the party as obsolete, since the proletariat had arrived at a new historical phase, one where it sought to 'substitute instead a meaningful creative activity with a social aim as the end and the exercise of its natural and required faculties as the means'.[91]

However, *Invading Socialist Society* is contradictory because while critiquing the Leninist party it did not argue for new organisational forms and was still wedded to the notions of a Leninist political party, demonstrating that the Tendency had not decisively broken with Trotskyism. This apparent contradiction can perhaps be explained by the fact that the Tendency at the time was negotiating its re-entry to the SWP.

What is at the root of the new historical stage which now required new forms of organisation? James writes:

Driven by the economic and social transformations (and the psychological responses engendered by these) the oppressed classes *turn away from the old political forms and seek to encompass the need of the all-embracing organisation*. History is and will be inexhaustible in its combinations. Soviets and the new party may appear together or in combined forms. The new content constantly appears in old forms.[92] (emphasis added)

For James, the proletariat's organisational political response to the new stage of capitalism and statification of production was mass self-mobilisation. This was a totally new conception in the Marxist movement which James was to define and develop further in 1948 in *Notes on Dialectics*.

The two levels at which the Tendency operated created a situation where they were attempting to fuse the transitional programme of Trotsky with the new political categories being created. For example, in spite of the notion of the proletariat's self-mobilisation in a new stage, *Invading Socialist Society* still proclaimed that 'the task of the Fourth International is to drive as clear a line between bourgeois nationalisation and proletarian nationalisation as the revolutionary Third International drove between bourgeois democracy and proletarian democracy'.[93] Although contradictory, *Invading Socialist Society* posits the major positions which James and the Johnson–Forest Tendency would explore in their subsequent works.

What were the influences which led James to these new conceptions? Writing in *Balance Sheet 1940–1947*, he discusses the history of the Johnson–Forest Tendency and notes that:

The Johnson–Forest Tendency became conscious of itself early in 1941 in the discussion on the Russian question ... Johnson and Forest, from the very beginning, considered a break with Trotsky on a fundamental question to be the most serious step imaginable for any Marxist ... we found in Russia the key to the most profound philosophic and abstract theories of Marx's analysis of capitalism ... we were convinced on a re-examination of Marx's capital that the solution to the economic ills of capitalism was the *human solution, not any reorganisation of property but the emergence of the proletariat ready to use the vast potentialities created by capitalism itself.*[94] (emphasis added)

Attempting to grapple with the phenomenon of state capitalism, James undertook a re-examination of classical Marxism. He brought to this project a mind trained in the Western intellectual tradition in a British colony. At the same time, he was deeply influenced by the life of ne'er-do-well Matthew Bondman who had played cricket under his grandmother's window and the nationalist self-activities of the Trinidad working class. The logic of state capitalism led him to new political forms. These he found in the activities of the proletariat in the United States. By 1947, nine years after arriving in America, James was ready to formulate an independent Marxist theory. Caliban had re-entered history, he was now about to rewrite it.

# CHAPTER 5

# James and the Race Question

In Chapter 3 we noted that in *The Black Jacobins* James had developed a position on race and class. For James, race was not incidental, and to think of it in those terms was to make 'an error only less grave than to make it fundamental'.[1] We also noted that the primary reason for James's lecture tour of the United States was because the SWP needed assistance on the race question: at that time the SWP had fewer than a dozen black members. This was reaffirmed in a letter Trotsky wrote to James Cannon: 'the party cannot postpone this extremely important question any longer. James's sojourn in the States is very important for the serious and energetic beginning of this work.'[2]

James's colonial background and anti-colonial work in London with George Padmore, his editorship of the *International African Opinion* and his colour made him the most suitable revolutionary of the Trotskyist current to intervene in the black liberation struggles in the United States. After the tour, James travelled to Mexico to begin discussions with Trotsky on the 'Negro Question'. This was critical to James's political evolution as it put him directly into dialogue with Trotsky.

## Black Struggle and Context in the United States

In the 1920s, there was a massive migration of African-Americans from the southern states where they had principally been employed in agriculture to the north. As economic expansion created a huge demand for industrial labour African-Americans took jobs in Pittsburgh steel mills, Detroit car plants and stockyards of Chicago. The migration not only increased the ranks of the black proletariat but doubled the size of the black population in many northern cities. In Detroit, for example, the black population swelled from 5741 in 1910 to 40,838 by 1921. Life in the north however was no paradise, as racial discrimination in industrial life was rampant.

In the immediate post-World War I period, a new political militancy was characteristic of the African-American population. In September 1919, after a 'race riot' in Knoxville, Tennessee, one newspaper commented:

the white inhabitants were anticipating great fun seeing negroes scurrying before them like so many rats driven by flames. They went, they saw, they were defeated. They saw fire, and volley belched forth from the mouths of rifles and revolvers held by the hands of *black men who now have stiff backs*.[3] (emphasis added)

The militant mood of the African-American population was summed up in a poem written by the Jamaican poet Claude McKay in 1919, 'If we must die'. In the 1920s, lynching was still prevalent. Between 1889 and 1922 the National Association for the Advancement of Colored People (NAACP) reported that 3436 blacks were lynched and in 1922 the Dyer Anti-Lynching Bill was defeated in the Senate. Within this frame of migration, proletarisation and militancy, many blacks attempted to join trade unions, but the labour movement, still in the grips of white racism, did not respond favourably. By 1917, according to Philip Foner, the 'AF of L had done nothing but discuss the problem created by the influx of black workers in industry ... nor was the record on the local level much better. Throughout the period evidence of discrimination by white unions mounted.'[4]

Racial oppression laid the basis for the independent organisations of the African-American population. In the domain of labour, before World War I, there was only one major independent black labour group. In 1917 an attempt was made to establish a confederation of black labour – the Colored Employees of America – which folded by the end of the year. In that same year A. Philip Randolph and Chandler Owen, both members of the Socialist Party, established a newspaper, *The Messenger*, to promote unionism and socialism among blacks. Another radical, Cyril Briggs, after leaving the Socialist Party in 1917 claiming that it was too moderate, particularly on the Negro Question, founded *The Crusader* and later formed the revolutionary black socialist organisation, The African Blood Brotherhood. This organisation advocated 'absolute race equality – political, economic, social and fellowship within the darker masses and with the class conscious revolutionary white workers'.[5] It also argued for the liberation of Africa from colonialism.

In 1925, Randolph formed the Brotherhood of Sleeping Car Porters (BSCP). The struggle of the BSCP for union recognition was epic. By 1926, it had mobilised the African-American community, and as Foner observes, developed a coherent strategy which involved working with other black organisations:

The NAACP and locals of the National Urban League endorsed the Brotherhood, and some black churches even permitted it to use their buildings for meetings. Most important of all, many black workers came to see the Brotherhood both as a symbol of the Negro's claim to dignity, respect and a decent livelihood and as a test of the ability of black workers to build and maintain an effective union.[6]

However, no organisation in this period expressed black militancy and the text of a nationalist response to racial oppression more than the Garvey movement – The Universal Negro Improvement Association (UNIA). Marcus Garvey launched the American chapter of the UNIA in 1916 and by 1921, according to Tony Martin, 'Garvey was unquestionably the leader of the largest organisation of its type in the history of the race'.[7] The basis for his success was his ability to tap into the vast wellspring of black nationalism. The main strength of the UNIA was its ability to inspire black pride globally and to bring together in organisation and motion the vast energies of black people. Its early programme had two major planks – the building of a free African nation and an uncompromising position in defence of racial and social equality for blacks internationally. In the United States the social backbone of the Garvey movement was the blacks who had migrated to the north and the recently formed black proletariat. Other organisations also benefited from this new militancy and by 1919 the membership of the NAACP, led by Dr W.E.B. DuBois numbered 91,000.

In general, the 1920s was a critical period in African-American history. Known as the period of the 'Harlem Renaissance', it was characterised by what Alain Locke described as the 'New Negro'. This 'New Negro' was defiant and his or her activities stamped a presence in American society. The core of these activities was the cultural and political awakening of African-Americans. One writer observes that it was

> the most important cultural movement which African-Americans had experienced since their ancestors had been extirpated from their African homeland; it displayed an increase in the artistic and literary productivity of the African-Americans such as had never been witnessed before. The literary movement was undoubtedly the result of the surge in group expression, self-assertion, and self-determination that were being sought by African-Americans during the years immediately following World War I.[8]

In the political domain, the myriad of African-American organisations added a fresh dynamic to black struggles. Participating in the revival were blacks from Africa and the Caribbean. In a profound way, Harlem in the 1920s as the black Mecca was the home for the most progressive thought in the black world.

It should be noted that the Caribbean segment of the black world contributed significantly to this cultural awakening. In the late nineteenth and early twentieth centuries, 25,000 Caribbean people migrated to the United States. In the 1920s at the height of the Harlem Renaissance, one quarter of the black population in Harlem were foreign blacks, the majority from the Caribbean.[9] DuBois had already noted that in the nineteenth century 'West Indians were mainly responsible for the manhood programmes presented by the race'.[10] This trend continued to some degree in the 1920s, not only with Garvey, but also through the literary work of Claude McKay and the political radicals, W.A. Domingo, Richard B. Moore and Cyril Briggs. In the late 1930s, therefore, when James began to study the race question, he was continuing in that black tradition which had helped shape the parameters of the African-American liberation struggles.

In 1922, both Briggs and Moore had joined the communist movement. In 1925 they were co-founders of the Negro Labour Congress. In 1930, Moore – by then a leading member of the party – was selected on the party's ticket for the position of Attorney General. Moore's position on the struggle against racial oppression was expressed in an article written in 1929 in the Communist Party's newspaper, *The Daily Worker*:

> The condition of the Negro masses in America grows steadily worse as the racial caste system spreads more and more into the north and west ... large sections of the white workers of Europe, America and Africa are bribed with a share of the imperialist spoils ... The social development of the system of racial caste oppression clearly proves that it is rooted in the economic exploitation of the capitalist imperialist class system. Race oppression is a form of capitalist imperialist class oppression. The Negro problem cannot be solved save through the solution of the labour problem. The labour problem cannot be solved unless the race problem is solved.[11]

The analysis linked labour exploitation and racial oppression. However, its core was class struggle and the struggle of the proletariat, typical of the analysis of the communist movement of the period. By the end of the 1920s, although West Indians were participating in the radical left movement in the United States, none had made a distinctive contribution to the analysis of race and class within the Marxist tradition. By the time James arrived in the United States the Garvey movement had declined. Within the labour movement, attempts were being made to organise blacks. One of the most significant of these was the organisation of black steel workers by the Steel Workers Organising Committee: several African-Americans became organisers.[12] At the forefront of the general organisational drive within the labour movement was the Congress of Industrial Organisations (CIO):

Beginning in 1936, the CIO conducted the most massive organising campaign in American Labour History. Unlike the traditional racial policies of the AF of L, the CIO's policy from the first was to open its doors to all black workers on an equal basis. There was no constitutional bar, no segregation of blacks into separate locals, no Jim Crow rituals. Black organisers were employed in all the initial CIO campaigns as the most effective way to demonstrate that the policy of non-discrimination was more than empty words and would be carried through.[13]

The CIO was supported by the independent National Negro Congress and several of their organisers became CIO members and activists. The NAACP also supported the CIO, proclaiming in an editorial that 'blacks had everything to gain and nothing to lose by affiliation with the CIO'.[14]

The African-American population numbered about 13 million in 1940. Their independent struggles in the 1920s and 1930s had been distinguished by their courage and innovation. However, racial oppression had been neither eradicated nor marginalised. James's arrival in the United States therefore ocurred within the context of growing independent activities of the African-American population, which would not only shape his conceptions of the black liberation struggle, but his political theory of self-determination too.

## Black Nationalism and Socialism – The Marxist Tradition

Marxism's legacy to nationalism has been a contradictory one. Marx and Engels, writing in the period of capitalist ascendancy, were influenced by Hegel's notions of 'historic' and 'non-historic' peoples. At the core of Marx's historical schema was the conception that each historical stage was an advancement over the preceding one. Since the schema was primarily extrapolated from European experience, there was a tendency in Marx's thinking to categorise countries as backward or advanced, and by extension, their population too. Influenced also by early anthropological work, Marx and Engels did not see any revolutionary potential in non-Western peoples or their civilisations. Indeed, in many instances, particularly in their early writings, they implied that the best thing for these countries was to catch up with the Europeans.[15] For example in 1850, Marx condoned the United States' attacks on Mexico, observing:

> that splendid California has been taken away from the *lazy* Mexicans who could not do anything with it. That the *energetic* Yankees by rapid exploitation of the Californian gold mines ... for the first time really opened the Pacific Ocean to civilisation.[16]
> (emphasis added)

The Irish struggles for self-determination changed Marx's and Engels's view on the nationality question, and by 1882 Engels was writing to Kautsky: 'An international movement of the proletariat is in general only possible between independent nations ... To get rid of national oppression is the basic condition of all healthy and free development.'[17]

Marx and Engels had paid no serious attention specifically to the racial oppression of African-Americans. The major references to African-Americans are in Marx's *Poverty of Philosophy* (1846) where he states:

> direct slavery is just as much the pivot of bourgeois industry as machinery, credits, etc. Without slavery you have no cotton, without cotton you have no modern industry ... Thus slavery is an economic category of the greatest importance ... Without slavery North America would be transformed into a patriarchal country.[18]

Another reference is in a letter of 1862 where Marx discusses the American Civil War and observes that 'a single Negro regiment would have a remarkable effect on southern nerves'.[19] Another comment is to be found in Engels's comments on slavery in 1864, where he notes that as soon as 'slavery – that greatest of obstacles to the political and social development of the United States – has been smashed, the country will experience a boom'.[20] In 1852, Marx wrote to Engels, on reviewing a book on the slave trade:

> The only thing of positive interest in the book is comparison between the former English Negro Slavery in Jamaica, etc. and the Negro Slavery of the United States. The present generation of Negroes in America, on the other hand, is a native product, more or less Yankeefied, English-speaking etc. ... and therefore *fit for emancipation*.[21] (emphasis added)

The obvious assumption is the notion that Africans were not civilised and were as a consequence non-historic people unfit for freedom. It is clear that Marx and Engels did not leave a consistent revolutionary legacy about national and racial oppression and were themselves prisoners of a traditional Western intellectual paradigm which did not consider Africans as fully human unless they were influenced by Western civilisation.

Within the early Marxist tradition, Otto Bauer's contribution on nationalism is significant. His *The Nationality Question and Social Democracy* (1907), departed from the traditional Marxist position on national oppression, to give it 'relative autonomy'.

The Russian Revolution opened another phase in Marxist conceptions on nationality. Lenin had consistently advanced the political position that Russia was a 'prison of peoples'. Although in 1903 he advocated a centralist party and fought against the Jewish Bund developing an independent revolutionary organisation, by the second congress of the Third International, having identified imperialism as the fundamental characteristic of the epoch, he openly supported national struggles. In 1919, in opening a debate on the national question, he asserted: 'What is important, the fundamental idea of our thesis? It is the difference between oppressed and oppressor nations':[22]

> The dialectic of history is such that small nations powerless as an independent factor in the struggle against imperialism play a part as one of the ferments one of the bacilli which will help the real power against imperialism to come to the scene, namely the socialist proletariat.[23]

This perspective was to become one of the major ingredients of James's conception of the black liberation struggle in the United States and its role in the American socialist revolution. If the early European-based Marxist movement ignored the 'Negro Question', the American movement could not. However, the left movement, immigrant in origin, developed a vulgar lack of sensitivity to the question. At the Socialist Party convention in 1901, no resolution condemned racism or any of its manifestations. Instead, guilty of economic reductionism, the resolution on black workers declared 'to the Negro Worker the identity of his interests and struggles with the interests and struggles of workers of all lands'.[24] Eugene Debs, the party leader, stated the party's position clearly when he declared: 'We have nothing special to offer the Negro and we cannot make special appeals to all races. The Socialist Party is the party of the working class of the whole world.'[25] Even though early socialism in the United States did not recognise racial or national oppression of African-Americans, this did not stop many black radicals joining the party, although the process was something of a revolving door:

> of the blacks who did join the SP, all at one time or another were critical of its racism ... W.E.B. Du Bois who joined in 1910 resigned in 1912 ... Du Bois wrote in the *New Review* that theoretical socialism of the twentieth century meets a critical dilemma in facing up to the problems of racism.[26]

It was clear that once socialist theory as a Western critique of capitalism had identified the historic agency for the overthrow of the system – the proletariat – it did not recognise the other social forces oppressed by capital, nor did it recognise the validity of the activity of these social forces. At work was a reductionist tendency as well as a Eurocentric focus, which had come to dominate Marxist theory. The result was the failure to synthesise socialism with the concrete political expressions of the black radical tradition which by then had emerged. When the Communist Party was formed after the 1919 split, the party's 1920 declaration on the 'Negro Question' paid no special attention to race but stated:

> The racial expression of the Negro is simply the expression of his economic bondage and oppression, each intensifying the other. This complicates the problem, but does not alter its fundamental proletarian character. The Communist party will carry on agitation among Negro workers to unite them with all class conscious workers.[27]

Wilson Record observes, however, that in practice there were significant differences between the Communist Party and Socialist Party political planks, and that 'whereas the socialists had regarded the Negro as a deterrent to effective organisation of the American working class – or else, for all practical purposes, had ignored him – the Communists regarded him as an asset'.[28] At the theoretical level, the Communist Party's position on the 'Negro Question' was to remain unchanged for almost a decade. Although the party paid some attention to the question, it did not recruit blacks in large numbers before 1928. That fact was recognised by the Comintern when its 1928 Congress declared that

> the party as a whole has not sufficiently realised the significance of work among the Negroes and that the Negroes should be considered not as a special task of the Negro comrades, but as one of the special revolutionary tasks of every communist of the whole Party.[29]

An earlier conference of the party had outlined its goals in relation to the 'Negro Question', specifically linking the 'racial demands of Negroes to economic and political struggles of the working class [and] to organise Negro workers under workers [Communist] Party leadership'.[30] While the party recognised the militancy of the African-Americans, it attributed to this militancy no fundamental revolutionary value outside the frame of communist control. What was operating here was not just reductionism, but organisational centralism.

In 1925, black trade unionists and progressive intellectuals organised, with the advice of the party, the American Negro Labour Congress. During the early 1920s, the party had conflictual relations with the mass-based UNIA, as party members in the UNIA were told to attempt to struggle against what many on the left called at the time 'Negro Zionism'.

In 1928 it was clear that black political militancy was a potent political force and this fact influenced the Communist International debate of the 'Negro Question' seriously. (It had done so earlier in 1922, but had not arrived at any major conclusions.) The 1928

Congress declared that the 'Negro Question' was a 'national problem' and therefore its solutions were to be based on the Leninist notion of national self-determination:

> African-Americans were not just a nationality, but a nation separate and distinct from mainstream white American society, and that in the economic and social conditions and class relations of the Negro people, there are increasing forces which serve as a basis for the development of a Negro nation.[31]

The definition of the African-American struggle as a national one meant that while advocating equal rights for African-Americans, the communist party would also now advocate national self-determination. Thus the party programme stated: 'The struggle for equal rights of Negroes does not in any way exclude recognition and support of their rights to their own special schools, government organs, etc.'[32]

To achieve national self-determination, the party programme demanded the confiscation of the large plantations in the South and the establishment of a Negro state in the Black Belt. The programme declared 'the complete and unlimited right of the Negro majority to exercise governmental authority in the entire territory of the Black Belt, as well as to decide on the relations between their territory and other nations'.[33] However, Wilson Record observes a dual approach by the party towards the resolution and comments that 'in publications, particularly the theoretical and directional organs, the Party placed great emphasis on the self-determination doctrine, but in its more practical day to day work among Negroes, it was obscured and even consciously played down'.[34]

Although black activists like Cyril Briggs supported the Black Belt proposal, and the party energetically defended it, African-Americans did not flock to join the party. There were three reasons for this. First, the area of the Black Belt – Texas to Virginia – had been fragmented by the waves of migration during World War I and in the 1920s. Second, the struggle for self-determination meant that the struggle of blacks could result in the formation of a nation. However, it could not be foisted on them. Finally, in a context where segregation and Jim Crowism were prevalent, such a plan from a predominantly white organisation, in spite of its 'revolutionary' nature, was viewed by many as another form of segregation.

Self-determination for the Black Belt was consistently advocated between 1928 and 1934, throughout the Depression, while party cadres worked tirelessly in organising black workers into unemployed councils. Mark Naison observes that:

in almost every city in which there was a large black community, Atlanta, Birmingham, Detroit, Chicago, Richmond, New York, black and white communist organisers went to the black unemployed and organised them into unemployed councils, sprouting a strange ideology that combined 'black and white unite and fight' with self-determination in the Black Belt.[35]

In 1935, the Comintern, reflecting the political domination of Stalin and preoccupied with Germany's threat to the Soviet Union, shifted its policy and developed the Popular Front. According to George Padmore this 'put a brake upon the anti-imperialist work of its affiliate sections and thereby sacrifice[d] the young national liberation movements in Asia and Africa'.[36] In the United States, the policy turn required the Communist Party to support liberal democracy. It also meant that activities critical of the American state and Roosevelt were either dropped or muted. As a result the party disbanded the Share Croppers' Union, and discontinued its paper, *The Negro Liberation*. By the time the news broke that the Soviet Union had sold arms to Italy during Italy's invasion of Abyssinia, the party's work on the 'Negro Question' was in disarray. The arms episode triggered resignations from the party's black members so that during the 1940s black membership became marginal, and by the late 1950s as the civil rights movement began to gather pace, the party was in no position to play a leading role. It was on the eve of World War II, and within the context of the failure of the Communist Party to integrate the race question as part of an integrated revolutionary strategy, the experience of the black masses in the early twentieth century in the Garvey movement and the emergence of the 'New Negro' that James began to develop his discourse on the African-American liberation struggle.

## James's Intervention

In 1933, Trotsky had advocated that the small Trotskyist movement undertake a study of the 'Negro Question'. In fact, in discussion he chided the movement, accusing his comrades of 'American chauvinism'[37] and suggested that blacks 'have full right to self-determination when they so desired'.[38] In April 1939, James – who by then had been in the United States for six months – led an SWP delegation to Mexico to meet Trotsky. Although he had begun to study the race question in America and had familiarised himself with the African-American community, James's major preparation for the meeting indicated that while he supported self-determination in theory, he was of the view that 'the Negro, fortunately for socialism, does not want self-determination'.[39] This early statement thus revealed that while James had operated in a dual political

capacity in England – the Trotskyist movement and the African
liberation movement – he had not yet broken with the mainstream
Marxist theory which viewed the social struggles of minorities as
of episodic value. His meeting with Trotsky confirmed this. The
discussion began with Trotsky agreeing with James's suggested
format. James's analysis suggested that the question of self-
determination was irrelevant in the American context:

> No one denies the Negroes' right to self-determination. It is a
> question of whether we should advocate it. In Africa and in the
> West Indies we advocate self-determination ... because a large
> majority of the people want it ... In America the situation is
> different. *The Negro desperately wants to be an American citizen.*[40]
> (emphasis added)

Turning to the Garvey movement and its role, James notes,
'Garvey raised the slogan "Back to Africa" but the Negroes who
followed him did not believe for the most part that they were really
going back to Africa'.[41] Claiming that one of the problems in 1919
was the absence of a white workers' organisation and the absence
of a revolutionary political programme calling blacks and white
workers to unite, James says, 'the Negroes were just back from the
War – militant and having no offer of assistance, they naturally
concentrated on their own particular affairs'.[42] He then makes the
point that 'nationalist movements have tended to disappear as the
Negro saw the opportunity to fight with organised workers and gain
something'.[43] In discussing the concept of a black state, James argues:
'for us to propose that the Negro should have this black state for
himself is asking too much from the white workers'.[44] He then
proposes:

(1) That we are for the right of self-determination;
(2) if some demand should arise among the Negroes for the right
    of self-determination we should support it;
(3) we do not go out of our way to raise this slogan and place
    an unnecessary barrier between ourselves and socialism;
(4) an investigation should be made into these movements;
    the one led by Garvey and the movement centering around
    Liberia.[45]

A number of issues are raised here. On self-determination for
African-Americans, James held to the traditional Marxist line,
demonstrating that he had not resolved the issue of nationality and
Marxism. Although recognising that African-Americans were
struggling to be 'American citizens', he did not consider this to be
the struggles of a nationality. Nor did James see at the time that it
was their exclusion from this process which could lay the basis for
a struggle of self-determination. His comment on 'Negroes ...

concentrating on their own affairs' is superficial and fails to see that this concentration was a necessary requirement for a broader political struggle and was not simply the result of a lack of a revolutionary party and the failure of the outreach of white workers. The position James advocated was inadequate, lacking both dialectical and historical imagination, and reveals him to be over-concerned with the role and support of white workers in the black struggle. This made him dismissive of the Garvey movement, although he advocated that the party should study it. In the main, James at this stage lacked an appreciation of the self-activity of oppressed peoples and Trotsky was sharply critical:

> I do not quite understand whether Comrade Johnson proposes to eliminate the slogan of self-determination for the Negroes from our programme ... As a party we can remain absolutely neutral on this ... I believe that the differences between the West Indies, Catalania, Poland and the situation of the Negroes in the States are not so decisive.[46]

Turning to the Garvey movement Trotsky notes:

> The American Negroes gathered under the banner of the Back to Africa movement because it seemed a possible fulfilment of their wish for their own home. They did not want to go to Africa. It was the expression of a mystic desire for a home in which they would be free of the domination of whites.[47]

Trotsky then advocates that if blacks wanted self-determination,

> it is not reactionary ... Comrade Johnson used three verbs – 'support', 'advocate' and 'inject' ... the idea of self-determination. I do not propose for the party to advocate ... but only to proclaim our obligation to support the struggle for self-determination if the Negroes themselves want it. It is not a question of our Negro comrades. It is a question of 13 or 14 million Negroes.[48]

James then affirms his agreement with Trotsky, but says, 'you seem to think that there is a greater possibility of the Negroes wanting self-determination than I think is probable'.[49] He suggests that even though the struggles of blacks for self-determination might be 'reactionary' since the 'idea of separating is a step backward so far as a socialist society is concerned, if the white workers extend a hand to the Negro, he will not want self-determination'.[50] Trotsky's response was sharp:

> It is so abstract because the realisation of this slogan can be reached only as the 13 or 14 million Negroes feel that the domination by the whites is terminated. To fight for the possibility

of realising an independent state is sign of great moral and political awakening.[51]

Although the exchange was unresolved, discussion moved on to organisational matters. At that level James proposed a black organisation and a programme of party work amongst the African-American population divided between theory and organisation. In the theoretical domain, the party was to study and produce documents which would examine the nodal moments of the black radical tradition – the emancipation process in San Domingo, the British Empire and the struggles against slavery and the civil war in the United States. At the organisational level James proposed a weekly newspaper and regular pamphlets, that the *International African Opinion* become a monthly journal devoted to theory, and that a group of black intellectuals and revolutionary activists be assembled to discuss the questions of the war and socialism. The organisation, while fighting as a 'Negro Organisation', had however to distinguish itself from 'Garveyism'.[52] One plank of the programme prefigured a modality of action which became successful in the later civil rights movement. This suggested that

> discrimination in restaurants should be fought by a campaign. A number of Negroes in any area go into a restaurant all together, ordering for instance some coffee, and refuse to come out until they are served. It would be possible to sit there for a whole day in a very orderly manner and throw upon the police the necessity of removing these Negroes. A campaign to be built around such action.[53]

The discussions with Trotsky helped shape James's interventions on the 'Negro Question'. However, there is a contradiction in James's early intervention: his movement from opposition to the concept of self-determination of African-Americans to his proposal of a black organisation. In the discussions, James had to convince Trotsky of the need for this political form, although Trotsky's analysis of the issue as one of nationality aided his conversion. But in James's case unless he was convinced of Trotsky's arguments on self-determination and nationality, the notion of a black organisation was illogical. If James had a positive view of nationality, why did he present a contrary position in the early discussions? Answers to this conundrum can only be speculative, but it is important to note that James's early exposition on the race question did not mark any significant new political departures.

By July 1939 James had begun to come to grips with black nationalism. In the resolution to the SWP which proposed the establishment of a 'National Negro Department', he writes:

The awakening political consciousness of the Negro not unnaturally takes the form of a desire for independent action uncontrolled by whites. The Negroes have long felt, and more than ever feel today the urge to create their own organisations under their own leaders, and thus assert not only in theory, but in action, their claim to complete equality with other American citizens. Such a desire is legitimate and must be vigorously supported even when it takes the form of a rather aggressive chauvinism. Black chauvinism in America today is merely the natural excess of the desire for equality and is essentially progressive while American chauvinism is essentially reactionary'.[54]

The resolution indicates that James was still working within the confines of traditional Trotskyism and that notions of independent black struggle and its valid contribution to socialism were not yet part of his political paradigm. It would take practical work with black sharecroppers in the South and an indepth study of the black radical tradition in the United States to break free of these strictures.

In December 1939, James published a major essay, *Revolution and the Negro* in which he asserted that the Negro's revolutionary history is rich, inspiring and unknown.[55] However, the central importance of this essay is James's assertion that 'what we as Marxists have to see is the tremendous role played by the Negroes in the transformation of Western civilisation from feudalism to capitalism'.[56] This became a pivotal argument: at each decisive stage of the evolution of the modern West, the struggles of blacks had played a central role. In developing his position, James was attempting to document an alternative discourse and suggest its impact on the dominant radical political discourse and the mainstream intellectual tradition. In doing so he was not only mapping new directions in the reading of revolutionary history, but overturning the intellectual basis of the assumptions which guided radical politics. James chose two episodes to demonstrate his position: the American Civil War and the Haitian Revolution. After describing the role of blacks in both, he states:

> Between 1871 and 1965 the proletariat revolution was dormant. In Africa the Negroes fought vainly to maintain their independence against imperialist invasions. But the Russian Revolution of 1905 was the forerunner of a new era that began with the October Revolution in 1917. While half a million Negroes fought with the French Revolution in 1789, today the socialist revolution in Europe has as its potential allies over 120 million Negroes in Africa.[57]

James then outlines the resistance activities of African peoples and proclaims that 'the Negroes in Africa are caged and ... against the bars continuously. It is the European proletariat that holds the key.'[58] The essay therefore also reveals that although James was conducting historical research which had shown him that African resistance had a life of its own, he nevertheless continued as an international socialist to subordinate these struggles to the activities of the European proletariat. This contradiction is brought into sharp focus when he writes at the end of the essay: 'in Africa, in America, in the West Indies, on a national and international scale, the millions of Negroes will raise their heads, rise up from their knees and write some of the most massive and brilliant chapters in history of international socialism'.[59] Clearly James had now moved to establish the critical moments of the black radical tradition and its relationship to decisive stages in the evolution of a tradition of Western political struggles. However, he had not yet come to grips with the specific validity of the black tradition or its importance.

In 1940 when James left the SWP, he began writing a weekly column for the WP's *Labour Action* titled 'The Negro Fight'. The column focused on racial discrimination, the war and the role of African-Americans. James's articles in this period were also anti-colonial and he used his extensive contacts to get Fenner Brockway and George Padmore to contribute to the paper. In 1941 James was assigned to political work in Missouri. The WP branch there had made successful contacts with predominantly black sharecroppers who were becoming restive. Sent primarily to cover the story for *Labour Action*, James's first articles described the poverty and racism in Missouri, as well as the Communist Party's domination of the union. In 1942 the sharecroppers went on strike and James wrote their strike pamphlet, *Down with Starvation Wages in South East Missouri*.

The pamphlet begins with the slogan 'Black and white unite and fight' and throughout there are appeals to black and white workers to unite in the struggle. James argues that unity is necessary since the 'landlords will try to start race riots', and that 'white and coloured together [are] like one race – the race of labour, united we stand, divided we fall'.[60] The pamphlet then makes an appeal to white workers, advocating that 'old prejudices' be forgotten and suggesting that the division between black and white workers was one factor which was responsible for the socio-economic conditions of the South. The pamphlet did not speak of any black independent organisation, but urged labour and racial solidarity. Years later James observed:

> This is a wonderful piece of work. I'll tell you why ... when the time came for us to have the strike, I called some of the leaders

together and said, 'we have to publish something', ... they said
yes. So I sat down with my pen and notebook and said 'Well
what shall we say' ... and I went through each of them, five or
six of them; each said his piece, and I joined them together.
Everybody said what he thought was important. I didn't write
anything ... They said what they thought and I put it together.[61]

Three elements emerge from the pamphlet and its production.
First was James's practice of keen listening, just as he had done in
Trinidad when writing his short story *La Divina Pastora*. The
second is the participant–observer style. This had important political
implications. For if the proletariat by their self-activity were the
embodiment of socialism as James suggested in *Invading Socialist
Society*, then the role of the revolutionary could not be that of
vanguard leader, but must be that of facilitator. At this time James
had not yet fully worked out this conception which would shatter
the old Leninist framework. The third element is that politically
the pamphlet does not say anything fundamentally new about the
nature of African-Americans' struggle. However, the experience
made a lasting impression on James and was the most successful
WP wartime mass activity.

For the next two years, James studied the race question and began
to modify his position. In a letter to Constance Webb written on
28 July 1944, he writes:

The book I shall write will be American history and the Negro
and I shall fit the Negro in the framework of history, American
economic and historical development. I have the outlines. I shall
have to study the literature and then when I have it all clear, I
shall write the political study. For politics embraces all forms
of the life of a community and a serious political study is
nonsensical without a grasp of the whole life of the community.[62]

In another letter to Constance Webb, in which James is describing
his meeting with the African-American writer Richard Wright, he
notes:

The Negroes represent a force in the future development of
American society out of all proportion [sic] to their members.
The repression has created such a frustration that this when
socially motivated will become one of the most powerful social
forces in the country. Finally, neither white America *nor black
America* has faced the Negro question for the deep fundamental
thing that it is in the life of the *nation as a whole*. He has worked
at it artistically, I through history. But our conclusions are
identical.[63] (emphasis in the original)

In the same letter, he notes:

the Negro is 'nationalist' to the heart and is perfectly right to be so. His racism, his nationalism, are a necessary means of giving him strength, self-respect and organisation *in order to fight for integration into American Society*. It is a perfect example of dialectical contradiction.[64] (emphasis in the original)

Importantly, James is still unclear about critical elements of a black response to racism. In the 1939 document to the SWP he labelled black nationalism 'black chauvinism' and in this letter, nationalist written in quotes seems to indicate that James still did not like the use of the word. His definition of black nationalist responses as racism seems to indicate too that at a theoretical level he still had not sorted out all the complex issues which are attendant in African-American struggles.

In a subsequent letter to Constance Webb, James traces the historical development of African-Americans' struggle and in outline form he notes that 'after the abolition of slavery Negroes join the Republican party, i.e., the revolutionary party. They seek complete citizenship. After reconstruction they recognise that there is no hope there.'[65] He then notes that African-Americans behave 'as if they were an oppressed nation'[66] and that 'the Negroes' relation to whites is part of the social relations – and the more capitalism develops and drags the Negroes into it, the sharper becomes the contradiction between the development of the productive forces and the social relation between white and Negro'.[67]

At the end of 1944, James was still working on the race question and its relation to capitalism and the socialist revolution. His starting point was a traditional Marxist position, but he was attempting, in studying American society, to grasp the concrete expression of this question. Tracing the historical development of the African-Americans and their unique role in American society, James, like DuBois, recognised that African-Americans represented a vital social force in American society and that their activities would have a bearing on the nation as a *whole*. What was missing from James's thinking at this time was an idea of the self-activity of blacks and the concept of the relationship between that self-activity and the struggle for socialism. This would come in 1948 once he had broken with the essential elements of Trotskyism and was on the verge of developing an independent Marxist tendency.

In January 1945, James published an important essay in the WP journal, *The New International* in which he outlined the ideas he had earlier expressed to Constance Webb and placed the 'Negro Question' within the trajectory of American historical development. New insights which later were to become critical to the famous 1948 position now began to emerge. After outlining the historical role of African-Americans, James notes:

Side by side with his increasing integration with production which becomes more and more a social process, the Negro becomes more than ever conscious of his exclusion from democratic privileges as a separate racial group in the community. *This dual movement is the key to the Marxist analysis of the Negro Question in the USA.* (emphasis in original)[68]

Identifying this struggle for the first time as that of 'an oppressed racial minority', James reviews the development of African-American activities in their attempt independently to establish their rights and he observes:

the main struggle of the Negro masses in the United States has been and until the achievement of socialism, will continue to be their struggle for their democratic rights as a *nationally oppressed minority.* Their entry into the ranks of organisation of labour does not lessen their sense of *national oppression.* On the contrary, it increases it and, in full accordance with their role in past American Revolutionary cases and the developing antagonisms of American society, this *independent action* of the Negro masses is already playing a role in relation to the American proletariat which constitutes one of the *most important elements in the struggle for socialism.*[69] (emphasis added)

The issue was the relation of this struggle of a national minority to the socialist struggle. On this point James is clear:

that the Negroes' struggle for democratic rights brings the Negroes almost immediately face to face with capital and state. The Marxist support of the Negro struggle for democratic rights is not a concession that Marxists make to Negroes. In the United States today, this struggle is a *direct part of the struggle for socialism.*[70] (emphasis added)

Despite this new insight, James was still arguing that nationalist movements were politically backward – 'the party wages a merciless war against the Negro nationalist movements, such as the Garveyites ... It demonstrates their fantastic and reactionary proposals for Negro emancipation'[71] – again revealing his contradictory appreciation of black struggle and lack of recognition that nationalist sentiments were a fundamental response to racial oppression, without which blacks would not have the self-confidence to struggle. This meant that James's notion of racial oppression was still incomplete. He had grasped the issue of racism as a social, political and economic problem, not an ontological one that required a redefinition of being. In this regard, black nationalism was not just a political response, but one that established the humanity of black people. This had been a major strength of Garvey and the UNIA, and a position which all radical black movements in the twentieth century have built upon.

James left the Workers' Party in 1947 and one year later he presented *Revolutionary Answer to the Negro Problem in the USA* to the SWP. This was the apex of his intervention in the black struggle. He begins by stating what was new in his thinking:

> We can compare what we have to say that is new by comparing it to previous positions on the Negro Question in the socialist movement. The proletariat as we know, must lead struggles of all the oppressed and all those who are persecuted by capitalism, but this has been interpreted in the past ... in the following sense: The independent struggles of the Negro people have not got much more than episodic value, and as a matter of fact, can constitute a great danger not only to the Negroes themselves, but to the organised labour movement. The real leadership of the Negro struggle must rest in the hands of organised labour and of the Marxist party ... We on the other hand, say something entirely different. We say, number one, that the Negro struggle has a vitality and validity of its own; that it has deeply historic roots in the past of America, and in present struggles, it has an organic political perspective, along which it is travelling, to one degree or another, and everything shows that at the present time it is travelling with great speed and vigour. We say number two, that this independent Negro movement is able to intervene with terrific force upon the general social and political life of the nation, despite the fact that it is waged under the banner of democratic rights, and is not led necessarily either by the organised labour movement or the Marxist Party. We say number three, and this is the most important, that it is able to exercise a powerful influence upon the revolutionary proletariat in the United States, and that is in itself a constituent part of the struggle for socialism.[72]

This was a breakthrough.

Clearly influenced by his studies of African-American history and the black radical tradition, as well as by his study of Hegel and the new universals espoused in his work *Notes on Dialectics*, the intervention remains one of the most perceptive Marxist analyses of black liberation in the United States. The events of the 1950s and 1970s, ranging from the civil rights movement to the formation of the Revolutionary League of Black Workers in Detroit, based upon black auto workers, and the impact of these movements and struggles on American politics, clearly vindicate the analysis. Viewed from the perspective of the evolution of James's political thinking, the document is a *leap*. Gone are the old conceptions of the 'struggle against Negro nationalism', or of the leading role of the party. Now the black liberation struggle can become a catalyst for socialist struggle and revolution. From the communist and leftist perspective on the race question, the document moved the parameters of the debate.

Traditionally, whether sympathetic or not, Marxists of whatever political current discussed black liberation struggles by posing the question, which was the more fundamental – the exploitation and oppression of blacks, racial oppression or class exploitation? In many instances, depending on what the answer was, it would be viewed as nationalist or socialist. Tony Martin has observed this tendency:

> The twentieth century has witnessed the world wide struggle of black people for freedom from colonialism and race prejudice … One of the most vexing problems, at both the theoretical and practical levels, with which most persons involved in this struggle have had to deal, is the question of the relative weights which should be assigned to the rival factors of race and class.[73]

Race and class, therefore, in the traditional paradigm of 'left' political theory, are seen as discrete and conflicting notions. In James's analysis the issue is not about which is primary or secondary, but rather that the self-activity of blacks brings them into conflict with the bourgeois state and that the dynamic of this logic is the struggle for socialism. In other words, the issue is one of moments in historical process. Race and class could not be separated into discrete, contradictory realities; they were an integral part of the experiences of the African-American population.

This approach represented a fundamental break with traditional Marxist thinking, and even though James based his argument on Lenin's thesis on nationalism, his analysis broke new ground. In Jamesian political theory, the struggles of those who were nationally oppressed were now of equal weight with the proletarian struggle for socialism. In the case of African-Americans, it was not only equal but a 'constituent part of the struggle for socialism', and in some instances could become the vanguard.

James ends the document evocatively:

> Let us not forget that in black people there sleep, and are now awakening, passions of a violence exceeding perhaps, as far as these things can be compared, anything among the tremendous forces that capitalism has created. Anyone who knows them, who knows their history, is able to talk to them intimately, watches them, watches them at their own theatres, watches them at their dances, watches them in their churches, reads their press with a discerning eye, must recognise that although their social force may not be able to compare with the social force of a corresponding number of organised workers, *the hatred of*

*bourgeois society and the readiness to destroy it when the opportunity should present itself, rests among them to a degree greater than in any other section of the population of the United States.*[74] (emphasis added)

It is a lucid statement of the validity of the black radical tradition, its anti-capitalist critique and revolutionary dynamic, in which James achieves the synthesis of Marxism and the black radical tradition. The achievement should be seen within the context of the trajectory which the Johnson–Forest Tendency had taken, expressed primarily in *Invading Socialist Society,* which explicitly critiqued the Leninist vanguard party, as well as positing the notion that mass mobilisation of the proletariat was the new universal of revolutionary organisation of the period.

In an interview given in 1971 in response to a question about the relationship of Marxism to the black liberation struggle, James answered:

There have been a lot of Marxists who have tried to keep them [blacks] down and make the movements subject to the Marxist movement, but that is not Marxism, not at all. Marxism deals with the revolution; Marxism deals with the ideas based upon the material circumstances and the political and social development. Marxism is not bound to be the doctrine of the people who are doing it.[75]

James's investigation of the race question opened up a new terrain of Marxist analysis. It demonstrated that for James, Marxism was primarily an analytical tool and a theory of revolutionary praxis. From his perspective, an oppressed people struggle against oppression, and such a struggle is valid and cannot be subordinated to the logic and demands of any other struggle. This kind of analysis prefigured political theorists of the 1970s and 1980s who sought to develop social and political theories which would specifically identify other social forces and their role in the revolutionary struggle. James's intervention on the race question stands today as one of the high points of his political and theoretical work. Caliban was now rewriting history, but from within his own tradition.

CHAPTER 6

# Breaking New Ground

By 1947, after operating as a minority within the Workers' Party, the Johnson–Forest Tendency had developed the essential elements of a coherent alternative revolutionary programme to that of traditional Trotskyism. However, the group still considered itself part of that and continued to argue for a unified Trotskyist movement. In April of that year, the unity talks between the Socialist Workers' Party (SWP) and the Workers' Party broke down when Shachtman declared that unity was politically incorrect. The Johnson–Forest Tendency disagreed, calling the position 'shameful, scandalous and utterly degrading ... [it] weakens the movement at a critical stage of its development'.[1]

Prior to the talks, James and others in the Tendency had reached a positive view about the SWP, stating in a Tendency resolution on the American Revolution that 'The SWP constantly makes the American workers aware of the coming social revolution in the United States.'[2] For James and the Tendency, the fact that the party stressed the possibilities of social revolution in America made it attractive, in contrast to the WP which increasingly accepted the political conception of the 'backwardness' of the American proletariat.

When the Johnson–Forest Tendency split from the WP in July 1947, it had a defined political shape. The group had grown from 3 to 74 and in many districts its members were operating as a faction within the party. At the theoretical level it had critiqued longstanding Trotskyist political postulates creating a trajectory which would take it outside the traditional Trotskyist movement. However, recognising the limitations of its size and to some degree unclear as to what its independent organisational path would be, the group decided to rejoin the SWP.

Superficially, the movement from the SWP to the Workers' Party in 1940 and back to SWP in 1948 could be viewed as political opportunism. While it is speculative to decide on cause, it is clear that in 1947 the Tendency had not worked out the precise organisational format for its alternative revolutionary politics. As a small group, it had developed a structure which facilitated theoretical work and attempted by ideas to influence others. It was uncertain about its organisational structure for two reasons. First, in 1947 it had not yet developed new political categories, and secondly, it did not see itself as the embryo of a Leninist political party. This was in contrast to many other tendencies in the Trotskyist movement, which split for doctrinal reasons as a political minuscule group and then re-establish themselves as a Leninist party, proclaiming to be the genuine inheritors of Lenin's legacy.

The direction of the Johnson–Forest Tendency led it to a transition phase, which it called the 'interim period'. As the internal 1951 report on the development of the Tendency noted, 'before we entered the Socialist Workers' Party we had an interim period of three months. This in itself was unprecedented. The work we accomplished set a new landmark in the revolutionary mobilisation of any vanguard grouping.'[3]

During this period, in addition to its weekly journal the Tendency published five major documents within the revolutionary Marxist tradition, thus laying the basis for their independent existence after their break with the SWP in 1951. These documents included some of the works previously discussed – *Dialectical Materialism and Fate of Humanity* and the *Balance Sheet of Trotskyism in the United States*, both written by James, and a path-breaking pamphlet on the white male American worker which detailed the factory life of a production worker and his opposition to the trade union bureaucracy. Although small, the latter was indicative that the Johnson–Forest Tendency was attempting to root its theoretical work in the practical experiences of the American proletariat. It is to this experience we now turn.

## The Activities of the American Proletariat

The 1940s was a period of mass activity for the American proletariat. The demands of war production required increased numbers of workers. Unemployment which stood at 14 per cent in 1940 had sharply declined by 1943. Factory life in 1943 was akin to Marx's traditional prognosis of production under a highly developed capitalism. One work on the period describes it thus:

> World War II era factories were gigantic, not only because of the great production requirements, but also because the technology of the assembly-line era massed together huge numbers of men, women and machines. In the aircraft industry, for example, 100,000 worked at the Douglas Aviation plants in El Segundo and Long Beach, California.[4]

High employment levels and assembly-line production had a profound impact on the nature of the American proletariat. There was mass migration from the South, radical upgrading of skills and what one writer called 'the most progressive redistribution of American wealth to take place in the twentieth century'.[5]

A major outcome of these changes was the 'Americanisation' of the proletariat. Historically, the American proletariat was comprised of different, primarily European, nationalities. However, the process of 'Americanisation' eroded these national cultures. Alongside this development was the entry of women into the labour market, thereby transforming their role in American society. As one woman worker noted,

> The seeds of my liberation and many other women's started with the war. The first intimation I had that it was taking place came when I was invited to a friend's house for Sunday dinner and I heard his mother and grandmother talk about which drill could bite into a piece of metal at the factory.[6]

Assembly-line production and speedups created conditions in which workers challenged the wartime no-strike pledge and attempted to establish their own working practices and disciplinary measures on the shop floor.[7]

For James, this mass activity of the American proletariat was an indication of the intense class struggle as well as the maturity of the American labour movement. The steelworkers' strikes of 1943 and the General Motors workers' strike of 1945 signalled to him and the Tendency that the self-activities of the American proletariat stood in sharp contrast to Nazism and totalitarianism. In other words, the degeneration of bourgeois society into Nazism and totalitarianism did not mean the degeneration of the American proletariat. The group was able to maintain this conception because the activity of the proletariat in all its forms became the distinguishing feature of its political outlook. A speaker at the Tendency's 1951 conference noted:

> We are distinguished from all others by the indissoluble way in which we connect the specific stage of *production* with the specific stage of the revolutionary *activity* of the masses. We have made the proletariat the centre of all our thinking and all our being. It is our social milieu. It is where we live, work, examine our theories and make new ones.[8] (emphasis added)

This close attention to the proletariat lay at the heart of James's revolutionary optimism during that period. Previously, in *The Invading Socialist Society* James and Forest had observed that 'the failure of world revolution' had recreated old dichotomies in social analysis, primarily between economics and politics, and from that they concluded that 'The proletariat on a higher plane, has drawn the ultimate conclusion. Its revolt is not against politics and the distribution of the surplus value; *the revolt is against value production itself*' (emphasis in the original).[9] Their conclusion was rooted in an analysis of capitalism and the social role of the proletariat in the mass factories of the period. James and Forest argued that:

> Experience in the factories has shown that it is precisely fundamental solutions that workers are ready to listen to ... the subjective factor, man as man, and not as the slave of capital, is now emerging as the decisive force in history and is organising itself to correspond.[10]

Drawing on their interpretation of Lenin, James and Forest returned to a notion of human agency within the Marxist tradition. To bolster their position further they posited a reinterpretation of Lenin's political activity; that 'Lenin with his incomparable concreteness placed before the masses the theoretical conclusions of Marx, that the solution to the problems of capital accumulation was a human solution'.[11]

This assertion was within the tradition of classical Marxism and reflected the impact of the *Economic and Philosophical Manuscripts*, restoring the role of human agency squarely within the tradition. For James and Forest, that agency was translated into the historic mission of the proletariat. This was not new ground. However, what was new was the Tendency's attempts to expand the notion of the proletariat's self-activities to include the activities of everyday life and to extrapolate new political categories from these actions. This would become their hallmark.

While traditional Marxists focused on the development of political ideas, or on the elaboration of a political programme for the proletariat, James and his group sought to discover interior movement within the proletariat. This required a close study not only of factory life, but also the subsequent integration of politics, economics and everyday existence. Nowhere is this methodology better seen than in the pamphlet *The American Worker* (1947).

## The American Worker

The preface to the pamphlet begins with a description of the crisis in contemporary society:

> Today, in all strata of society, a search is going on for the way to create a world, one world, in which men can live as social and creative individuals, where they can live as all-round men and not just as average men. Out of this search a *new philosophy of life is being created*. Neither The Christian Revolution nor the Protestant Revolution, the only comparable milestones in the history of Western civilisation, can parallel in depth and scope, the process of evolution and re-evaluation now going on in the activity and in the thoughts of men.[12] (emphasis added)

Asserting that the pamphlet written by a worker is a fundamental contribution to this evaluation, it continues: 'As the working class today is the only class which can reconstruct society or new beginnings, so everything that it thinks and does provides the key for all those who seek in the modern barbarism for a unifying principle by which to understand the past and build the future.'[13]

For James and the Tendency, the working class was an *active subject* and the American proletariat was an advanced social force which, by its activities, 'provide[s] the foundation for an analysis of the economic transition from capitalism to socialism or the concrete demonstration of the new society developing within the old'.[14]

These formulations represented a fundamental break with traditional revolutionary politics where revolutionary and socialist consciousness was the active property of a vanguard group, which was then transmitted to the proletariat. Within this frame, if workers did not conform to a prior pattern of political behaviour determined by the vanguard, they were labelled politically backward. Such a conception tended to focus on the convential political forms of working-class activity. James and the Tendency's analysis began with what the proletariat itself did, not what they thought it should do. It made valid the self-activity of labour.

For the Tendency, the proletariat by its practical activity would rethink old concepts and create a new philosophy of life. This represented a view of history which saw purpose and meaning in human activity. It took Marx's statement that philosophy had to become proletarian seriously. Since in the Marxist paradigm only the proletariat could create the new society in which real human history and freedom would begin, a philosophy of life developed by the self-activity of the proletariat would necessarily form the empirical and intellectual basis for this new society, answering some of the age-old questions of political theory and philosophy. The context of the mass production of American capitalism framed the new political categories. The pamphlet equated the radical self-activities of the workers with a reclamation of themselves as human beings:

> The American worker today is facing his real conditions of life, and his relations with his kind ... The suddenness with which millions of workers have had their lives revolutionised by production ... has transformed the American worker from an easy-going practical empiricist into a thoughtful, questioning, investigator into the realities of the society around him ... nowhere more than in the United States do the workers, in putting forward their claims as workers, also put forward their claims as human beings.[15]

Using labour and its activity as their fundamental base, the pamphlet then explored some of the basic elements of classical Marxist analysis and their applicability to American labour. These included the notion of alienation, the examination of human nature and a critique of bourgeois politics. With reference to the last of these, the preface comments on the classical Marxist paradigm of human emancipation, noting that:

> In striving for complete emancipation, men go through the stage of political emancipation because it represents a progressive step over the domination of men by the opiate of religion. Religion gives men the illusion of democracy only in the heavenly Kingdom; political democracy at least brings the Kingdom closer to earth ... but political emancipation is the reduction of man on the one side, to the member of bourgeois society, to the egoistic independent individual, on the other side, to the citizen, to the moral person.[16]

The creation of fragmented individuals and their alienation would later become a major theme as James grappled with the meaning of society as a social totality and its relationship to individual freedom.

From a discussion of human emancipation, the preface then switches to an interpretation of Marx's notion of socialism and restates Marx's classical view of the state where, with the emergence of socialism, 'politics and the state could wither away, because it would no longer be necessary to maintain the illusionary political community'.[17] This was radically different from the traditional Marxist-Leninist movement whereby, contrary to the withering away of politics and the state, the political became more pronounced as the state grew in both size and scope, as was the case of the Soviet Union. The Trotskyist movement also supported a strong and highly political state in socialist society. James and the Tendency were moving in the opposite direction. They perceived the state in all its contemporary forms as an obstacle to human freedom in accordance with a tendency in classical Marxism which posited a new society, drawing inspiration from ancient Greek democracy and the Paris Commune.[18]

At the core of this conception was James's preoccupation with the separation of the state from civil society – a feature of Hegel and Marx. However, like Marx, James asserted that fundamental to this separation was the nature of the social and production relations under capitalism. The state and politics therefore became instrument and activity – the requirements of bourgeois society. Socialist society would replace the state and politics and reconcile the fragmented nature of human beings. James, like Marx, agreed with the Aristotelian postulate that man by nature is a political animal. The fundamental difference for both James and Marx with Aristotle was that when the citizen and the state were reunited, politics would become the administration of things and the state as its locus would be redundant.

James and the Tendency subscribed to a particular Marxist analysis of the Paris Commune. In this analysis the mass democratic character of the Commune went beyond the traditional conceptions of liberal democracy. The state did not become stronger but rather was replaced by alternative forms. For James, in 1947, the moment had arrived in human history when the proletariat was capable of abolishing the state and ending pre-history.

## Revolutionary Organisation

One of the major features found in the documents and bulletins of the Johnson–Forest Tendency during the 'interim period' was its preoccupation with revolutionary organisation. Still advocating a Leninist notion of the party, the Tendency continued to search for new ways to apply this formulation to the American labour movement. At its trade union conference in July 1947, a resolution confirmed that the Tendency's main task was to recruit and integrate workers. It spoke about 'the penetration of our Marxist ideas which they have already begun to grasp in instinctive action and thought'.[19] This indicated that while searching for new forms of organisation, the group was still wedded to Leninist conception. Sometimes, the contradiction in the group's political outlook was recognised, as the resolution continues:

> The workers have a great deal to say. For Marxists to recruit workers from all strata means that we must understand the extent of all they have to say. We must not for example, expect contracts, Negro workers, young factory workers ... coming to us from factory schooling to fit right in our ways ... the socialism in the proletariat today is very powerful but it is not clearly expressed politically.[20]

The debate on revolutionary organisation was the single most discussed item in the bulletins of the interim period. In the final bulletin (September 1947, no. 12), James wrote:

> Our work has been rooted in the experiences of the workers in the caucus. For years now our young comrades have gone eagerly into the factories all over the country, not as a duty or a task, but seeking to learn, to correct inevitable differences of a group like ours and to find themselves as revolutionaries. The percentage of proletarians and proletarianised in our caucus is between sixty and seventy percent.[21]

James ends the article by encouraging the Tendency to disband its caucus status and integrate itself into the Socialist Workers' Party.

In this interim period, the Tendency's membership grew by seven. At the end of the three months the organisation had members located in the following areas:[22]

New York – 11
Newark – 2
Cleveland – 2
Chicago – 1
West Virginia – 9
Philadelphia – 11
San Francisco – 7
Detroit – 10
Los Angeles – 7

In the final bulletin, the debate continued about the nature of revolutionary organisation and in particular the nature of workers' consciousness. In a letter, Phil Romano, co-author of *The American Worker*, expressed the problem in the following way:

> I want to take the opportunity to say also that, in my opinion, an 'advanced worker' is one who has been subjected to the modern factory system to such a degree, that the multitude of contradictions vested in him prepare him for immediate reception of socialist propaganda.[23]

Clearly, if the proletariat was revolutionary by everyday instinct, then it should be prepared in significant numbers to make the socialist revolution. Although there was an explosion of working-class activity at the time, this did not develop into revolutionary struggles. What the Tendency ignored was the character of hegemonic ideology and the role it plays in human consciousness. Secondly, while searching for new forms, the Tendency was still hemmed in by Trotskyist traditions and the demands of polemical internal left manoeuvrings. Thirdly, although the Tendency leadership had mastered *Capital*, the group had not yet mastered the dialectic. This would happen in 1948, when James's *Notes on Dialectics* formed the basis of study for the group. However, while *Notes on Dialectics* established the new universal political categories, the groundwork, the classification of the character, both of the epoch and of social revolution in that period, was to a large extent work honed in the interim period. All the notions which came to distinguish James's political thought – state capitalism, revolutionary organisation, an integrative vision of the proletariat, the independent perspective of the Black Liberation struggle in the United States, human freedom and historical development – were debated and discussed in the Tendency's internal bulletins.

Let us look at the issue of the Black struggle and the Tendency's perspective during this period.

## The Black Struggle

In a comprehensive essay, William Gorman has elaborated the notion of the centrality of the race question to the American socialist revolution. Tracing the impact of African-American struggles on political events in American history, the War of Independence and the Civil War, Gorman notes that:

> The civil war known in popular terms as the war between the North and the South, was in reality only a climax to the two and a half centuries of murderous warfare between the master and his slaves. This is demonstrated most convincingly and dramatically by the Negroes themselves ... Those within the revolutionary movement who would deny the Vanguard role of the Negroes in the coming American Revolution, must consciously or otherwise join in maintaining the role of Negroes in the American bourgeois revolution. Past history and present politics are identical on this point.[24]

Within such a framework, the self-activity of the slaves had a political impact. In the North it influenced the abolitionist movement and, as Gorman explains:

> It was the Negro abolitionists, because of their subjective experiences as chattel slaves, who were in the most compelling position to explain to the white workers and farmers the vital need for a bold war against the slavocracy. It was the Negro abolitionists who were able in advance to develop an insight into the relation of chattel slavery to wage slavery ... it was not accidental that Frederick Douglass on his trip to England should speak at working class meetings, to leaders and to the leaders of the movement for Irish Independence.[25]

However, the relationship between the white proletariat and African-Americans on the question of slavery was problematic. Dominated by the fear that emancipation would mean lower wages and therefore unemployment for white workers, the workers' movement allied itself in its early struggles with the slave-owners, a phenomenon which has had a tortuous history and ramifications in American revolutionary politics. Recognising that their demand for land in the Reconstruction period was a revolutionary one, and rejecting William Garrison's plan for colonisation, the ex-slaves demanded the reconstruction of Southern society and hence were the most radical forces in the period of radical populism in American politics.

Moving from the nineteenth to the twentieth century, Gorman notes that although African-Americans entered industry, they were alienated from society. And this alienation took on a specially extreme form and became the basis for the Garvey movement. He writes:

> Marcus Garvey ostensibly proposed the return of the Negroes to Africa. But for the Negro millions in the Garvey movement, Africa was only a symbol of the Negroes profound aspirations to reconstruct *The United States* ... just as the forcible separation of the Negro from chattel slavery by flight prior to the Civil War indicated his deep desire to reconstruct the whole United States ... If in the twenties the Negro was in the vanguard of the whole country in his aspirations for the reconstruction of American society, the organisation of CIO indicated that the same aspirations existed in large sections of the working class.[26] (emphasis in the original)

An appreciation of the struggles against slavery and racial oppression was therefore critical to the American socialist revolution, since African-Americans historically had engaged in an independent struggle, which in turn impacted on and influenced other sectors. These elements of Gorman's essay were integrated into James's resolution on the Black Question, and showed how far he and the Tendency had moved from traditional Marxist-Leninism with regard to race.

## Other Trends

It is interesting to note that the early post-World War II period witnessed the growth of two major European intellectual currents: existentialism and the Frankfurt School of Critical Theory. Both had a profound impact on Western radical critique of capitalist civilisation.

In France, a radical interpretation of Hegel and the publication of Marx's *Economic and Philosophical Manuscripts* were decisive. As David McLellan notes, they 'gave the impression that a very different form of Marxism was available ... that could enter into fruitful dialogue with the increasingly popular philosophies of phenomenology ... and existentialism'.[27]

Within this milieu, thinkers like Henri Lefebvre, deeply influenced by these developments, produced major works on the nature of alienation. The problematic of alienation dominated French philosophic discourse in the immediate post-war period, and was popularised in the novels of Albert Camus and the writings of Jean-Paul Sartre. In the late 1950s Sartre attempted to reconcile existentialism with Marxism and in *Critique of Dialectic Reason* he sought to develop a methodology which would 'not allow the dialectic to become a divine law again, a metaphysical fate, it must proceed from individuals and not from some kind of supra-individual ensemble'.[28] Central to Sartre's methodology was material production: 'As soon as there will exist for everyone a margin of real freedom beyond the production of life, Marxism will have lived out its span; a philosophy of freedom will take its place.'[29]

Sartre's attempt to synthesise Marxism and existentialism was a major project, but it did not address the fundamental question of what social forces would lead the reconstruction of society. Other writers like André Gorz attempted to develop arguments about the features of a new working class. While one stream of radical critique was preoccupied with the notion of alienation and the emergence of a new working class, another stream, influenced by the work of Max Horkheimer, focused on the nature of authoritarianism in the political domain and on psychoanalysis and aesthetics. Developing what became known as Critical Theory, these thinkers, influenced by Marx, Hegel and Freud, probed the human condition within Western civilisation, against the backdrop of a devastated Europe, the rise of fascism and the defeat of the European labour movement. In this scenario there seemed to be no social force capable of reconstructing society.

As a consequence, the current focused on theoretical rather than political issues – and Western Marxism 'came to concentrate overwhelmingly on [the] study of superstructures'.[30] Within this frame, major advances were made in the domain of aesthetics. Although influenced by the experience of mass culture in the United States, Critical Theory perceived mass culture as an imposition on the masses by the ruling elite. This was a radically different perspective from that of James and the Tendency.

For James, mass culture was a positive phenomenon which allowed the individual to develop social relations critical to proletarian revolution. The key to this difference lay in the nature of the American proletariat and the European labour movement and the conclusions drawn by Johnson–Forest Tendency about the precise characteristics of the American proletariat.

Marx had written when capitalism was in the ascendant. At the turn of the nineteenth century, the United States was fast becoming the most powerful capitalist society, and by the end of World War II, it had emerged as the world's leading capitalist power with its proletariat an active social force. James was therefore operating at a time when the new forces in the American proletariat were making an impact. In Europe by contrast the proletariat had not only been devastated by war, but the rise of Nazism and the consolidation of Stalinism had turned revolutionary hope into defeat and disillusion. Just as Marx, in an earlier period, could extrapolate the laws of capital reproduction by examining the political economy of England, so, James, immersed in the analysis of the American proletariat, laid the basis for the development of new revolutionary universals. In this, his keen eye and fascination with the lives of ordinary people were critical tools.

## The Johnson–Forest Tendency

Throughout this chapter, the focus has been on the political work of the Tendency. While James was its leader, the Tendency's leadership operated collectively through a division of labour. James was the theoretical and political leader. Grace Lee (Ria Stone) wrote primarily on philosophical matters and attempted to situate the development of the American working class and mass production within the movement of history. Forest focused on labour and the nature of state capitalism, and was co-political leader with James. William Gorman focused on history, in particular plotting the revolutionary trajectory of American history. Harvey (Martin Glaberman) focused on trade union work and the general organisation of the group. James sought to develop the strengths that each one brought to the leadership. His leadership style was one which facilitated the development of individual talents. A letter to Constance Webb gives us his own assessment of his style:

> Look at how I am handling Grace – my last letter was hard. It was an indictment. But I told G. she would see that I was full of concern for her. I keep up our studies, etc. I want her to correct herself, but I do not want to have any wounds. I do not want to crush her spirit. It is because I think all the time of our little organisation.[31]

Martin Glaberman noted on the group's leadership:

> for twelve years the three top leaders of our organisation were, a woman born in Russia, an American woman of Chinese descent and a Black man from Trinidad. There has never been an American Organisation like that and I suspect probably never will again.[32]

For several years, James and the Tendency worked at developing an alternative conception of revolutionary politics. Establishing itself first as a minority Tendency in the WP and organising around the notion of state capitalism, the group developed a corpus of Marxist analysis which sought to update Marxism for the immediate post-war period. Rooting themselves in the mass activity of the American proletariat, they argued against the theory of 'American exceptionalism' and developed a framework for the socialist revolution in America. The fact that the group was led by a West Indian black is of fundamental significance. From as early as 1931 in his first anti-colonial work, *The Life of Captain Cipriani* James had noted that the Black West Indian outlook was 'of Western Civilisation modified and adapted to their particular circumstances'.[33]

In the United States, James found social forces adapted to Western civilisation, and not limited by size or the feudal relations of the old world. His political skills and literary imagination honed in the West Indies reached their peak in the American revolutionary socialist movement. To validate his identity Caliban was now a pioneer.

# CHAPTER 7

# The New Universals

We have documented that between 1940 and 1948, C.L.R. James and the Tendency studied Marxist economics and politics and developed and defined a theory of state capitalism as a new phase in world capitalism. This analysis of revolutionary Marxist politics was rooted in the post-World War II developments of the American labour movement. Although initially the group studied philosophy, this attempt was primarily guided by Marxist categories of political economy and historical materialism. Thus, the Tendency did not root their political analysis within an explicitly philosophical framework, perhaps reflecting Marx's statement in *The German Ideology* that 'the philosophers have only interpreted the world in various ways; the point is to change it'.[1]

It has been ably documented the extent of Hegel's influence on Marx's early work. As a consequence reveals strains of a teleological conception of human nature and society: as the movement of history reconciled individual alienation and social being into a higher unity. Both classless society and communism – the locations in which the real history of human beings and human freedom begin – were central for Marxist political theory.

Following James, Marx argued that capitalism had created the conditions in which humans could see their real human essence, making communism the negation of the history of pre-humanity. James operated within the Aristotelian tradition of infusing human activity with *telos*. He attempts to avoid the teleological trap by explaining that the purpose of human beings is not given, but instead is extracted from the empirical observation of their existence: 'Purpose, not in the religious sense, but in the sense that if we examine man's history through the centuries, he has sought those aims.'[2] Purpose was thus a developing idea. James's efforts to free himself of teleology were never entirely successful and his political thought would not completely overcome it. Indeed, it would become more evident as he began to analyse the works of Hegel.

In 1947 James and the Tendency were continuing their exploration of certain fundamental issues which would distance them from Trotskyism. The logic of the theory of state capitalism had led to a rethinking of traditional political categories, which eventually would result in their reviewing other Marxist conceptions of human society and its possibilities. In 1948 James himself set about investigating philosophy as the framework for these new categories. His work resulted in *Notes on Dialectics* (1948). Martin Glaberman recounts its impact on the Tendency:

> When I first saw it I was on the night shift machining crank shafts for the Buick division of General Motors ... and this thing would come in the mail in pieces ... every once in a while I would come home from work at midnight or one o'clock and my wife would say, – 'Well, the mail came and we have another chapter'. And we would sit till two or three in the morning reading sections of *Notes on Dialectics*.[3]

James himself became obsessed with the work. In a letter to Constance Webb he notes: 'It is 20 years since I have worked like this. I feel no mental or manual fatigue – absolutely none. I have ... mastered at last the Hegelian logic.'[4] This preoccupation with mastering Hegel was a well-tested route which many Marxists before James had travelled.

In 1914, after the outbreak of World War I, Lenin revisited Hegel's work when he was assessing the political behaviour of the Second International and their betrayal of a cardinal principle of Marxism – proletarian internationalism. Consequently, he noted: 'it is impossible completely to understand Marx's *Capital* and especially its first chapter without having understood the whole of Hegel's *Logic* ... half a century later none of the Marxists understood Marx'.[5] It is obvious, that, in spite of Marx's notion of the 'end of philosophy', there was a tradition in Marxism after Marx which sought explanations for new developments of social reality in philosophical discourses. After a decade in the United States, James set himself that task.

## *James and Hegel*

From a Marxist perspective, history, knowledge and human nature are interconnected. James's philosophical discourse begins with a radical statement which announces a rupture not only from Trotskyism, but traditional Marxism-Leninism. In *Notes on Dialectics*, he proclaims:

> Truth can only be where it makes itself its own result. Truth in our analysis, the total emancipation of labour, can only be achieved when it contains and overcomes its complete penetration by its inherent antagonism, the capital relation. At this stage of actuality in the labour movement I come inevitably to the conclusion that there was no further place in the labour movement for the *party*.[6] (emphasis added)

This is the central political thesis of *Notes on Dialectics* – the abolition of the political party as a progressive political organism. Here James is attempting to establish the political requirements demanded by the new stage of state capitalism and the labour movement which he and the Tendency had elaborated. At the core of his methodology is the application of Hegelian categories to the evolution of the labour movement. He begins by restating the dialectic and notes that Hegel's dialectic 'is new, a new way of organising thought – not of thinking, but of knowing what you do when you think'.[7] Tracing the evolution of the Johnson–Forest Tendency, and why they embarked on the study of Hegel, he comments that the group had now arrived at a stage where it felt the need to systemise knowledge, within a philosophical framework. Critical to this process, James notes, was the dialectic and its relation to thought:

> Thought is not an instrument you apply to content. The content moves, develops, changes, and creates new categories of thought and gives them direction ... philosophic cognition of it means not philosophy about it but a correct cognition, a correct grasp of it in its movement. The labour movement takes certain forms – the commune, The Second International, the Third International, the Unions, CIO, IWW, etc.[8]

James says that the error made in revolutionary political analysis was to ossify particular forms of the labour movement, turning them into absolutes instead of recognising that all forms were transient, since they are an expression of movement. James notes that Hegel makes the point that 'understanding' was thinking in finite categories and that '*all error in thought comes from this*' (emphasis added).[9] Reason, on the other hand he argues, is when individuals 'know how and why they move',[10] while understanding 'makes determination and maintains them'.[11] James then says that Marxist revolutionary thought had been stuck at the level of understanding and makes the point that

> understanding makes determination and maintains them. There is a reformist international, Mensheviks, a revolutionary international, Bolsheviks, there are general strikes, Soviets (1917 model) a Bolshevik party, etc. We fit what we perceive into these categories. At every plenum we study them, we clarify them and we change them a little. In reality, the old categories hold us by the throat, especially thinkers.[12]

James's task, then, was to destroy the old categories and establish the new revolutionary universals of the labour movement for the period. Achieving this would require a fundamental comprehension of the nature of knowledge and its application to the object of study. Stating a simple schema of cognition based on Hegel's methodology,

James defined the three divisions of knowledge as: '[the] simple, everyday commonsense vulgar empiricism, ordinary perception; understanding; and [the] Dialectic'.[13]

James, not unaware of the critique of Hegel as a idealist philosopher attempts to define consciousness and posits that 'consciousness is to know the concrete, but to know it dialectically'.[14] He also stated that thought was the 'link between human beings and things',[15] and the study of logic was 'the analysis of this movement of philosophic cognition'.[16] Such a methodology and its application would obviously lead to the creation of universal categories, a fact James was keenly aware of:

> You must know categorisation in general, movement in general, changes in categories in general, and then you can examine the object ... and work out its categories, its form of movement, its method of change etc., always conscious of the general laws as exemplified in the particular concrete.[17]

From this basis, James seeks to explain political phenomena, such as Stalinism. He suggests that as a phenomenon it was not a deception or the betrayal of the labour movement, but a necessary part of the nature of the movement: 'Stalinism is a necessary, inevitable form of development of the labour movement. The workers are not mistaken. They are not deceived. Not in any serious sense of these words. They are making an experience that is necessary to their own development.'[18]

Such a perspective was not only new to the Trotskyist movement, but demonstrated a characteristic of James's thought – an emphasis on the notion of necessity. This tendency was present early and we have noted it in a review of his previous essay, *The Philosophy of History and Necessity: A few words with Professor Hook* (1943). In James's political thought, necessity was equated with logical developments where each moment revealed a further essence of the object. Present as well within this conception was the teleological notion of individual happiness as purpose. For many Marxists, notions of necessity and teleology trapped them into old political categories. For James, neither the Commune nor the Soviet were the final forms of the emancipation of labour, but were the expressions of labour's essence in a particular context and period. The method allowed him to examine empirically the nature of revolutionary forms and to prepare for new ones.

In developing an analysis of the labour movement, James operated from the standpoint of an empirical examination of the actions of the proletariat and from within the confines of a particular stream in the Marxist tradition. James and Antonio Gramsci had a common approach to the philosophy of Marxism and history. For Gramsci, 'Certainly the philosophy of praxis is realised in the concrete study of past history and in the contemporary activity of creating new history.'[19] With regard to the role of necessity in human history, both attempted to distinguish between necessity and inevitability, and as Gramsci observed:

> Necessity in history is closely connected to that of 'regularity' and 'rationality'. 'Necessity' in the historical concrete sense! Necessity exists when there exists an efficient and active premise, consciousness of which in people's minds has become operative ... In the premise must be contained already developed or in the process of development, the necessary and sufficient material conditions for the realization of the impulse of collective will.[20]

While Gramsci explored the notion of hegemony and its role in consciousness as one factor which confronted the proletarian revolution, James's focus in 1948 was on the political and organisational forms of the labour movement. His project was different and required new questions. The issue was not why the labour movement had been defeated, but rather what the activities of the proletariat signified within the frame of the new stage of state capitalism. His categorisation of Stalinism as a necessary form of the labour movement demonstrated that for James, once the Russian Revolution had been defeated, its legacies had been transformed. In the Gramscian sense, the legacy of 1917 would become a significant part of workers' consciousness, resulting in support for those who claimed to be the inheritors of the legacy. The critical importance of this analysis for Jamesian thought was that in revolutionary praxis, the issues could no longer be reduced to correct revolutionary leadership, but rather that the proletariat was creating a necessary experience which was inevitable after the degeneration of the October Revolution. The issue obviously was more complicated than this and the weakness in James's position is that he did not pay attention to how ideological hegemony was constructed and its functions in capitalist society.

However, from the Jamesian perspective the American proletariat, given their traditions, need not be weighed down by the necessity of creating this experience. They would break free, creating the new revolutionary political forms demanded by the new age.

## The New Categories

The framework for James's enquiry consists of the categories developed in Hegel's *Science of Logic and the Phenomenology of Mind*. The conceptual apparatuses used are the doctrine of being and the doctrine of notion, combined with the dialectic. Trotskyism as a revolutionary theory is the first object of the analysis. James notes that

Trotskyism, as far as thought is concerned, is the use of the categories, etc. of Lenin's practice, 1903–1923, pressured in their essential clarity and transferred to a period for which they became day by day more unsuited. Between 1933 and 1936, they became absolutely unsuited.[21]

The basis of Trotskyism as a political framework for the period was, therefore, wrong. James records that the debates between Stalin and Trotsky occurred post 1917 and that Trotsky's mind 'was on other wheels. Lenin's monopoly capitalism, private property, reactionary international for private property, all the categories of 1917: these he lived in'.[22] James argues that political categories changed while Trotsky's analysis stood still; as a result Trotskyism degenerated into analysing political movements as 'tools of [the] Kremlin'. The fundamental philosophical error of Trotsky's political thought James argued was synthetic cognition. Using Hegel's idea of cognition, he states:

Synthetic cognition transforms the objective into notions, but gives [them] the form of the notion-determination, and then has to look for and analyse separately by themselves, the individuality of the object ... Similarly, synthetic cognition finds propositions and laws and shows their necessity, but not as a necessity of the case in and for itself. No. The laws it finds are not laws that spring from the notion. It creates laws from the determinations of the fixed particular in which the universal happened at one time to find itself ... For us this is a terrible truth. Taking these particular forms in which the universal for a brief period found a determination, Trotsky has drawn from them laws of his own which end by threatening the foundations of Marxism itself.[23]

Empirically, this meant that the core thesis of the Trotskyist analysis of the then Soviet Union as a degenerated workers' state, was flawed. James writes:

He taught that only the revolutionary proletariat can nationalise properly and plan. This was the concrete situation in Russia, 1917. This fixed, limited, finite, particular determination, he made into a universal, despite Lenin's warnings. Ignoring what was specifically proletarian was the Soviet and the Soviet alone.[24]

James's critique of Trotskyism reveals his own understanding of socialism. Contradicting the notion that 'nationalised property was the basis for socialism', he writes confirming that the self-activity of the proletariat was the basis for socialism. In a new society, 'only the proletariat can free the plan; otherwise the plan reproduces with intensified murderousness all the evils of value production ... only free humanity, socialism, can develop nationalised property'.[25]

While Trotskyism was an inadequate revolutionary theory, for James, Leninism expressed the impulses of the proletariat. Here his admiration for Lenin is underscored. In 1947, in reviewing Lenin's work, James observed that after 1914 Lenin set out to find the basis of the 'betrayal' of the Second International and created a new category, the 'bourgeoisified worker'. In 1948, conventional analysis of Leninism attributed two central notions to Leninist thinking – the vanguard party and imperialism. James, by contrast, argues:

> Lenin's conception of the party was a conception of the party in bourgeois society ... Lenin never bothered himself about the struggle for socialism in Russia. Even up to 1917 he did not. That would come after. But up to 1914, periodically the concrete Russian struggle would lead him to make abstract generalisations about socialism drawn from the concrete ... he had to wait for a word from the workers to become as positive about socialism as he had been positive about bourgeois democracy in Russia. This came in 1917 with the Soviets – concrete socialism ... It was the workers who did the theoretical work on the Soviet. They thought over the Soviet. They analysed it and remembered it and within a few days of the February revolution they organised in the great centres of Russia this unprecedented social formation.[26]

Here James posits that Lenin's notion of socialism, his major contribution to revolutionary thought, was his ability to discern the evolution of the Soviet and then establish the new political universal of the Soviet state. He argues that the essence of Lenin's *State and Revolution* was that 'the armed workers, all of them, form a new type of state'.[27] These armed workers then 'carry out universal accounting and control of production and distribution, and this universal accounting and control is the distinguishing mark of the new society in production. This universal accounting and control is a *new productive force*' (emphasis in the original).[28] James suggests that revolutionaries who read *State and Revolution* and did not understand this had a limited conception of socialism. He argues that the Soviet form replaced the commune and became the determinate form of the dictatorship of the proletariat. From there James makes a leap forward:

> The party *had* disappeared. For Lenin not only in pure theory, but concretely to the Russian people, Lenin was saying – Every worker, 'to a man' had to learn to govern the state, and to administer the economy ... The armed workers, all the workers, all the workers administering the state, all the workers administering the economy. The party as such disappears. For

a party which consists of all the workers, armed cooks and all, is no longer a party as we knew it.[29] (emphasis in the original)

James goes on to lament the fact that Lenin's real programme was not carried out. 'The few workers in the poverty-stricken country isolated by the failure of the revolution in Europe, *did not administer the state*. The division between politics and economics came back with renewed force' (emphasis in the original).[30] He dates the turning point of the nature of Russian society from that period of the trade union debate in 1920 and then notes that, 'The turning point theoretically was the 1920 trade union discussion ... the workers as workers, he said must in their unions protect themselves, their economic and cultural interests, against the workers acting in their party as rulers of the state.'[31] He suggests that from then until his death, Lenin argued about how to preserve the core of the Soviet in a different context. All these conceptions were well within the Marxist tradition of post-bourgeois society: not only was politics transformed, but the mysteries of state power were illuminated.

Drawing on a comparison between Lenin's era and his own, James notes that in the same way that Lenin's conception of socialism changed in 1917, so too in this era must there be a new notion of socialism. From this perspective, he sees the different struggles of the proletariat and the creation of new forms as the preparation of the classes for the transformation of capitalist society. The distinguishing political feature of the proletariat, James argues, is the organisations which have represented it. And he observes that the capitalist contradiction expresses itself within the proletariat by the corruption of these organisations.[32] James then expresses the classic Leninist view of the party and notes that 'the proletariat is the only historical class to which the party, the political party, is essential'.[33] The vanguard party as the knowing of the proletariat is the climax of a particular stage of thought within Marxism-Leninist theory. In bourgeois society, James claims that the proletariat needs the party, as a consequence he establishes a historical sequence where politics, thought and philosophic tradition interact. He writes:

Kant: Without human thought there is no cognition.
Hegel: Man without thought is nothing, i.e. an animal. He is man through the faculty of thought.
Marx: Man without labour is an animal. He is man through the faculty of labour.
Marx: Proletarian man is revolutionary or he is nothing.
Lenin: (1907–17) Proletarian man politically must have a political party or he is nothing.[34]

Moving on from the notions of great thinkers, James then traces the history of the proletariat and states that 'The proletariat revolutions of 1848, the Commune, the political general strike, the 1905 Soviets, the 1917 Soviets, there the proletarian impulse ... created new forms and new knowledge.'[35] Sticking closely to the Hegelian philosophic categories of 'knowing' and 'being', James again notes what we have already observed – within Marx's thought, there is abolition of politics. James adds to this that the socialist revolution would mean that the difference between manual and intellectual labour would vanish and socialism would eradicate the distinction between knowing and being. In *Notes on Dialectics*, following this line of argument, he draws a dramatic conclusion: 'Now if the party is the knowing of the proletariat, then the coming of age of the proletariat means the abolition of the party. That is our new universal.'[36]

Such a rupture from traditional Leninist thinking had profound implications. But James himself was unclear. When does the party disappear? Is it before the revolution, or after? What are the forms and instruments of struggle before and during the revolution? Continuing his argument, James states 'when the whole labouring population becomes the state. That is the disappearance of the state.'[37] This holds true too logically for the political party, and in attempting to develop this position, James observes that 'the dominating political conception of our time [was] the one party state'.[38] He has in mind the rise of fascism and notes that the 'one party state is the bourgeoisie's attempt to respond to contemporary necessity for the fusion and transcendence of class, party, state'.[39] James also argues that since the 1930s 'the proletariat has been trying to abolish the old party ... in France in 1936 it went into the factories and joined the unions, four million in three months ... the CIO is no union. It is the American tentative approximation at a mass party.'[40] Given this analysis, for James, the universal revolutionary was a new political category: 'The Party and Revolution. That is our leap. That is our new universal.'[41] In arriving at this conclusion James also examines the class Roots of the political party in Western political history.

James roots the formation of the Leninist vanguard party in the role of the petit-bourgeois class in European history. Tracing the historical evolution of that class, he periodises their evolution into the following stages:

(1) The English Revolution where the petite parliamentary bourgeoisie created democracy.
(2) The French Revolution where the class is no longer farmers and artisans, but includes the intelligentsia. This grouping led by Robespierre and Saint Juste developed a dictatorship which

attempted to 'retain the revolutionary character against the bourgeoisie and reaction, but equally served to subordinate and restrain the masses while keeping intact their revolutionary energy'.

(3) Russia, according to James, where Marxism fought 'petite-bourgeois anarchist theories'.

(4) A transition from Menshevism to Stalinism. He then notes that 'the Stalinist party of 1926 is the identity of the labour bureaucracy using the proletariat against big bourgeoisie'.[42]

Here we see James moving from a Hegelian understanding of the philosophic roots of Stalinism to its historic class roots. He even observes that the reformist petite bourgeoisie in the post-World War II era is not a defender of private property, 'even the Catholic Conservative element of the petite bourgeoisie which so rapidly organised the Mouvement Republicain Populaire in France was ready for nationalisation'.[43] At the core of this new economic form of the petite bourgeoisie was the new stage of capital – state capitalism. The political circle was now complete. Moving from the category of state capitalism James had now developed a complete theory of Marxism for his time. State capitalism required a new political universal – the abolition of the party. The immediate question was what the role of Marxists would be in this new context.

## New Tasks

In the same work, *Notes on Dialectics*, James recognised that a Marxist grouping in bourgeois society was still a vanguard and that it 'organises itself as it always had ... it forms its own propaganda group or circle or *party* and propagates the destruction of the bureaucracy' (emphasis added).[44] This is a critical statement because it displays a lack of clarity in James's thinking at this stage. Here he does not argue against a party, but notes that it can be one of the organisational forms of the Marxist group. He also seems to be saying that the validity of the party is based on the understanding of its own abolition in post-revolutionary society. Nevertheless, James's suggestions of concrete tasks were limited. The analysis contained in *Notes on Dialectics* deconstructed Trotskyism, yet James remained organisationally a part of the Trotskyist movement. This contradiction was also partly responsible for the weakness in his concrete organisational programme.

In a series of interviews given in 1980 and 1981, James states that he considers his most important work to be *Notes on Dialectics*. Referring to the events in Poland in the 1980s, he argues that this work foresaw the situation where the proletariat in a mass form would intervene in political life. He also makes the point that both the events in Hungary in 1956 and the actions of the Polish workers signalled the death of the Leninist vanguard Party. Yet organisation was necessary, and always central to Marxist political thought was this necessity. The deconstruction of the party did not mean the end of organisation but the abolition of one form of party organisation. James's new universal, 'The Party and Revolution', has been critiqued, particularly his notion of the abolition of the party which has been regarded as not only a rupture with Marxism/Leninism but a fundamental departure from Marxist political theory. Let us examine this in more detail.

## The Marxist Theory of the Party

The Marxist theory of social and political change is rooted in the notion of classes and class struggle. From this perspective, political parties are representative of a specific stage of the growth of classes. Political parties defined in the Marxist sense are therefore organisations and institutions which reflect class developments. As John Molyneux notes, 'parties are moments in the development of classes'.[45]

There are four major thinkers within the classical Marxist tradition whose writings attempt to develop the notion of the political party. Marx himself, writing the *Communist Manifesto*, states that 'The Communists do not form a separate party opposed to other working class parties.'[46] Here he stresses the role of communists as distinct from all other representatives of the working class by the fact that they are:

> The most advanced and resolute section of the working class parties of every country ... theoretically, they have over the great mass of the proletariat the advantage of clearly understanding the line of march, the conditions and the ultimate general results of the proletarian movement.[47]

Marx's formulation establishes a dichotomy between *class* and party, and it is obvious that the theoretical knowledge of the communist group means that it operates at a higher level of political consciousness. From this formulation it follows that a mechanism is needed which will bring this consciousness to the proletariat. Marx's formulation also contains what has become a central dilemma of the Marxist theory of the party – the relationship between consciousness, class and party. In many of Marx's writings the emphasis is on the emancipation of the working class being an act of self-emancipation. The communists as a specific group work within the working-class movement to facilitate its logical development. Overall, however, Marx's preoccupation was not with the development of an independent revolutionary organisation, but more with the self-organisation and activity of the working class, and finding the new elements of this activity which would demonstrate the revolutionary nature of the class. His theory of the party was therefore general and his formulations, although posing the contradictions, do not attempt to answer them. If he left any organisational legacy, it is the internationalism of the working-class movement. From the Communist League to the First International, the organisation of the working class was international in nature.

The growth of socialist movements and parties, and the development of social democracy, particularly in Germany, were the next stages of proletarian political party development. The social democratic party was the forerunner of mass political parties and the German model became the ideal for all revolutionaries. Karl Kautsky, the leading Marxist theoretician of the period, took Marx's formulation of the political consciousness of the communists to its negative logical conclusion, and stated that socialist consciousness could only be brought to the working class from agencies external to it. This formulation became the core of Lenin's theoretical justification for the formation of the vanguard party. This combined with the specific factors of Russian society, an authoritarian state, shaped organisational conceptions as outlined in Lenin's *What is to be done?* In this pamphlet Lenin recognised that:

> In an autocratic state, the more we confine the membership of such organisation to people who are professionally engaged in revolutionary activity and who have been professionally trained in the art of combating the political police, the more difficult will it be to unearth the organisation.[48]

He concluded that in such a situation the traditional democratic electoral practices were impractical. 'Under conditions of political freedom our party will be built entirely on the elective principle. Under the autocracy this is impracticable for the collective thousands of workers that make up the party.'[49] Lenin's solution to this was the notion of democratic centralism, which raised fundamental issues of political organisation, particularly the relationship between consciousness and advanced political thought. In this regard, he notes:

> Working-class consciousness cannot be genuine political consciousness unless the workers are trained to respond to all cases of tyranny ... class political consciousness can be brought to the workers only from without, that is, only from outside the economic struggle, from outside the sphere of relations between workers and employers.[50]

Here starkly posed were all the dilemmas of the Marxist theory of the party. What is the relationship of the class to the formation of consciousness? Who has this consciousness and how is it attained? What is the relationship between the economic and political struggle? According to James, Lenin understood revolutionary struggle and change as organically connected to the party up to 1917. But influenced by the Soviets in 1917, Lenin changed his position about the nature of working-class consciousness, although he never formally repudiated the vanguard notion of the party.

The inherent dangers in Lenin's formulations were dissected by Rosa Luxemburg. In her work *The Russian Revolution and Leninism or Marxism* she writes:

> But the movement as a whole does not proceed from the economic to the political struggle, nor even to the reverse. Every great political mass action, after it has attained its political highest point, breaks up into a mass of economic strikes, but also to the revolution as a whole ... In a word, the economic struggle is the transmitter from one political centre to another ... cause and effect here continually change places here.[51]

Luxemburg's approach is dialectical and grasps the relation between class, party and consciousness as a dynamic process in which class activity propels the party forward. Consciousness, in her view, was not brought to the working class from outside, but was a result of their own class experiences. She writes: 'A high degree of political education, of class consciousness and organisation ... cannot be fulfilled by pamphlets and leaflets, but only by the living political school, by the fight and in the fight, in the continuous course of the revolution.'[52]

The mistakes of mass working-class self-activity were better than an efficient party central committee. As Luxemburg notes: 'Let us speak plainly – historically, the errors committed by a truly revolutionary movement are infinitely more fruitful than the infallibility of the cleverest Central Committee.'[53] From her perspective the central problem of the Marxist theory of the party was consciousness. For Lenin, consciousness was brought to the class externally, thereby developing a dichotomy between the politics of the working class and Marxist politics. Luxemburg rejected the dichotomy and rooted consciousness in the self-activity of the class. However, it was the Italian Marxist Antonio Gramsci who systematically studied the nature and role of consciousness in the working-class movement. He writes that:

> Man is above all else mind, consciousness – that is, he is a product of history – not nature. There is no other way of explaining why socialism has not come into existence already, although there have always been exploiters and exploited ... Such awareness was not generated out of brute physiological needs, but out of

intelligent reasoning, first of all by a few and later by entire social classes who perceived that causes of certain social facts and understood that there might be ways of converting the structure of repression into one of rebellion and social reconstruction. This means that every revolution has been preceded by an intense labour of social criticism, of cultural penetration and diffusion.[54]

A consequence of Gramsci's analysis was the relation of consciousness to objective social reality; as he notes, 'Man does not enter into relations with nature just by being himself part of nature, but actively, by means of work and technique. Furthermore, the relations are not mechanical. *They are active and conscious*' (emphasis added).[55] There is, therefore, a dialectical reciprocity between objective reality – man and consciousness. From this standpoint Gramsci defines spontaneity and consciousness, and notes that there is no pure spontaneity, and that in the most spontaneous movement it is simply the case that the elements of 'conscious leadership' cannot be checked and have left no reliable document.[56] He further argues that common sense is the fundamental element of spontaneity. He defines common sense thus: 'Its most fundamental characteristic is that it is a conception which, even in the brain of one individual, is fragmentary, incoherent and inconsequential.'[57] However, he notes that common sense is not in opposition to great systems of thought. The proletariat therefore begins with common sense, and the passage to consciousness is through a struggle of political hegemonies. Hence, consciousness is a spiral in which progressive self-consciousness is the site for the unification of theory and practice.

Critical to this transition is the role of intellectuals and ideology. According to Carl Boggs:

> During the long struggle for ideological hegemony, the revolutionary intellectuals would have to take the initiative on many fronts ... in bourgeois society, however, given the prevailing definition of intellectuals as either scientific-technical experts or learned men of culture, this form of ideological combat always threatens to become elitist and even obscurantist ... Gramsci's way out of this dilemma was the formation of groupings of 'organic intellectuals' that could be both 'leading and representative' in the critical aspect of being part of the everyday social existence of the working class.[58]

For Gramsci, this conception meant a new definition of the Marxist party and its role. The party came into being as an expression of the independent nature of the proletariat seeking its own self-consciousness. However, Gramsci himself falls prey to the dilemma of what role proletariat self-activity plays in consciousness because he also notes that 'in the initial stages, innovation cannot flow from the masses'.[59] In the end his work does not resolve the dilemma but sharply poses the questions. We therefore see that the history of the Marxist theory of party has contradictory elements. James recognised this from 1937 when in his first full-length Marxist work, *World Revolution 1919–1936*, he wrote: 'There is no specific answer for this problem. It is perhaps the greatest of the many bows that the revolutionary Ulysses will have to bend.'[60]

In 1948, operating from the perspective of the archetypal figure of Matthew Bondman, James came to the conclusion that the conditions and self-activity of the proletariat led it to create new forms. Increasingly, as the 'invading socialist society' approached, the proletariat would seek to intervene in the political sphere. His posing of the problem in 1948 was not narrowly organisational, but was an attempt to chart the political requirements for a new stage of capital. From James's perspective within the Marxist tradition, the conception of the party was a consequence of early capitalist development. This context had changed by 1948. No other major Marxist thinker of the 1940s had subjected the Leninist party to the rigours of the Hegelian dialectic. But James's focus on the self-activity of the proletariat and the new forms which emerged from this self-activity still left a void in his political theory. What was the precise characteristic and nature of the revolutionary organisation in the modern period, and how was political power to be seized? The issue was further compounded, because what if the self-activity of the proletariat did not reveal Revolutionary conciousness?

James would argue that his concern in 1948 was to create new political categories; the precise organisational form of a Marxist organisation would come later. His focus was to make central what was then missing in Marxist political theory: the nature of the self-activity of the proletariat and the historical evolution of this self-activity as regards the Socialist Revolution. In doing this, James changed the co-ordinates of the party and class debate and shifted the focus to the new context and the precise activities of the proletariat.

## State capitalism, World Revolution and the Party

By 1950 the critical properties of a Jamesian political theory were in place. Perhaps James himself would react to this assertion like Marx before him – I am not a Jamesian – however, his and the Tendency's contributions were distinct. In his work *State Capitalism and World Revolution* (1950), he presented his last major document to the Trotskyist movement. In it he refines the critique of Trotskyism, stating categorically that:

Our position is that the chaos in the International is due to the fact that Trotsky's method of analysis and system of ideas are wrong and that the chaos in the International will continue to grow until a new system is substituted for the present one.[61]

He then states his own political position not only on state capitalism and the nature of Soviet society, but on the fundamental characteristic of the socialist revolution, the role of intellectuals and the historical processes of social change. In the traditional Marxism-Leninist paradigm, the socialist revolution was marked by the proletariat seizure of state power. For James this was not the case. Martin Glaberman writes in the Preface to *State Capitalism and World Revolution*:

The Revolution is not the means by which workers achieve new socialist institutions to replace the old bourgeois institutions. The revolution is the means by which the socialist institutions emerge and destroy the bourgeois institutions which restrain them.[62]

The core ideas of the workers achieving socialist consciousness by their own self-activity, and that bourgeois society is an obstacle to this, are central to a Jamesian theory of revolutionary politics. The basis for this is James's belief that Marxist analysis of the growth of capital was based on the presumption that the 'proletariat is always increasing in numbers and is united, disciplined and organised', that is, they are prepared socially for its task, by the very mechanism of capitalist production itself.[63]

For James, increasing conflict consequently created a 'socially prepared proletariat'. To set this statement in context, James addressed the mode of labour in the Soviet Union and United States. From this examination he developed a theory of the bureaucracy in the international labour movement. Defining the term bureaucracy, James begins with a quote from Lenin:

This is why and the only reason why the officials of our political and industrial organisations are corrupt – or more precisely, tend to be corrupted by the conditions of capitalism, why they betray a tendency to become transformed into bureaucrats, i.e. privileged persons divorced from the masses and supervision of the masses.[64]

The essence of a bureaucracy was therefore the divorce of the masses from the officials. Within the American economy, James notes the development of Taylorism and the increased rationalisation of production, which reached its peak as Fordism. This new tendency created in its wake a new tier of workers, who James says, burst into revolt in the CIO. The CIO in its inception aimed at revolution in production. The workers would examine what they were told to do and then decide whether it was satisfactory to them or not. This rejection of the basis of capitalist economy is the preliminary basis of a socialist economy. The next positive step is the total management of industry by the proletariat.[65]

What holds this step back is the creation of a labour bureaucracy.

> The history of production ... is the corruption of the bureaucracy and its transformation into an instrument of capitalist production, the restoration to the bourgeoisie of what it had lost in 1936, the right to control production standards. Without this mediating role of the bureaucracy, production in the United States would be violently and continuously disrupted until one class was undisputed master ...[66]

The aim of this bureaucracy is to 'substitute the struggle over consumption, higher wages, pensions, education, etc., for a struggle in production'.[67] A similar situation existed for the mode of labour in the Soviet Union and James observes that 'the Stalinist bureaucracy is the American bureaucracy carried to its ultimate and logical conclusion ... The rulers of Russia perform the same functions as are performed by Ford, General Motors, and their huge bureaucratic staffs.'[68]

James's conclusions in *State Capitalism and World Revolution* are based on a study of the process of bureaucratisation in the Soviet economy between 1924 and 1936. His definition of bureaucracy and its roots in capitalist production allowed him to distinguish his Tendency from the traditional Trotskyist notion of the bureaucratic degeneration of the Soviet Union. For James the degeneration was rooted in production; for Trotsky it was in the political sphere. Hence, the programmatic calls of Trotskyism for the restoration of democracy, while James's programme was for socialist revolution and the release of the creative energies of the proletariat as the basis for a new society. James's theory of the bureaucracy and its role in the labour movement is critical since the successful march of the 'invading socialist society' was stopped only by this group. His programmatic response was to encourage the self-activity of the proletariat in production against the traditional unions and the officials of labour. The issue of the bureaucracy was related also to the nature of the Leninist party.

Criticising Stalin's position on the party, James states:

> The Stalinist theory and practice of the Party is the direct result of the Stalinist conception of the Plan. The Party consists of the elite, the most efficient, the most loyal, the most devoted, etc. The Party mobilises the proletariat, politically, economically

and morally to *carry out the plan* ... their conception of the party becomes the essence of bureaucracy, bureaucratic administration, bureaucratic organisation, the bureaucratic party.[69] (emphasis in the original)

James then places this perspective within a philosophical framework of rationalism and the role of intellectuals, observing that:

Rationalism is the philosophy of bourgeois political economy ... and that production is a division of labour between the passive masses and the active elite. Rationalism has reached its end in the complete divorce and absolute disharmony between manual and intellectual labour, between the socialised proletariat and the monster of centralised capital.[70]

Stalinism and the corruption of the party and the plan were expressions of rationalism reorganised to look like a new revolutionary doctrine. Refining the notions developed in *Notes on Dialectics*, James states that it is the modern petit-bourgeois intellectual who has become the representative of rationalism:

The anti-Stalinist, anti-capitalist petty bourgeois intellectuals themselves the victims of the absolute division between mental and physical labour, do not know where to go or what to do. Unable to base themselves completely upon the modern proletariat, they turn inward, pursuing a self-destructive, soul searching analysis of their own isolation, alienation and indecision.[71]

Revolutionary intellectuals now had to overcome the division between themselves and the proletariat – 'philosophy must now be proletarian'. James comments that 'there is no longer any purely philosophical answer ... philosophical questions ... can only be solved by the revolutionary action of the proletariat and the masses'.[72] James had arrived at a coherent revolutionary political theory which would make Matthew Bondman the *core* of a new society. His political theory and sense of history was now firmly rooted in a dialectic and the political and ideological forms of the oppressed classes. From this base he would develop a notion of freedom as

The end towards which mankind is inexorably developing by the constant overcoming of internal antagonisms. Freedom is *not* the enjoyment, ownership or use of goods, but self-realisation, creativity based upon the incorporation into the individual personality of the whole previous development of humanity. *Freedom is creative* universal – not utility.[73] (emphasis in the original)

*Notes on Dialectics State Capitalism and World Revolution* represented the final theoretical break with Trotskyism. West Indian nationalism, the self-activity of the American working class and a sensibility honed to the passions of human life had driven James to the new revolutionary universals.

Caliban had not only entered history, but was walking where few others dare.

CHAPTER 8

# James, Marx and the Notion of Happiness

*Notes on the Dialectics* cleared the path for new directions in James's political theory. It did so within the general context of the theoretical ossification of Marxism as Soviet state ideology and the pessimism which characterised Western intellectual thought in the post-World War II period. The new directions became a pole of optimism for James and the Tendency. At this time James's political theory represented an alternative to mainstream Marxist-Leninist thought which was influenced by the Soviet theorist Zhalanov, who reduced major questions of philosophy and political theory to the dogmatic repetition of Lenin's *Materialism and Empiro-Criticism*. For many communists, the existence of the Soviet Union settled all the fundamental questions of revolutionary politics, a consequence of the division of political thought into two opposing camps, bourgeoisie and proletariat, with the latter defined by Stalin.

The Stalinisation of intellectual life affected the Western communist parties in bizarre ways. For example, the French Communist Party with its vast array of journals, launched an assault on the discipline of psychoanalysis. The French communist writer Roger Garaudy equated human freedom with the Stalinist plan in the Soviet Union. Outside the traditional communist movement, three major trends developed in the immediate post-World War II period. In France, Jean-Paul Sartre continued his work on the philosophy of existentialism, and in America psychoanalysis became an important feature of intellectual life. The third trend was the emergence of the notion of totalitarianism. Overarching all three streams was the idea of crisis in intellectual thought. Daniel Bell encapsulated the pessimism in 1949 when he stated:

> For out of the confusions and exhaustions of war, a new non-political attitude is spreading, typified by the French 'je m'en fiche' (I don't give a damn) and the Italian 'fanno schiffo tutti' (they all stink) in which the sole desire of the great masses of people is simply to be left alone. Conscripted, regimented, manipulated, disoriented in the swirl of ideological warfare, the basic and growing attitude is one of distrust. And for the

intellectual, the seed bearers of culture, the feeling is one of betrayal by power and the mood is one of impotence.[1]

The English poet T.S. Eliot summed up this mood when he wrote in 1948, 'We can assert with some confidence that our own period is one of decline; that the standards of culture are lower than they were fifty years ago; and that the evidences of this decline are visible in every department of human society.'[2] Surveying the human landscape, many Western intellectuals came to the conclusion that society was in deep crisis. Frank Füredi observes that 'after the end of the second World War, it was not possible to think of a return to a normal past, on the contrary, the past embodied in the inter-war years was one to be avoided. After Hiroshima and Nagasaki the future did not appear brilliant either.'[3]

In this context the earlier rise of Nazism and Stalinism seemed to confirm totalitarianism as a specific feature and stage of human society. Writers on the subject were divided into three schools of thought. First, there were those who divorced totalitarianism from capitalism. Second, there were those like James Burnham, who, while recognising totalitarianism as a form of capitalism, demonstrated similarities between the state structures of Nazi Germany and Stalinist Soviet Union. The third stream was the most developed, elaborated by Hannah Arendt in *The Origins of Totalitarianism* (1948). Arendt conceptualised totalitarianism as a specific stage in human society. She posited the notion that the rise of totalitarianism was a result of the breakdown in class society and that 'the totalitarian movements aim at and succeed in organising masses – not classes. Totalitarian movements are possible whenever there are masses who for one reason or another have acquired the appetite for political organisation.'[4]

The German social theorist Herbert Marcuse, in describing the ideological elements of totalitarianism, noted its strong universalist tendencies and its conception of totality. He suggested that the need for totalitarianism was a weakness in traditional capitalist society and suggested the necessity for rational planning. However, Marcuse notes that the totalitarian society did not rectify this weakness:

> for in the totalitarian theory of the state, the foundations of this society, i.e., the economic order based on private property in the means of production, are not attacked. Instead, they are modified to the degree demanded by the monopolistic stage of this very economic order. In consequence, all contradictions that inhere in such an order and make a real totality impossible, are carried over into the new stage and its theory. Realising the desired unifying totality would in truth be an economic task.[5]

As Stalinism developed, studies of the nature of totalitarianism became concerned with the character of individualism as its opposite. At another level, the debate about totalitarianism became part of the Western ideological arsenal in the Cold War. As H. Stuart Hughes observes:

> In the early 1940s and early 1950s, the term served to ease the shock of emotional readjustment for Americans or Englishmen – or Emigrés, who had just defeated one enemy and were now called upon by their governments to confront another. If it could be proved that Nazism and Communism were very much the same thing, the cold war against the late ally could be justified by the rhetoric that had proved so effective against the late enemy.[6]

In filling out this contextual picture of the streams of intellectual thought, it should also be noted that particularly in Europe the period was also characterised as 'The Age of Anxiety', a phrase taken from W.H. Auden's 1947 work of that title. A number of themes merged in this period. There was not only the question of the existence of God, but four pillars of the Enlightenment and modernity were at stake. The experiences of Nazism and Stalinism generally weakened faith in science, reason, progress and history. The fate of history was particularly dubious since it was the totalitarian who seemed to capture the idea of history, using it as a powerful instrument. With scepticism in history came the idea of the decline of the West and cynicism about progress. Arnold Toynbee wrote of the period:

> this swift succession of catastrophic events on a steeply mounting gradient inevitably inspires a dark doubt about the future, and this doubt threatens to undermine our faith and hope at a critical eleventh hour which calls for the utmost exertion of these saving spiritual faculties.[7]

All evidence suggests that the old West – Europe – after two world wars was on the verge of collapse and had lost confidence in itself.

In summary,sections of the Western World in the late 1940s and early 1950s were characterised by the ossification of Marxist studies as Stalinisation consolidated itself; the development of theories of alienation, primarily existentialism; the emergence of the theory of totalitarianism; and the collapse of the idea of historical progress and the emergence of the notion that society was in regression. All this was accompanied by a pervasive pessimism.

## The United States Context

In profound contrast to this, the post-war period was hailed, in the words of Henry Luce, as 'The American Century'. One writer observes that by the end of the 1940s the average American enjoyed

[an] income fifteen times greater than that of the average
foreigner ... by 1947, the United States produced half the
world's manufactures; 57% of the steel; 43 percent of the
electricity; and 62 percent of the oil ... At the same time,
America's global economic dominance, together with its
technological advances contributed to a period of unrivalled
affluence at home ... Swelling families, new suburban homes,
televisions, and above all, big powerful shiny automobiles
symbolised the hopes and possibilities of the era.[8]

While the mood in Europe was one of pessimism, in the United
States the economic boom generated optimism and the Cold War
itself became the rhetoric which facilitated a major pillar of economic
boom: arms production and military spending. Further, it provided
the elements of an ideological construct which facilitated the
dominance of American values. The expansion of the American
economy, the growth of consumer durables and the development
of communications created a fundamental new context for the
American proletariat. The arrival of migrant labour to fill jobs in
the secondary labour market and the movement of industries from
traditional centres also added to the changes that were taking
place. The American proletariat was also unencumbered by the fact
that the American mainland was not a theatre of war or of Nazism.
All these factors confirmed to James and his Tendency the capacity
of the American proletariat to create new revolutionary forms of
proletarian action in both politics and culture.

Following his charateristic methodology, James had studied the
different aspects of the American working class. From as early as
1943, he was profoundly impressed by certain features of American
society, and his ten-month tour of the country had made a deep
impression on him. James's method of observation operated on many
different levels. At one level, it meant studying books and journals,
while at another, he was absorbed by the daily lives and activities
of people. In the latter his studies were facilitated by the novelist's
keen eye for personalities and their unique features. In 1943, he
wrote to Constance Webb that he was beginning to go to the
cinema regularly: 'The only thing that keeps me quiet is the movies.
So at all hours of the day or night I go where there is a picture,
often the nearest. That is why I see some over and over again. *I
am learning America plenty*' (emphasis added).[9] James spent years
attempting to gain a comprehensive understanding of the American
working class. For him, capitalist society had fragmented human
beings, and at a fundamental level the revolutionary response had
done the same, positing the political person, the social person and
the cultural person. James now was seeking to come to terms with
the new dimensions of political and social life, as well as working

out his own artistic and literary instincts. At some stage both processes would have to be fused. His contact with the American working class and his relationship with Constance Webb, who was ambitious to become an actress, had revived his artistic and literary instincts which, he claimed, had been drained out of him by his revolutionary activity in Europe. But by the late 1940's the expression of his artistic and literary instincts had been honed by years of political and social observations and experiences in various countries.

In a series of letters to Constance Webb, in 1944, James attempts to grapple with the nature of human fragmentation. He states that it is a uniquely human response which is central to an integrated perspective: 'But you have to feel like them ... you must have inside the *common simple human responses*' (emphasis added).[10] Increasingly, the expression of James's artistic side needed to be integrated into a holistic view of society. In another letter to Webb he writes:

> My life is political, a very special branch ... As you see poetry is for me a very living, a very vital part of my life ... all the creative instincts I have had to suppress or ignore are alive in me again in you ... I have particularly during the last four years made a complete examination of the whole theory, helped by some splendid people. And from the theory has come insight into the movement in economic, in philosophical in *human* terms. It is during the past 4 years that I have learnt to know what it is to need ... I become more and more interested in all aspects of life, as in our modern society all aspects of life become more closely inter-related.[11] (emphasis in original)

This perspective of society as a totality had at its centre human beings:

> The problem is not a higher standard of living or no employment. The problem ... the strictly scientific economic problem, the solution of the capitalist crisis, lies in precisely the recognition of man as Man. That is Marxism, that is Marx's philosophic theory, that is his economic theory, that is his political theory. The acting out of revolution makes him man.[12]

The shape of James's Marxism in the late 1940s was fundamentally different from the traditional Marxist/Leninist currents. Beginning with the early works of Marx, James had woven together the threads of an integrative radical critique of capitalism. With the United States as his context each part of the theory was shaped in relation to fundamental political questions. First, it was the nature of the Soviet Union – state capitalism; then it was the nature of the Trotskyist movement; and then the philosophic roots of Marxism, followed by grappling with the revolutionary forms of the proletariat at each of its historic junctures. The next step was the integration of all these streams – of the condition of modern society in 1950 – into a theory of modern civilisation and a prognosis for its evolution. In the early months of 1950, James wrote the manuscript *Notes on American Civilisation*.

## Notes on American Civilisation

*Notes on American Civilisation*, alternatively called *The Struggle for Happiness*, marks a watershed in James's political evolution. In its unpublished form, it was a proposal written for the clarification of his key ideas. This resulted in a textual unevenness with the general lines of argument sometimes becoming lost in unnecessarily long quotations. James apologised for this and promised to remove the surplus quotations in the finished text. His writing methodology had been established during this first American period, and the text was written for the members of the Tendency, to be critiqued by them before publication. In the Preface he notes: 'The person who has this copy … is asked to make marginal notes or make comments in any other way, preferably writing.'[13] This was also a fundamental aspect of Jamesian political methodology. Although he was the leader of the Tendency, the final product was usually the result of discussion and debate. He himself acknowledged this and consistently refers to the trio of Grace Lee, Raya Dunayevskaya and himself.

*Notes on American Civilisation*[14] is a systematic attempt to elaborate a Marxism of the period as a radical critique of Western civilisation using the United States as the point of departure. After the three major revolutions of the eighteenth century – American (1776), French (1789) and Haitian (1791) – within the trajectory of Western political thought, the concepts of liberty, individual freedom and equality had become the basis for human association. For over a century the precise meanings and clarification of these terms preoccupied traditional political theorists.

But within the Marxist perspective, normative political theory was discouraged, following the line that the existence of the Soviet Union had answered all these questions. Importantly, Marx's writings had critiqued the early proclamation of these political values as limited by bourgeois politics and the market economy. Marx had also declared that these political values were ideals which would be transformed in communist society. Marx's notion of freedom involved the subordination rather than the exaggeration of politics. However, the evolution of society and the continuous development of ideas meant that individuals lived according to many of these values. Traditional Marxist-Leninist analysis ignored the common conceptions of these values and their importance to human consciousness, whereas James, in his attempt to construct political theory for the period, took these conceptions and how people acted them out into consideration. Thus the core of Part I of *Notes on American Civilisation* was a rupture from conventional radical Marxist political analysis.

James begins the text by dividing American civilisation into two symbolic stages – the Declaration of Independence represented by George Washington, and mass production represented by Henry Ford:

> The Declaration of Independence enshrines life, liberty and the pursuit of happiness. To this day, nowhere in the world is there such a struggle to grasp at all the elements of life and liberty. Nowhere has happiness been pursued with such uninhibited energy and zest ... In fact, life, liberty and the pursuit of happiness and mass production are today not distinguishable. They form an entity. For the spokesmen of American civilisation, this entity is the basis of all the benefits and possibilities which they propose to maintain and extend to a disintegrating world as the only hope of its salvation.[15]

For James, a study of American civilisation could lead to a comprehensive grasp of the general crisis in thought, in economic and social life in the post-World War II period. The manuscript not only elaborated a Marxist methodology for the period, but merged it with the intellectual tradition of writers like de Tocqueville and other classical political theorists within the Western tradition. This feature of James's work was central and raises the issue of what influences facilitated his departure in Marxist political analysis. Was he returning to his earlier readings of classical Western political theory, as well as returning to a tradition of history which was expressed in the radical egalitarian groups of the English Revolution of the 1640s, the popular movements of the French Revolution and the Paris Commune?

In the manuscript, James's task seemed to be to study American civilisation within the framework of readings of the categories of political value, freedom and equality, transposed to America and expressed in American popular movements. As such *Notes on American Civilisation* should also be considered as a major contribution to radical American political theory. In the work James identifies what he perceives to be a dilemma – the bankruptcy in thought and crisis in American society within the context of great material wealth. Thus he notes that in spite of its great wealth 'the fact remains that this civilisation is ridden with conflicts over economic, social, political, racial [issues,] over elementary human relations, love and marriage'.[16] Why this was so and how it had come about, James proposed to examine as a

stranger who has lived in the United States for twelve crucial
years. I propose to analyse the concepts of liberty, freedom,
individuality, the pursuit of happiness as I observed them and
studied them in the past history and actual lives of the
American people.[17]

What were the factors which James brought to this project? Two
were critical. First was the sensibility of the littérateur, and second
was the fact that he was an outsider, a black person operating
within a radical tradition. Cedric Robinson in his work *Black
Marxism* (1983) makes the point that the 'Renegade Black intellectual
within the radical Black tradition not only had to master the
requirements of Western civilisation, but critique it'.[18] James
confirms this in speaking of the Caribbean poet Aimé Cesaire: 'So
when Cesaire wrote his tremendous attack upon Western civilisation,
in *Return to my Native Land* he was able to make this ferocious attack
because he knew it inside out.'[19] Robinson observes that the
achievement for black intellectuals was wider than the notions of
political struggles, viewed from traditional Marxist paradigms.
This was particularly so for Caribbean intellectuals. One aspect of
the intellectual efforts of the West Indian population was that it
captured, revised and creolised Western intellectual traditions as
part of a development of an *authentic* Caribbean experience. Hence,
many Caribbean intellectuals have been called 'children of the
Enlightenment'.[20] Thus, James like Cesaire was equipped to
transpose the core values which emerged from the revolutionary
experiences of Europe to America.

## The Text

James asserts that America in 1950 represented a new departure
in human civilisation. He notes that the development of mass
production had

> created a vast populace, literate, technically trained, conscious
> of itself and of its inherent right to enjoy all the possibilities of
> the society ... no such social forces have existed in any society
> with such ideas and aspirations since the citizens of Athens ...
> the modern populace decides not by votes, but by the tickets
> it buys and the money it pays. The result has been a new
> extension of aesthetic premises. The popular film, the radio, the
> gramophone, the comic strip, the popular daily paper and far
> more, the popular periodical, constitute a form of art and media
> of social communication ... and constitute a departure in the
> twentieth century as new in civilisation as the art of printing in
> the fifteenth.[21]

He counterposes this development in popular culture to the writings of traditional intellectuals and writers of the period and notes that:

> It is possible to say that it is in the study of these and the outbursts of American social and political action ... that there can be seen the beginnings of tendencies ... the literary and social expression of the popular arts in the United States with all their defects, assume therefore a symbolical significance which raises them far beyond the status they occupied in estimates based on other premises.[22]

Using this as one element in his methodology, James then proceeds to examine the central political and social concerns of the period – the nature and characteristics of totalitarianism. He observed that while the vast majority of the American people feared totalitarianism, there were tendencies in American life which were totalitarian and suggested that totalitarianism is a universal phenomenon of the modern age:

> the apparently irrational and stupefying behaviour of people in totalitarian states is a product of modern civilisation, not merely in terms of the preservation of property and privilege but as the result of deep social and psychological needs of man in modern society.[23]

His definition of totalitarianism is very specific:

> In this volume there is made an identification of the regimes of Hitlerism and Stalinism under the common name *totalitarian*. It must be understood that this implies no identity of the regimes. The characterisation has been made merely to emphasise the ultimate social consequences of any kind of regime which does not develop along cooperative lines, developing the creative spirit of the mass. Politically speaking, the differences between Stalinism and Fascism particularly on a world scale, are of immense, in fact decisive importance.[24] (emphasis in the original)

Here James attempts to distance himself from the Cold War ideological debates and from other social and political theories of totalitarianism of the period. Describing totalitarianism as a stage in human society, not the specific forms of fascist Germany or Stalinist Soviet Union, his argument is that it is a tendency in Western civilisation, which is present in all 'developed capitalist societies'. As a phenomenon it is not narrowly the result of monopoly capitalism in a specific stage of growth, but rather the maturation of tendencies ever present in Western civilisation and thought. A central feature of his project therefore was to unravel the history and evolution of that tendency and to indicate the social forces which could counter it. To do this James divides the work into four major sections.

The historical development of the American Spirit, according to James is:

> the peculiar development of the United States ... allows the ideals of eighteenth century Europe to be expressed in a manner ... close to reality. This development, different from that of Europe, allowed for a profound practice in democracy and the creation of the free individual.[25]

It is critical to note here that the concept of the individual as a political and social notion in Western civilisation was a revolutionary one and that its ascendancy resulted in the transformation of the basis of society from that of family or tribe to that of the individual self. The notion of human freedom was separated from its social dimension and human freedom in Europe became *individual* freedom. For James, the 'American Spirit' was the clearest expression of this notion. He quotes de Tocqueville's description of American traders as 'heroic' and notes that:

> Freedom, initiative, adventure, self-expression in pursuit of trade and industry. The foundations of the American character are being solidified. The original stocks are bold, adventurous, handy to make the journey at all. The historical and geographical circumstances form an environment which develops these qualities to the full.[26]

Politically, James contends that this spirit expressed itself in the movement of 'Jacksonian Democracy'. In American history, the achievements of this period were starkly different from those in Europe: 'In contrast with the tremendous intellectual speculations and achievements of Europe, we have in the United States a rough untutored empirical achievement in actuality of the most advanced speculations of the old world.'[27] Then James argues that the American intellectuals of the nineteenth century – Walt Whitman, Herman Melville – and the work of the abolitionists raised the fundamental problem of the modern age – the nature of individualism and its relationship to human freedom. James's focus was now leading him into new realms where traditional Marxist thought had not delved and thus into paths where answers would be novel and complex.

Discussing Walt Whitman, James shows how Whitman's work expressed American individualism and that his fundamental conception was 'his conviction of the worth of the individual as an individual in work and play and all aspects of the life, and the recognition that this individual would only find his fullest expression with other individuals equal to himself'.[28] On the other hand, the work of Herman Melville, particularly his book *Moby Dick* was different. James notes:

> He described with absolute precision various individuals in their social setting, the work they did, their relations with other men. This led him to see that individualism in certain sections of America had become one of the most dangerous vices of the age and would destroy society.[29]

Recognising Melville as one of the greatest writers of the period, James comments, 'a great artist is not a politician and his social and political ideas are to be deduced from his artistic work'.[30] In Melville's portrayal of the character Ahab in *Moby Dick*, James says that this is 'the only serious study in fiction of the type which has reached its climax in the modern totalitarian dictator'.[31] James dissects Ahab's personality and notes that:

> Ahab represents not merely man in general, but the individualistic man of the nineteenth century at a stage where he faces the insoluble nature of his problems both with nature and society. That is where modern man has reached today ... today we have reached a stage where this consuming rage with the social and psychological problems of society is eating away at the whole of humanity.[32]

In such a crisis, individualism drives some, who base themselves on the ordinary needs of human beings, to feel that they are chosen and above the law. Out of this crisis a personality like Hitler arises who, James suggests, 'is not only an individual. A man like Hitler could only appear when an essential number of people, representing the type, had become a social grouping, representing vast social forces.'[33] James then argues that the totalitarian personality is present in Ahab and is representative of the modern age:

> in his frantic morbidness he at last came to identify with him, not only his bodily woes, but all his intellectual and spiritual exasperations. The White Whale swam before him as the monomanic incarnation of all those malicious agencies some deep men feel eating in them.[34]

The fundamental importance of *Moby Dick* was that it expressed 'the immense vitality and dangers of the individualism which was about to rise to a new and unprecedented stage'.[35] Turning from writers to political activists, James examines the work of the Abolitionists and comments that:

> With the Abolitionist intellectuals, we touch a new dimension, intellectuals whose whole intellectual, social and political creativity was the expression of precise social forces. They were

the means by which a direct social movement expressed itself, the movement of the slaves and free negroes for freedom.[36]

He defines the main planks of the Abolitionists' programme as: the immediate emancipation of the slave, the pacifism of the movement, the disapproval of the constitution as pro-slavery, a belief in mass activity, their internationalism, their belief in gender equality, and their political intolerance. James says that the Abolitionists represented a specific American phenonemon:

> But one thing emerges. Out of America, with no assistance from any alien tradition but from the very genesis of the country, emerged this clearly recognisable replica of the early Christians, the Puritans, and later the early Bolsheviks, types which have appeared only when fundamental changes are shaping a society.[37]

Having set the stage and indicated individualism and mass revolution as two tendencies in American society, James, always the dialectician, begins to pose both the problem and its negation in the remainder of the text, discussing how these tendencies play themselves out in the America of the 1950s. With the historical framework established, James poses the fundamental question in sharp relief. What is freedom? He notes that at the official level the notion of freedom 'revolves around the thesis of the freedom of the individual in business enterprises'.[38] At the same time, he observes that there is a fundamental contradiction in the notion of freedom and argues that 'the economic and social structure of the United States has created so huge an apparatus of economic, social and political institutions that the freedom of the individual except in the most abstract terms does not exist'.[39] As a result the American state had shifted the debate from the notion of freedom to that of 'security'.

It is here that the work becomes assertive and sustained major analysis and definitions are lacking. In the section on freedom, James does not offer a definition of freedom; he only asserts that individual freedom is part of America's tradition and that it is expressed in the 'heroic frontiers man, trader, sailor and artisan striving to be a capitalist of the early days'.[40] Here there are some obvious similarities between James's and Marx's conceptions on the context for the emergence of individual freedom. However, engaging in debate about the nature of the state and its relation to the individual citizen, James posits that the welfare state which was emerging was contradictory to individual freedom and association. Here again he seems to be following the tendency in Marxist thought which pursued freedom only in a classless and stateless society. At the same time there seemed to be a libertarian strain in James's thought. Nevertheless, this would be misleading for two reasons: first, James

sees freedom as the reconcilation of the individual and society –
the dissolution of the fragmented individual; and secondly, James's
notion of direct democracy emphasised a synthesis between the
individual and community. In other words, the tension between
individual freedom, democracy and equality which is apparent in
liberal political theory is resolved in James's vision of the proletariat's
activities, which abolishes alienation at the point of production,
establishing a new productive system and a new society. James
therefore posits that the American population were

> faced now with the question of what has happened to individual
> freedom and freedom of association? The simplest way to state
> (1) that freedom has been lost in modern industrial production
> (2) that the outstanding social fact of the United States is that
> the population has gone a long way on the road to recognising
> that freedom has been lost.[41]

From this perspective he concludes:

> The specific feature of American heavy industry is the
> transference from man to machinery of the bodily and mental
> activities which formerly distinguished craftsmen or skilled
> labour. The modern worker is a cog in a machine. All progress
> in industry consists of making him more and more of a cog and
> less and less of a human being. The process has now reached
> a breaking point.[42]

In describing this process, James was returning to the earlier works
of Karl Marx. In the *Economic and Philosophical Manuscripts of 1844*,
Marx had postulated that human alienation manifested itself in
three ways: alienation from the object of one's labour, self-alienation
and alienation of human beings from each other and from humanity
in general. In describing the alienation of labour, Marx had noted
that

> [The] alienation of the worker in production meant not only
> that his labour becomes an object, an external existence but that
> it exists outside him, independently, as something alien to him,
> and that it becomes a power on its own, confronting him. It means
> that the life which he conferred on the object confronts him as
> something hostile and alien.[43]

James's analysis of industrial production and its fundamental role
in American society as well as the forms and ways in which the
American proletariat attempted to control the production process
itself, redefining the nature of work, was the critical link and
passage between economics, politics and culture. All the central
political questions now had to be posed from this perspective.
More importantly, the issue of political values which had been central

to human association could now be resolved, not mediated and therefore limited. But there was one additional element. While many Marxists studying the labour process would focus on political and economic struggles and then attempt to extrapolate political and social demands, James would add the new dimension of American popular culture.

Before turning to this, James offers his final assessment of individual freedom, industrial production and the American people:

> Upon a people bursting with energy, untroubled by feudal remains or a feudal past, soaked to the marrow in a tradition of individual freedom, industrial security, free association, a tradition which constantly held before them as the basis of their civilisation, upon this people more than all others has been imposed a mechanised way of life at work, mechanised forms of living, a mechanised totality which from morning till night, week after week, day after day, crushed the very individuality which tradition nourishes and the abundance of mass produced goods encouraged.[44]

From here James then moves into a new terrain of Marxist analysis by studying the responses of the American proletariat by means of a critical examination of popular culture.

Culture has always been an arena of controversy in Marxist studies and in the main has been subordinated to politics, with revolutionaries always questioning how culture could serve politics. Leon Trotsky, makes this point clearly in *Literature and Revolution* (1925) when he notes that 'literature ... from the point of view of an objective historical process ... is always a social servant and historically, utilitarian'.[45] James's perspective was fundamentally different and yet quite similar in some respects to Gramsci's who wrote:

> Culture is something quite different. It is organisation, discipline of one's inner self, a coming to terms with one's own personality; it is the attainment of a higher awareness, with the aid of which one succeeds in understanding one's own historical value, one's function in life, one's own rights and obligations.[46]

Popular culture was therefore the attempt by the masses to grapple with the inner logic of their existence. It did not serve politics, revolutionary or otherwise, but was the concrete expression of their world-view. James's approach was not utilitarian, but rather one which grappled with the precise nature of the phenomenon, and what is said about the needs and aspirations of the ordinary person. Such a methodology facilitated significant insights into the nature of popular culture and its relation to the social totality.

## Popular Culture and Individual Freedom

As noted before James's description of popular culture and its role is strikingly different from the traditional Marxist view. Formerly,

> we had to look at the economic relations of society, the political and social movements and the great artistic expressions to get a whole, complete and dynamic view of society, while as far as the great mass was concerned, we had to guess; today it is not so. The modern popular film, the modern newspaper (*The Daily News* not *The Times*), the comic strip, the evolution of Jazz, a popular periodical like *Life*, these mirror from year to year the deep social responses and evolution of the American people in relation to the fate which has overtaken the original concepts of freedom, free individuality, free associations, etc. To put it more harshly still, it is in the serious study of above all, Charles Chaplin, Dick Tracy, Gasoline Alley, James Cagney ... genuinely popular novels like those of Frank Yerby ... that you find the clearest ideological expression of the sentiments and deepest feelings of the American people and a great window into the future of America and the modern world.[47]

Here James is proposing that the products of popular culture were critical to an understanding of the inner feelings of the ordinary person and thus for an understanding of American civilisation. It was this dimension that needed to be examined.

Tracing the history of the entertainment industry and its turn to violence, sadism and cruelty, James suggests the rationale for it was the 'release of aggression immediately after the consciousness of the depression had seized hold of the country'.[48] He notes that this runs contrary to the traditional view, which suggests that 'to believe that the great masses of the people are merely passive recipients of what the purveyors of popular art give to them, is in reality to see people as dumb slaves'.[49] Popular film, James says, represents 'the deepest feelings of the masses, but represents them within the common agreement of no serious political or social questions which would cause explosions'.[50] According to James, the detective stories in particular were characteristic of the tension in modern American life:

> The film, strip, radio – drama are a form of art which must satisfy the masses. The individual seeking individuality in a mechanised socialised society where there is no certainty of employment, far less of being able to rise by energy and ability or going West as in the old days. In such a society, the individual demands an aesthetic compensation in the contemplation of free individuals who go out with the world and settle their problems by free activity and individualist methods. In the end 'crime does not

pay' but for an hour and a half, highly skilled actors and a huge organisation of production and distribution have given to many millions a sense of active living, and in the bloodshed, the violence, the freedom from restraint to allow pent up feelings free play, they have released the bitterness, hate, fear and sadism which simmer just below the surface.[51]

Next he argues that American and world society in general was in crisis. In so far as the conflict between formal social conceptions and those of ordinary persons were at such odds with reality, the result was bewilderment. In such a state, masses of people responded by turning to irrationalism and mysticism. Charlie Chaplin's work was different. Stating that the 'artistic achievements of films up to 1932 are the most remarkable of our age', James observes that Charlie Chaplin represented something new and the future:

Chaplin has been called the one universal man of modern times, appealing to all intellectuals and populace alike ... First of all, as a social figure, for this is the most important thing about him. The tramp was an individual. He defied the growing mechanisation and socialisation of life ... secondly Chaplin represented the ideals of the society in their constant conflict with reality.[52]

Claiming that the Depression had put an end to a particular genre of comedy, James states that only the Marx brothers and the work of Walt Disney are of any significance within the genre. He writes of the early films:

In its first contact with the masses and aiming solely to make money by pleasing them, there emerged the most remarkable artistic heritage of the times. It was killed by the depression ... instead we have a complete inversion, the mass exposing its rage, anger and hostility, its desire to smash the impasse in which it finds itself, and making this the outstanding new characteristic.[53]

James then makes a definitive statement about the nature of the film as an artform: 'The film is essentially the art of the masses, the working classes, the dwellers in remote agricultural areas and small towns, the lower middle classes.'[54] For James, this artform represented a new stage, and indicated in general the relationship between art and the masses. It also raises the issue of the definition of art.

James suggests that the distinction between serious art and popular art could no longer be maintained. In particular the emergence of the movie star system was representative of personalities which expressed the mood of the period. Film and the other popular artforms in early twentieth-century America were fundamental to any social analysis. In conclusion:

> It would seem that deprived of any serious treatment of the problem which overwhelmed it since 1919, the modern masses have reacted in two main ways. They have fostered on the one hand an individualistic response to violence, murder, atrocities, crime, sadism; and on the other, they have pertinaciously fostered and encouraged by their money and interest this creation of synthetic characters. Through them they live vicariously, see in them examples of that free individuality which is the dominant need of the vast mass today.[55]

Here James is using cultural analysis to make a major political point. The young man who at 21 had directed an operetta and had written short stories was returning to his original impulses but with a profound difference; he had absorbed both revolutionary politics and the foundations of Western thought. It was the latter which decisively shaped his conceptions of art and culture and their specific relationships to society:

> I have been emphasising the fact that the great mass of the modern population now is the object of modern popular art ... it will astonish ... to be reminded that practically the whole of the able-bodied population of the free citizens of Athens went to the theatre to see the plays and decide by their votes who was the prize winner.[56]

James then observes that the Greek conception of democracy was an integrative one and in:

> modern popular art, film, radio, television, comic strip, we are headed for some such artistic comprehensive integration of modern life, that the spiritual, intellectual ideological life of modern peoples will express itself in the closest and most rapid, most complete, absolutely free relation to the actual life of the citizens tomorrow ... It is being done in the totalitarian states already. But whereas among the Greeks free expression was the basis of intellectual life, the integrated expression of the totalitarian states is the result of the suppression of free expression.[57]

In applying this analysis to America, James would note that the contradiction between the conception of social life as it is and what people thought it should be, particularly in a society which had individualism as its framework would lead to ruin and totalitarianism. The implicit assumption therefore was that an elemental drive existed in human beings for universalism and integration in social relationships. James then asserts that the attraction of the totalitarian states was superficial universalism. The danger which faced American society was that this fragmentation would lead to rage and frustration and a popular appetite for blood-letting, which was a central feature of the totalitarian state:

> The possibility of totalitarian power arises only when the suppressed hatreds, antagonism, frustrations burst irrepressibly into the open. At this period it is clear that the social, political ideas of the old regime are exhausted and recognised as such by the vast majority. The function of the totalitarian state is to substitute a new state organisation and a new ideology for the old.[58]

The notion of fragmentation is central to James's political thought. He begins as Marx did with the examination of individuals in society within the framework of social relations, and as a result it is within this framework that individuals achieve their purpose. In this, James's thinking was similar to elements of Greek political philosophy. James characterised societal development as evolutionary: in the earliest phase, social and individual relations appear natural and unified, while in the phase of capitalist society, a dissolution occurs between the individual and social relations, and individualism becomes the norm. For James, the basis of individualism is capitalist ownership of the means of production and the alienation of labour in the productive process. Within this evolutionary schema, capitalism and its contradiction then lead to another phase in which the individual appropriates his or her labour, is reunited with it and reclaims universality. The individual then becomes a 'communal individual'.

In his 1947 essay *Dialectical Materialism and the Fate of Humanity,* James had postulated notions of the relationship of the individual, community and universality. As he states, 'the nature of man, therefore, becomes the search for this completeness and the overcoming of the obstacles which stood and stand in its way'.[59] In modern society this search resolved itself into the proletarian negation of the bourgeois state, and 'the modern state being what it is and the modern masses being what they are, the resolution of the antagonism implies the substitution of the masses for the state'.[60] When this occurs the quest for universality is completed. James observes this quest as one 'which constitutes the past history of humanity ... quest for concrete conditions of life adequate to man's real humanity'.[61]

James's conception of fragmentation therefore informs his political understanding of totalitarianism. He claims that the great need of modern man is for integration, and that his quest for universality required a new relationship between individual and community. In the next stage of *Notes on American Civilisation* he attempts to address this new sense of community and relate it to the struggle for happiness.

## The Quest for Happiness

James faces the problem of the quest for happiness by asking, 'What is it that people want?'[62] Traditionally this question would elicit a response like a 'better life'. Both liberals and revolutionaries would define this better life as one that increased the material welfare of the majority. Indeed many reform programmes have been based on this. Starting from a different perspective, James proclaims that the most important aspect of the proletariat's existence is work and notes that there is a duality within the proletariat:

> The same workers who express, as far as general politics are concerned, conservative and even reactionary sentiments will immediately turn around and express with regard to their daily work sentiments with the most revolutionary implications conceivable.[63]

At the core of this duality is a fundamental conflict:

> There is on the one hand the need, the desire created in him by the whole mighty mechanism of American industry, to work, to learn, to master the machine, to co-operate with others, to work out ways and means to do in two hours what ordinarily takes four, to organise the plant as only the workers know how. And on the other hand, the endless frustration of being merely a cog in a great machine.[64]

This conflict, James claims, shapes labour and compels the proletariat to action:

> At the other end of the scale are the mass walk outs, the continuous wild cat strikes ... the bitterness, the frustration, accumulated anger at times reach such a stage that the particular issue on which the strike is called is an issue and no more than an issue.[65]

The solution to this conflict is 'in the most abstract terms, the solution is that somehow the creative energies of modern man, the sense of personality of hundreds of millions of modern men must be made to function in their daily work'.[66] The solution to the labour–capital conflict was therefore not higher wages or greater material rewards, but the integration of the proletariat with work. In everyday language, James was describing the process of alienation and its resolution as the direct control of production by workers. By the 1950s, the control of production by the proletariat itself without mediation was a critical element of Jamesian political thought, and he felt that this tendency of the proletariat was recognised by both the bourgeoisie and reformist labour leaders.

In reporting a debate between the labour leader Walter Reuther and a union delegate, James comments that workers' councils were referred to sympathetically by Reuther, because he recognised this dynamic and because historically it was the programme of the Industrial Workers of the World (IWW), and the workers themselves were aware of that tradition. Comparing the labour leaders John Lewis and Reuther, James saw that the critical difference between the two was Lewis's conception of conflict, which was 'that workers and the industrialists must fight out these problems themselves without government interference'.[67] Since James's efforts were organised around a comprehensive view of American society, in the text, after discussing the proletariat, he moves on to the other social groups. He suggests that American farmers were a social group ready to take action, as were the lower sections of the middle class. The work then takes up the four other issues: women, blacks, sexuality and the role of the American intellectual.

On the question of blacks and their pivotal role in American society, James restates the position he had developed in the 1948 SWP resolution which established the independence, validity and the contributing characteristics of the black struggle to American civilisation and the role they would play in the American revolution.

On women, James argues that there is a dilemma:

> Today however, equality is not an industrial need or the subjective passion of a few intense or rebellious people. From every point of view it is a social necessity in the modern world ... The husband who goes forth and the little woman at home. The public and the life of the home, the old restrictions have been shattered ... by the blows of modern civilisation ... hence the sense of bitterness and the frustration and a feeling of the burdens placed immediately upon women. Many women who are indifferent to civil rights burn with rage and impotence at this antagonism between theoretical and practical life which touches them so clearly.[68]

To resolve the problem of the inequality of women, James advocates 'a revolution in individual relationships so great as the revolution pointed at in the labour process'.[69] He then makes the overturn of these relations contingent on a revolution in economic relations and identifies gender oppression and its resolution as a critical factor in the revolutionary process. In 1950 this was a major step.

Next James turns to sexual relations, particularly homosexuality. He views this as abnormal and derived from the fact that the American male in his passion for human relationships has not been 'able to establish this relationship with women'.[70] However, his explanations are woefully inadequate.

In an examination of the American intellectuals of the period he notes that not only are they powerless to halt the development of totalitarianism, but that they contribute to it:

> The intellectuals contribute to it and then either drown themselves and their doubts and hesitations in it or desperately seek a retreat in their own individual psyches. Existentialists in France or psychoanalysis in the United States.[71]

Noting that the intellectuals in the modern world were a result of the division of labour he says:

> Thus the development of society itself has created a situation where on the one hand is the increasingly undifferentiated mass, and on the other, the organisation of science, technology, social, political and administrative management which becomes the preserve of the intellectual worker.[72]

James argues that while the European intellectual developed a literary and philosophical movement, the American counterpart seeks

> refuge ... in psychoanalysis and the examination of themselves as individuals, their internal conflicts the unplumbed depths of their consciousness where they hope to find peace of mind ... The sickness is the same, a sickness in face of society.[73]

Intellectuals who become political, James notes, join the Stalinist movement where they accept the totalitarian doctrine. The acceptance of this doctrine answers their needs and James comments that:

> The intellectuals feel accumulated in themselves, tremendous knowledge, science, technique, means. They have to fasten on to certain social purposes and ends. The rationalist premises of their scientific method make them hostile to the Catholic humanists. And in the party they find all the vulgar materialist ends of power over nature, social relations and a science of man.[74]

Stating that this doctrine is the rationalism of Descartes, James concludes that it placed

> body and mind in separate compartments, i.e. the mass of ordinary men on one side and the intellect knowledge, science, method on the other. It heralded the division of the human personality by the individual process of capitalism ... the Stalinists have not the slightest use for totally integrated social man as a unit, economic and political, of a completely new

reorganisation of society. They, without pretence seek to join the intellectual as intellectual, worker as worker.[75]

This creates an intellectual elite and a homogeneous belief system administered by the elite. Analysing the writings of Norman Mailer, James comments that while his work paints a picture of negativity, it does not recognise the social forces that are able to redress that negativity. Therefore as a writer Mailer is lost. But Mailer's dilemma is characteristic of American intellectuals and their inability to understand the social forces which could change American society. Hence hopelessness or the acceptance of Stalinism prevails. In concluding the manuscript James expresses the view that:

> The American people are the most highly civilised people on the face of the globe. They combine an excessive individualism, a sense of the primary value of their own individual personality, with an equally remarkable need, desire and capacity for social co-operative action.[76]

Finally, James outlines a political and social programme for the resolution of the crisis in the United States and for capitalist countries as

> complete control and management of industry by workers; complete technical education for all men and women, so as to abolish the distinction between management, suspervisors, office workers and mechanised workers ... I believe in the instinct of humanity to survive and that this is the only way it can survive. The modern world is organising itself scientifically at such a speed that either it must be ruled in a totalitarian fashion or by a new conception of democracy beyond anything we have known.[77]

He quotes Lenin on democratic participation and Karl Marx on revolution, ending the text on a note of revolutionary optimism.

## Conclusion

*Notes on American Civilisation* is outstanding as a revolutionary work. First, in breaking the traditional mould of Marxist studies, James begins not with a traditional historical survey, but with a definition of individualism as a critical social and intellectual tendency. He makes the point that it is the fragmentation of the human personality which is at the root of totalitarianism. This was a novel approach, one that broke away from the traditional concepts of Marxist political economy. James instead attempts to root the problem in the process of the evolution of human society, human responses and their expression in ideas. This developed into a key tenet of his independent Marxism.

In James's notion of socialism, workers' control of production belongs to the tendency in the Marxist movement of 'socialism from below'. His portrayal of the forces of the American revolution – blacks, workers, women and homosexuals – combined with the notion of direct democracy was far more advanced than any other Marxist political thinker in 1950. It is also obvious, having formulated the new political category of the 'party and the revolution' in *Notes on the Dialectics*, that James was attempting to write a popular work for an American audience which would place squarely before them a contemporary Marxist analysis stripped of the baggage of traditional Marxist conceptions and language. The work therefore does not mark a break in James's political thought in the sense that he was no longer a Marxist. All his major political categories remained Marxist. What was novel was his application, which ventured into spheres where many had not trod. As a consequence, new political categories were created and a methodology refined. It is this methodology which would lead James away from a central aspect of Marx's thinking on human nature.

Perhaps the most fundamental feature of this manuscript is James's definition of the essence of a human being:

> We have so far made clear above all two things. We refuse to treat man as statistics, more wages, more leisure less unemployment, more goods for consumption, etc. For large numbers of the population these things are still necessary ... but men have in the past suffered from far greater privations with less sense of frustration, social crisis and doom. It is how they work, every day, the material circumstances of their lives; that shape their consciousness; the things by which they live and their sense of perspective, confidence, belief in a social order, its politics, its ethics, etc.[78]

This conception of human nature was at the core of James's social and political theory and was in conflict with a Marxist interpretation of human nature. Norman Geras has successfully pointed out that a distinction needs to be made between 'human nature' and the 'nature of man'.[79] Human nature restricts itself to what Marx identifies as biological needs – food, drink etc. Although Marx also writes about social needs, particularly the need for 'social intercourse',[80] he asserts that 'life involves before everything else, eating'.[81] Material conditions, therefore, are central to freedom, and liberation is a historical and not a mental act, it is brought by historical conditions, the level of industry, commerce, agriculture and intercourse.[82] This is not to place Marx within a tradition of vulgar materialism, but instead to point to a specific tension between

James and Marx. Marx's realm of freedom begins 'only where labour which is determined by necessity and mundane conditions cease. Thus in the very nature of things it is beyond the sphere of actual production.'[83]

Unquestionably, therefore, to suggest – as James does – that people's consciousness is more central to freedom is to revise Marx. Such a 'revision' was necessary because James was attempting in *Notes on American Civilisation* to explore ideas and political values and how individuals and humanity acted them out. In the end James posits a theory of the nature of man which is adaptable in spite of material limitations. From this perspective the content of human freedom was possible and at all times shaped by historical circumstances. This particular theme would become a source of intellectual conflict in James's thought and would arise and be further compounded by teleological schema of history which he never fully discarded. The Johnson–Forest Tendency's project was to distil the entire range of human activities and expressions. By doing so James would add and revise new dimensions to Marxist thought and open new lines of enquiry. Totalitarianism never gained a foothold in American society and by the 1960s, the new social forces which James had identified were attempting to reconstruct America. That they failed is not the subject of this volume. What is important is the political insight of James at that time. Caliban was now marking the signposts for the future.

# CHAPTER 9

# James, Independent Marxism and the Marxist Tradition: A Summary 1934–53

James did not complete his project on American civilisation, but the manuscript *Notes on American Civilisation* demonstrated that he was grappling with the nuances of an independent Marxist political and social theory. His other major published work of this period, *Mariners, Renegades and Castaways* (1953), an analysis of the writings of American author Herman Melville, built on the themes in *Notes on American Civilisation*. James wrote this work while placed in detention on Ellis Island by the US immigration authorities. In the Introduction he continues his discussion on totalitarianism:

> The totalitarian madness ... swept the world first as Nazism and now as Soviet Communism; the great mass labour movements and colonial revolts; intellectuals drowning in the incestuous dreams of psychoanalysis – this is the world the masses of men strive to make sense of. This is what Melville coordinates – but not as industry, science, politics, economics or psychology, but as a world of human personalities, living as the vast majority of human beings live, not by ideas but by their emotions, seeking to avoid pain and misery and struggling for happiness.[1]

James locates Melville's importance in modern literature. He describes Melville's *Pierre* (1852) as the 'finest and most profound study'[2] in the existence of what the Freudians call the 'neurosis', and notes that although Melville was not influenced by Freud, neurosis was not part of human nature. Instead he suggested that it was a sickness confined to a special class, 'chiefly intellectuals and the idle rich who cannot decide what attitude they should take to a changing society'.[3] James argues that the crisis of neurotic intellectuals was not so much 'that they commit incest, but that they preoccupy themselves unceasingly with incestuous desires, father-complex, mother fixation as the foundation of human personality and human behaviour'.[4] This statement reflects a tendency to be dismissive of ideas which probed human relations and which sometimes could not be reduced to immediate political explanations. It did not happen often to him, but it is one of the tensions which characterise Marxist thought, and James could also fall into this reductionist trap.

James's analysis of great writers is the subject of a critical chapter in *Mariners, Renegades and Castaways,* starting with the now familiar theme of Greek society and its features. James observes that ancient Greek civilisation hailed great writers. The reason, he states, is the fact of the creative imagination of the great writer and his or her capacity for profound insights into the human condition. In discussing how Melville achieved this, he comments:

> What Melville did was to place within the covers of one book a presentation of a whole civilisation so that any ordinary human being today can read it in a few days and grasp the essentials of the world he lived in. To do this a man must contain within his single self at one and the same time, the whole history of the past, the most significant experiences of the world around him and a clear vision of the future. Of all this he creates an ordered whole. No philosopher, statesman, scientist exceeds him in creative effort.[5]

James then places Melville alongside the Greek Aeschylus and the English playwright, William Shakespeare. Both, he claims, wrote at moments when the old society into which they were born was crumbling and changing. Within this perspective, the great writer

> creates a world of human beings and an environment to correspond. He has read and absorbed how great characters in previous critical situations acted ... But what matters in his work is what is new and that he must dig out for himself. What matters to us in Ahab is not his heroic determination. It is the sense of purpose, the attitude to science and industry, the defence of individual personality, the attitude to the men around him.[6]

For James, the genius of Herman Melville lay in his consistent portrayal of the human personality of the totalitarian type. This analysis was firmly rooted in his studies of popular cultural forms of the late 1940s and 1950s in the United States, and in his theoretical conception that an understanding of society required one to grasp the basic text of its human impulses. *Mariners, Renegades and Castaways* confirms James's return to literary criticism. It also affirmed the new contours of his political theory which were grappling with new issues from the standpoint of social relations rather than an orthodox Marxist political economy. The work again demonstrated his conviction that at the core of Western civilisation was totalitarianism. This civilisation, James argues, was destroying the human personality and could only be stopped by the reordering of economic and social relations. In this analysis,

James was participating in an historic debate about the nature of the West. That debate has always been central within the black radical tradition. James's argument about the irrationality of totalitarianism was perhaps made possible by his understanding of the racial character of the West and its evolution. Such an analysis marked a rupture from traditional Marxist categories, themselves a result of a specific tradition within the Western intellectual tradition. Reviewing Jamesian thought we see a notion of totality emerging. The conception of a totality facilitated James's analysis of the totalitarian personality and leader within the Western civilisation. Cedric Robinson, in an astute insight, argues that in James's work on Melville,

> James had fused the bureaucratic strata of a theory of state capitalism with Hegel's 'world historical' heroes, whose passionate belief in the legitimacy of their own private aims and interests is such that they cannot abide any disparity between what they desire for themselves and what the public morality and legal system demand of men in general.[7]

This was the basis of James's notion of totality and informed his literary and political analysis in the 1950s; it would later become a central point of his political theory in the 1960s.

The major political purpose of *Mariners, Renegades and Castaways* was to convince the US immigration authorities not to deport him and to that end hundreds of copies were distributed to leading political and social personalities. However, the hysteria of McCarthyism proved too great and James was deported in 1953. James's involvement with the US immigration authorities had begun in 1948, and throughout that time he continued to lead the Johnson–Forest Tendency. When the Tendency formally broke with Trotskyism and left the Socialist Workers' Party, it had established its own political style and immediately published *The Balance Sheet Completed*. The document, signed by 14 members, characterised the SWP as politically degenerate, and critiqued the party's activities on key political questions. It noted that for the Johnson–Forest Tendency:

> The party is the vanguard. The first necessity is to educate the party. The SWP leadership with its abstract programme ... cannot educate the party, because it is itself uneducated in Marxism. Search the publications of twenty years and you will not find a dozen articles on the proletariat in the United States worth printing ... the rank and file worker comes to the party to find out about himself and the potentialities of his class. He finds nothing.[8]

The Tendency also was critical of the SWP's work on the 'Negro Question', noting that the party finds all 'sorts of fantastic reasons for the fact that so many Negroes joined the party and left it'.[9] The document proclaims that 'all politics in the United States are expressed most sharply on the Negro question',[10] and complains of the constant conflict between the Johnson–Forest Tendency and the party on this question. It also accused the SWP of abandoning the dialectic methodology. It is important to note that the theory of state capitalism was critical to the break as it had been in 1941. On this the Tendency noted:

> state capitalism for us is that of capitalism in which not the labour aristocracy but the labour bureaucracy as such becomes the main enemy. The specific type of proletarian revolt is the political form corresponding to the socialisation of production. *The aim is to destroy bureaucracy as a category.*[11] (emphasis added)

It was clear that the Johnson–Forest Tendency could no longer live in the traditional Marxist-Leninist house. Its logic of development and study had led it to new boundaries. The break was therefore inevitable. Emerging from its split from traditional Trotskyism, the Tendency developed into an independent organisation called 'Correspondence' which subsequently underwent a series of internal splits. In 1956, Forest split from the group and established the Marxist-Humanist Tendency. From this, James, now resident in England, formed 'Facing Reality' with Grace Lee and Martin Glaberman. In 1962, a second split led by Grace Lee reduced the Tendency to five. By the 1970s, a period when many of the new social forces recognised by James were becoming active, the group numbered 25 and its active political life was in jeopardy. Martin Glaberman, then de facto organiser and political secretary, took the decision to dissolve the group. His reasons were obvious: 'It became clear to me, however, that 25 persons could not sustain the minimum activity required to maintain a serious political group.'[12] In spite of James's objections, the group dissolved.

Never a mass political formation and operating always on the fringe of radical political life in the United States, the Tendency had nevertheless developed a body of distinctive ideas, and constructed a theory of Marxism for the immediate post-World War II era.

C.L.R. James was the central political and theoretical figure in this project. His deportation from the United States marked the end of the second but most important period in the trajectory of his political activity. In the United States, all the central questions of revolutionary politics for the period were raised and James's answers provided a theoretical framework from within the Marxist tradition but also expanded it. We now turn to summarising the essential elements of his theory as it had evolved by 1953.

So far, this study has attempted a theoretical investigation of the major elements of the political thought of C.L.R. James between 1934 and 1953, James's most fertile period of sustained organisational revolutionary politics. In this effort, the objective was to isolate critical elements and to identify what was particularly 'Jamesian', as well as to locate the fundamental properties of James's thought within specific intellectual traditions. For the purpose of the present analysis, James's thought can be divided into two areas – social and political theory, and philosophy. These categories are, however, artificial, since James's theory was a totality. Therefore our analysis will proceed on two levels. First, we will isolate the specific areas of James's contributions to these two domains and then we will attempt a synthesis of the notion of totality in James's thought and its location within an intellectual tradition.

## James's Philosophy

Alrick Cambridge states that:

> C.L.R. James was among the first self-consciously humanist Marxist in the post-war era ... James was amongst the first ... to pose the issue of how to make political judgements on philosophical positions ... James's work concerns the original status of Marxist philosophy and may then be read as a return to the authentic Marxism of Marx and Lenin.[13]

James's methodology has to be situated within a current inside the Marxist tradition, which in times of crisis returned to the philosophical roots of Marxist social theory. While thoroughly familiar with the works of Marx on political economy, a prerequisite for the development of the theory of state capitalism, it was James's study of Hegel and philosophy which led to the creation of the new Marxist universals for the Johnson–Forest Tendency and finally established an independent Marxism. Philosophy has a special role within the Marxist tradition. For Marx, the development of the social theory of historical materialism brought abstract philosophic thought to an end and he continued to be influenced by Hegelian methodology. Some Marxist commentators have pointed out differences between Marx's structure of the *Grundrisse* and that of *Capital*, with the former grounded in Hegel's notion of the absolute idea and the development of logical categories, while the latter was

> Wholly subordinated to the empirical task of investigating capitalism. The structure of Capital is radically anti-Hegelian;

it culminates, not in the reconciliation of contradictions in a higher unity, but in the class struggle into which the movement and the smash-up of the whole business resolves itself.[14]

The work of Marx that is most strongly influenced by Hegel's methodology and categories is the *Economic and Philosophic Manuscripts of 1844*. Here, Marx's concept of human beings and history is that of a 'species-being' in active relationship with the world through labour. He notes that:

> It is just in his work upon the objective world ... that man really proves himself to be a species-being ... Through this production, nature appears as his work and his reality. The object of labour is, therefore, the objectification of man's species life: for it duplicates himself not only as in consciousness, intellectually, but also actively in reality, and therefore he sees himself in a world he has created.[15]

This concept of human beings and of labour consistently transforming and re-creating humans as they strive towards self-realisation became a fundamental tenet of classical Marxism. Beginning with the labour process, Marx developed a specific notion of alienation and posits that the resolution of this alienation establishes a new stage of human society. In this, his methodology and process are similar to those of Hegel. As Alex Callinicos observes, 'the structure of process is the same in both Marx and Hegel; original unity, self-estrangement, reconciliation in a higher unity'.[16] This obviously can lead to a teleological view of history and an inflexible role for the notion of necessity.

C.L.R. James's theory of the nature of human society and history rests squarely upon these foundations. In an article replying to the American philosopher Sidney Hook, James had declared that 'Marx used the Hegelian method to discover the "necessity" of historical movement and its "purpose". Then, seeing the forces which comprised the "necessity", he elaborated a philosophy which was a guide to action for the working class.'[17] And in *Dialectic and History* (1947) James had written that:

> Marx's fundamental hypotheses were not hypotheses in general ... They were logical abstractions organised according to the *Method* of Hegel and reflecting the movement of human society ... Both Hegel and Marx in their different ways believed that man is destined for freedom and happiness ... They came to this conclusion by examining man's history as a totality. Man for Marx was not Christian man nor the man of the French revolution. The concept of man was a constantly developing idea which was headed for some sort of completeness.[18]

Here the nature of human beings and history are integrated and linked to the notion of self-actualisation in freedom and happiness. James views society as being in constant transformation and the strivings of human beings as the agents of that process. History for James is progressive and has a purpose that defines the content of human nature. In *Notes on American Civilisation*, he writes: 'we refuse to treat men as statistics ... It is how they work every day, the material circumstances of their lives, that shape their consciousness: the things by which they live are their sense of perspective.'[19]

As in Marx, the labour process is fundamental in James's thought. However, unlike Marx, James focuses not only on the notion of self-actualisation and the end of alienation, but on the consciousness of human beings, and he constructs notions of freedom and happiness which are constantly changing. For James, the beginning of real history does not mean human freedom and the end of class exploitation, but *complete* happiness. The content of freedom and happiness, he argues, would constantly evolve until real history began.

In James's political thought, universality was equated with freedom and democracy and was possible only with the achievement of socialism. Within this framework his theory of history is not open-ended. While for Marx real history after the dawn of communism did not stop the motion of human society, for James there is a completeness of history with the advent of socialism. Because he defines socialism as humanity's complete ultimate stage and universality, James automatically limits human possibilities since for him with the advent of socialism, history comes to an end. His theory did not address certain questions: What occurs after the ultimate stage? If the nature of human beings is constantly transformative and in motion, how can one define completeness? By what criteria is the *ultimate* stage judged? Because these questions remain unanswered, at one level James's theory of history is a *self-contained science of society*. This is further validated if one examines the influence of Greek thinking on his thought. Arguing that classical Western thought began in ancient Greek civilisation, James takes note of two particular aspects of that society – democracy and the notion of the social individual. He writes in *Notes on American Civilisation* that Greek democracy:

> had no bureaucracy, it had no organised priesthood, every citizen took part in the government, took part in debates, voted, served on various assemblies. A man was supposed to take part in everything ... Everything concerned the state, and thus everything concerned the individual man ... with this idea of universal man the Greek citizen had a peculiar attitude to the

state ... the state was all powerful, controlling everything, but he was the state.[20]

James's notion of universality therefore contains within it the idea of the social individual of the Greek *polis*. His theory of history and his notion of completeness suggest that the ultimate stage of history is humanity's return to the social individual. It is important to note that in 1953 this theory of history was firmly rooted in a study of Western civilisation. In other words, at this time James drew his theoretical conclusions from one stream of study of human society. James's political theory constantly shifts from alienation in the labour process to the role of the individual in society. But in the final analysis his theory of history traces human beings as individuals, split from their social moorings after the collapse of Greece, to the seeking of universality through Christianity, to the development of the conditions in modern capitalism, where 'man faces his real conditions' and then the possibilities of universality again with the advent of socialism, a new stage but a *complete* one. This is clearly seen when he writes:

> it is 'only at the end' of bourgeois society that we can see what man is in very truth. Thus it is in the contemporary barbarism that can be seen most clearly what is the 'real' nature of humanity. The need and desire for socialism, for democracy, for complete freedom, that is the 'real' nature of man.[21]

James therefore operates within an end-of-history paradigm, and his Hegelian methodology leads him to dissolve Hegel's absolute idea into a notion of the completion of history. In spite of this, within James's theory there is rich flexibility of the many determinations which create the synthesis of historical moments and their movement, making the question of agency critical, and giving James's political theory a complex richness of human activity and interaction. Since human agency is fundamental, within the context of capitalism the self-emancipation of the proletariat is *the* critical agency of transformation. James's ontology is of human beings changing their nature through self-activity which culminates into the self-emancipation of the proletariat. As he states in *Notes on Dialectics*, 'The task today is to call for, to teach, to illustrate, to develop spontaneity – the free creative activity of the proletariat.'[22] The self-emancipation of the proletariat in James's thought would complete history.

## Methodology and Epistemology in James's Thought

James's epistemology is the dialectic and the unity of theory and praxis. He writes:

The dialectic is a theory of knowledge but precisely for that reason it is a theory of the nature of man. Hegel and Marx did not first arrive at a theory of knowledge which they applied to nature and society. They arrived at a theory of knowledge from their examination of men in society.[23]

In *Notes on Dialectics*, we again discern the conflation of a theory of knowledge with that of historical movement: 'thought is not instrument you apply to content. The content moves, develops, changes and creates new categories of thought and gives them direction.'[24] In these formulations knowledge is organically linked to historical movement and the concrete praxis of human beings. This feature allows James to use the dialectic creatively in exploring new social and political realities. It makes his Marxist studies concrete and his methodology a search for the historical movement of a subject. His use of Hegel's concept of the different levels of knowledge also allows for sociological and political insights into social and political realities.

A central problematic in Marxist philosophy is that of consciousness, especially that of the proletariat. James's epistemology allows him to construct from proletariat self-activity, in all human spheres, a social and political theory about the modern nature of the proletariat. In this regard he was not guilty of using phrases like 'the backward nature' of the proletariat, but instead attempted to dissect the world-view of the proletariat as a totality with progressive meaning and not reduce it to crude political formulae. The application of dialectics rescues James's political thought from being highly deterministic and allows his theoretical narrative to understand society as a totality with an ensemble of relations. In James the dialectic was not reduced to crude contradictions, and history was not regularity, normality and uniformity. Add to this conception the notion of the centrality of human beings' activity in the historical process, and we then comprehend how James viewed the modern age and the central questions which faced it in the post-World War II era. As he wrote in *Invading Socialist Society*:

> It is precisely the character of our age and the maturity of humanity that obliterates the opposition between theory and practice, between the intellectual preoccupations of the educated and of the masses. All the great philosophical concepts, from the nature of the physical universal (atomic energy) through the structure and function of productive systems (free enterprise), 'socialism' or 'communism' the nature of government (the state versus the individual), to the destiny of man (can mankind survive?), these are no longer 'theory' but are in the market place, tied together so that they cannot be separated, matters on which the daily lives of millions upon millions depend.[25]

Philosophy for James in the 1940s had truly become proletarian. It was the creative, concrete self-activity of the proletariat which would rescue society and provide the solutions to the profound social and philosophic issues of the day. The responsibility of the Marxist was to recognise that self-activity and organise around it.

## James's Social and Political Theory

By 1953 there were nine distinctive elements of James's social and political thought:

- a theory of state capitalism;
- a theory of race and class and the independent validity of the black liberation movement;
- a theory of freedom and labour;
- a theory of organisation, revolution and the self-activity of the masses;
- a theory of the role of the individual in historical and political action;
- a critique of Western civilisation;
- a theory of democracy;
- a theory of mass society and popular culture;
- a theory of the role of bureaucracy in modern life.

All these elements coalesced into an independent Marxism. Beginning with the theory of state capitalism as a new stage of capital, James and the Johnson–Forest Tendency charted new frontiers of radical political thought. The theory of state capitalism was entirely new and would explain the rapid growth of monopolies in the post-World War II era as well as the expanding role of the state. In an era where the state was powerful and the notion of totalitarian was current, state capitalism was a theory which reconfirmed that social revolution was possible. Its principal thesis was the central organising theme of James's political thought, the self-emancipation of the working class, the basis for his independent Marxism.

After 1948, the formulation of the new universals in *Notes on Dialectics* opened the way for a distinctive political critique of world society. In the United States in the 1950s, James's work on entertainment, popular culture and the nature of American civilisation prefigured works like that of David Riesman's *Lonely Crowd* which attempted to analyse mass society, and discussed similar themes to those of social theorists of the Frankfurt School, in particular, T.W. Adorno. In *The Authoritarian Personality* Adorno discusses the authoritarian syndrome in the United States. Like James he rooted this tendency in the bankruptcy of Western civilisation, However Adorno was influenced by Freud, and also located it as 'deriving from a sadomasochistic resolution of the Oedipus complex'.[26]

By the early 1960s, as television became increasingly popular, commentators became more concerned about the nature of 'mass culture' and many developed the theme of alienation/passivity/fantasy in entertainment. Writing on the role of television, one commentator explained the rationale of this school of thought: 'First the obvious reason: the passive pleasure of being entertained, living a fantasy, taking part vicariously in thrill play, identifying with exciting and attractive people, getting away from real life problems.'[27] James's understanding of popular entertainment was that it was not diversion:

> investigation has already shown that these serials, ridiculous as they are, mean more than mere idle passing the time to the women who listen, overburdened with domestic work, the care of children, illnesses. They should be listened to and examined in the light of the fact that art has now assumed a very intimate relation to the daily lives of the great masses of people.[28]

James equated socialism with democracy and notes that 'the struggle for socialism is the struggle for proletarian democracy. Proletarian democracy is not the crown of socialism. It is the basis.'[29] Because of his deep admiration for ancient Greek civilisation, James's notion of democracy is a form of direct democracy. The nature of direct democracy changes constantly and with the arrival of the proletariat as a distinct class in society, it was their democratic forms which would represent complete direct democracy. By this argument, the Soviets in 1917 and the Workers' Councils in Hungary in 1956 were specifically proletarian contributions to human emancipation. James's notion of democracy was therefore integrated with that of the creative self-activity of the proletariat.

James's judgement on the legacy of Lenin was primarily based on his reading of Lenin's 1923 articles, particularly 'Better Fewer, But Better' and 'How We Should Reorganise The Workers and Peasants' Inspection'. He remarks in *Notes on Dialectics* that during civil war in Russia, Lenin placed all hopes of saving the revolution on the workers who were organised not in the party, but in their factory committees. James's theory of history posits that the fundamental element of universality is direct democracy which has been mediated historically at junctures since objective circumstances have led to its incompleteness.

The bureaucracy was counterpoised to democracy both in the labour movement and the state. This bureaucracy had become a central phenomenon and was the logical climax of the division between mental and manual labour in capitalist society – an idea reinforced in *State Capitalism and World Revolution*, where James argues that 'the crisis of production today is the crisis of the antagonism between manual and intellectual labour. The problem of modern philosophy from Descartes in the sixteenth century to Stalinism in 1950 is the problem of the division of labour between the intellectuals and the workers.'[30] James sees the philosophy of rationalism as supporting this division, and bureaucracy was the fundamental obstacle holding back the development of both the American and Soviet proletariats in the 1950s. The central factor which gives this special role to the bureaucracy is the 'centralisation of bureaucracy' into state capitalism. James's contribution to understanding the race/class question was unique. It was summed up in November 1971 when he stated:

> Black people have a right to struggle against oppression. They don't have to be stimulated by the communist party; they needn't be socialist; they needn't be subject to any of these doctrines, but to struggle against oppression is their absolute right; it is their duty; and that right and that duty is established and urged upon them by Marxism.[31]

This position for independent black struggle was advanced within the context of Marxism and the black liberation struggle in the 1950s. James's position that the black struggle would influence other social movements has been validated by the history of the civil rights and black movements of the 1960s. Here again the central theme is the self-organisation of ordinary people. Criticism of James's political thought has focused on the fact that his concentration on the self-activity of ordinary people means that his position on organisation is 'spontaneous'. Alex Callinicos, in his study *Trotskyism* (1990), locates James within the trajectory of the socialist thinkers who operate from the perspective of 'socialism from below', and says that James's analysis of the 'emerging socialist society at work within it in spontaneous shop floor revolts, reflected James's Hegelian confidence in a historical process which would inevitably subvert the existing order using the most unlikely of instruments'.[32]

While it is true that James's Hegelian methodology traps him into a notion of inevitability, Callinicos does not appreciate James's theory of organisation, which is not a theory of organising *for revolution* or *how to seize state power*. His theory of organisation was an elaboration of how, at different historical junctures, the self-activity of the proletariat developed different forms of organisation. James's notions of organisation can be divided into two phases:

• A traditional Marxist-Leninist phase where he argues for the development of a Leninist Party as a critical instrument for leadership of the world socialist revolution.

- A phase in which the vanguard part is debunked and where James claims that, while revolutions previously aimed at achieving social emancipation, 'today revolution must begin with social emancipation'.[33]

Beginning from this standpoint, James suggests that it is in the nature of contemporary struggles for the proletariat to develop organisations similar to those of the Paris Commune and the Soviet. However, Marxists obviously had to organise themselves, and it was not until 1958 that James elaborated a position on how a Marxist organisation should function, based on the political activities of the Tendency. James argues though that this kind of organisation is fundamentally different from the proletarian organisation and institutions at the moment of revolution. He saw his task as separating the Leninist Party as a proletarian organisation from the organisation developed by the proletariat itself. Thus he redefined proletarian organisations as those created by the mass self-activity of the proletariat at specific historical moments. All this was as a result of the central theme of James's political project – comprehending the modalities of the self-emancipation of the working class.

## The Notion of Totality

In Western political thought, the notion of totality has its origins in Greek thought. One concern of Greek political philosophy was the unity of human society and the concept of the *holōn*. Aristotle, the Greek political philosopher, contends that the state 'by nature is clearly prior to the individual, since the whole is prior to the parts'.[34] He further makes the point that the 'individual when isolated is not self-sufficing; and therefore is like a part in relation to the whole'.[35] However, Martin Jay argues that while having a concept of totality, the 'Greek lacked a belief that history could be understood as a progressively meaningful whole with a beginning, middle and end'.[36] In Marxist thought, the notion of totality is pervasive. Marx himself consistently writes of the 'whole'. In the *German Ideology* he writes:

> Our conception of history depends on our ability to expound the real process of production, starting out from the simple material production of life and to comprehend the form of intercourse ... as the basis of history ... to explain the whole mass of different theoretical products and forms of consciousness, religion, philosophy, ethics, etc., etc. and trace their origins and growth, by which means, of course, the whole thing can be shown in its totality.[37]

In Marx, the notion of totality merges with the theory of history and a dialectical method. Totality, therefore, means the total relations in society and their historical evolution. James adopts this concept of totality but takes it further with a notion of totality that has three features. First, as in Aristotle, is the element of the relation of the individual to the community. James's vision confirms that self-actualisation of the individual was only possible within the context of a relationship to the community and, as he argues, the success of totalitarianism derives from its superficial construction of this total community. Secondly, as in Marx, James argues that the historical development of society and the development of capitalism created a crisis which was represented by labour and its alienation. The reconciliation of this alienation created the basis for the social emancipation of labour. The third feature marks James's extraordinary contribution to Marxist social and political thought. His suggestion is that totality is not simply all the relations of society, but instead an entire *civilisation* and its trajectory. In other words, carrying the historical process further, James's *notion of totality gives him a broad historical sweep and therefore fundamentally makes his political thought a radical critique of Western civilisation.*

Marx, writing in the nineteenth century, was still influenced by notions of the 'civilising' nature of capitalism. James, on the other hand, wrote in a context where Western civilisation which had dominated the world was now in a fundamental crisis. While Marx worked in the era of consolidation of capitalist civilisation, James worked during the period of its profound crisis and in an era where the empires on which European civilisation was built were collapsing. He could therefore see the whole clearer. James would argue that the brutal regimes and the totalitarianism which were features of the period were integral to the nature of Western civilisation; as such the crisis was complete. Its solution required the reorganisation of society under the creativity and self-activity of the proletariat – a fundamental break from conceptions which lay at the core of the construction of Western civilisation and society. This formulation of the problematic in terms of the history of civilisation was fundamentally different from other currents in Marxism. By the 1950s, this represented for James himself a different approach to many issues. This can be seen when we compare his discussion of fascism in *World Revolution* in the 1930s with his analysis of world politics in the 1950s.

What were the factors which facilitated James's notion of totality, and his location of specific studies of societies within that context and frame? The answer might well be found in the relationship of James's thought to the black radical tradition. As a native intellectual within a colonial context, he had absorbed the literature, history and ethos of Western civilisation. However, becoming an anti-colonial rebel required at least a critique of that civilisation. As a Marxist, by the late 1930s, the anti-colonial tradition in him had merged with a current of radical critique in Western thought. Developing this further, we can discern the critical currents which shaped James's political thought by returning to earlier discussions in Chapter 1.

James stands within a specific Marxist trajectory which in the post-October 1917 period runs from Rosa Luxemburg to Antonio Gramsci. Included in this tradition are the council communists. This segment of the Marxist tradition took issue with Lenin on the character of Bolshevik party rule. Georg Lukács, who flirted with the current, expressed its kernel when he wrote in *History and Class Consciousness*:

> The workers' councils spells the political and economic defeat of reification. In the period following the dictatorship it will eliminate the bourgeois separation of the legislature, administration and judiciary. During the struggle for control, its mission is two-fold. On the one hand, it must overcome the fragmentation of the proletariat in time and space, and on the other, it has to bring economics and politics together with true synthesis of proletarian praxis.[38]

James saw in the IWW, the CIO and the mass strikes of the American proletariat the potential form of new workers' organisation. After the Hungarian Revolution, he would posit the notion of 'government of workers' councils'. However, there is specific conflict in James's political thought – between vanguard Leninism, workers' self-activity and his radical democratic and egalitarian impulses. One current of Leninism is centrality and homogeneity, which was perhaps shaped by Tsarist Russia. James attempts to go beyond this current by focusing on Lenin's advocacy of the Soviet form. His efforts, though, are not entirely successful and although James sees Lenin as a complex political character, there can be no doubt of Lenin's centralist tendencies. On the other hand, James draws from his experiences of the Trinidadian proletariat, his understanding of Greek democracy and a reading of history which highlights radical egalitarian movements, and he was firmly on the side of a form of radical democracy.

Increasingly, James stopped using the phrase 'dictatorship of the proletariat' and in *Invading Socialist Society* he writes, 'today from end to end of the world there can be no turning back. But the democratic instincts and needs of hundreds of millions of people are crying out for an expression which only the socialist revolution can give.'[39] For James, socialism was the framework for radical democracy. Therefore, while James operated within the Marxist tradition, Marxism was the modern frame for the expression of his radical, democratic and egalitarian impulses. This carried him out of the Trotskyist movement and led to his development of an independent Marxism.

The question we now face is, why have his contributions been underated or ignored? Part of the answer lies in his fifteen years of obscurity in the United States, and his involvement in small revolutionary groups. But for the larger part, the answer rests with the nature of the Marxist tradition itself. As an intellectual heir to the European Enlightenment, Marxism and its legacies came to be viewed as a distinct Western phenomenon, notwithstanding that some of its advocates were not Westerners. Further, radical political theory and Marxism only recognised the 'other' social forces when those social forces acknowledged the centrality of Marxism. So thinkers and activists who do not fall within this mainstream are outside the tradition, and their validity is not recognised except in relation to the tradition and its canons.

The lacuna in Western political thought regarding the importance of the black struggle and its impact on the nature of politics again puts black political thinkers outside the Western intellectual tradition and its radical legacies. Consequently, the conceptions of Western Marxism are white and European, and literature on Marxism after Marx does not mention black thinkers or the nature of the racial question. Yet it is the works of C.L.R. James and W.E.B. DuBois which raise some of the fundamental issues of Western society about the nature and limitations of equality, freedom and democracy, because the nature of the black radical tradition in all its heterogeneity is both a critique of and a fundamental enquiry into these classical notions. The universality of the Enlightenment stopped short on race. The black radical tradition offers a larger dimension to these issues.

While James's radical democratic and egalitarian impulses are oftentimes expressed in his understandings of European history, *The Black Jacobins* reflects a fundamental expression of his political thought – where revolution releases the creative energies of the oppressed and enslaved people, shattering all conceptions that purported the nature of blacks to be non-human.

In other words, it is the Haitian revolution which gives universality to the slogan 'Liberty, Fraternity and Equality'. This is a feature of the black radical tradition in the Americas and one which is present in Jamesian political theory. James continued to engage himself in political thought after his departure from the United States, adding further dimensions of his political theory. In 1953 James was deported from the United States and he returned to England. This completed one phase of his political life and opened a new one, centred on the emerging social forces of the 1960s and 1970s. For the next thirty-six years, James involved himself in the Caribbean independence movement and federation, African independence and the black liberation movement in the United States. He also served as the theoretical guru for sections of the New Left. At the same time, he would produce his masterpiece *Beyond a Boundary*, and continue to develop notions of popular culture. But fundamentally he would continue to search for new forms of proletarian self-activity and the constituent elements of world revolution from the perspective that the self-emancipation of Matthew Bondman is the central tenet of human emancipation, mapping new cognitive space. As such Caliban's freedom was his own work, creating and shaping new signposts in the struggle for human freedom and happiness.

# Notes

## 1 Issues in James's Political Thought

1. C.L.R. James, in *C.L.R. James: His Life and Work*, ed. Paul Buhle (London: Allison & Busby, 1986) p. 164.
2. C.L.R. James, unpublished draft writing programme (New York: Schomburg Center for Research on Black Culture, 1950).
3. Ibid.
4. Cedric Robinson's significant book *Black Marxism* (London: Zed Books, 1983) raises the notion of a black radical tradition. I have used this notion and its dynamic to probe further both the context and character of James's political thought.
5. C.L.R. James, incomplete fragments of his biography in *The C.L.R. James Archive: A Reader's Guide*, ed. Anne Grimshaw (New York: C.L.R. James Institute, 1991) pp. 52–3.
6. John Molyneux, *What is the Real Marxist Tradition?* (London: Pluto Press, 1985) p. 65.
7. Ibid, pp. 65–6.
8. Karl Mannheim, *Diagnosis of our Time* (London: Kegan Paul, 1943) p. 7.

## 2 The Making of a Marxist

1. Selwyn Ryan, *Race and Nationalism in Trinidad and Tobago* (Toronto: University of Toronto Press, 1972) pp. 17–27.
2. Bridget Brereton, *A History of Modern Trinidad 1793–1962* (Kingston: Heinemann, 1982) p. 91.
3. Ryan, *Race and Nationalism in Trinidad and Tobago*, p. 28.
4. Rupert Lewis, 'J.J. Thomas and Political Thought in the Caribbean', *Caribbean Quarterly*, vol. 356, nos 1 & 2 (June 1990) p. 46.
5. Ibid.
6. C.L.R. James, interview with Sebastian Clarke, 'The Literature of Politics' *Front Line* (Nov./Dec. 1981).
7. C.L.R. James, Letter to Constance Webb (New York: Schomburg Center for the Research of Black Culture, 1944).
8. Ibid.
9. C.L.R. James, 'Discovering Literature in Trinidad in the 1930s', in *C.L.R. James: Spheres of Existence* (London: Allison & Busby, 1980) p. 37.
10. Anna Grimshaw, *The C.L.R. James Archive: A Reader's Guide* (New York: C.L.R. James Institute, 1991) p. 48.
11. C.L.R. James, *Beyond a Boundary* (London: Hutchinson, 1963) p. 37.
12. Ibid., pp. 17–18.

13. Ibid., p. 31.
14. Ibid., p. 14.
15. Radio Interview with Olga Comma-Maynard, Trinidad, 1989.
16. Tony Martin, *The Pan-African Connection from Slavery to Garvey and Beyond* (Cambridge, MA: Schenkman, 1983) pp. 63–94.
17. Kwesi Solomon Aggemony, 'A Study in Radical Political Thought in Colonial Trinidad'. MPhil thesis, University of the West Indies, St Augustine, Trinidad, p. 9.
18. Kelvin Singh, 'Economy and Politics in Trinidad (1917–1938): The Influence of Ethnic, Class and Imperial Factors', PhD diss., University of the West Indies, St Augustine, Trinidad, p. 7.
19. Ibid.
20. Bukka Rennie, *History of the Working Class in Twentieth Century Trinidad and Tobago* (Toronto: New Beginning Movement, 1974) p. 32.
21. Reinhard W. Sander, *The Trinidad Awakening: West Indian Literature of the 1930s* (Connecticut: Greenwood Press, 1988) p. 21.
22. Aaron Gonzales, *Self-Discovery Through Literature: Creative Writing in Trinidad and Tobago* (Port-of-Spain: Aaron Gonzales, 1972).
23. James, *Beyond a Boundary*, p. 27.
24. Paul Buhle, *The Artist as Revolutionary* (London: Verso, 1988) p. 26.
25. Radio interview with Olga Comma-Maynard, Trinidad, 1989.
26. For a discussion on Marxism and literary criticism, see Raymond Williams, *Marxism and Literature* (Oxford: Oxford University Press, 1977); Terry Eagleton, *Criticism and Ideology: A Study in Marxist Literary Theory* (London: Verso, 1978). The term 'aesthetic ideology' is taken from Eagleton's work.
27. Edward Said, 'Figures, Configurations, Transfigurations', *Polygraph*, no. 4 (1990) p. 9.
28. C.L.R. James, *Notes on Dialectics* (London: Allison & Busby, 1980) p. 9.
29. Albert Gomes, *Through a Maze of Colour* (Port-of-Spain: Key Publications, 1974) p. 18.
30. Sander, p. 82.
31. *The Beacon*, vol. 1, no. 1 (March 1931) p. 32.
32. Ibid., p. 22.
33. Ibid., pp. 17–18.
34. *The Beacon*, vol. 1, no. 4 (July 1931) p. 30.
35. *The Beacon*, vol. 1, no. 5 (August 1931) p. 6.
36. Ibid., p. 7.
37. Ibid., p. 9.
38. Ibid., p. 10.
39. Grimshaw, *The C.L.R. James Archive*, p. 48.
40. *The Beacon*, vol. 1, no. 6 (September 1931) p. 17.
41. Ibid., p. 22.
42. Ibid.
43. Ibid., p. 21.
44. *The Beacon*, vol. 1, no. 5 (August 1931) p. 19.
45. C.L.R. James, *The Life of Captain Cipriani: An Account of British Government in the West Indies* (London: Nelson, 1932) p. 40.
46. Ibid., p. 10.

47. C.L.R. James, *The Case for West Indian Self-government* (London: Hogarth Press, 1933) p. 31.
48. Ibid., p. 37.
49. C.L.R. James, 'The Case for West Indian Self-government', in *The C.L.R. James Reader,* ed. Anna Grimshaw (Oxford: Blackwell, 1992) p. 52.
50. Reinhard W. Sander, 'Interview with C.L.R. James', in *Kas-Kas Interviews with Three Caribbean Writers in Texas:* Ian Munro and Reinhard W. Sander (eds), (Austin: African-American Research Institute, 1972) p. 33.
51. Sander, *The Trinidad Awakening*, p. 101.
52. Sander, 'Interview with C.L.R. James', p. 33.
53. Ibid.
54. Sander, *The Trinidad Awakening*, p. 102.
55. John La Guerre, *The Social and Political Thought of the Colonial Intelligentsia* (Kingston: ISER, University of the West Indies, 1982) p. 86.
56. Ibid.
57. Cited in Grimshaw, *The C.L.R. James Archive*, pp. 52–3.
58. James, *The Literature of Politics*.
59. James, *Beyond a Boundary*, p. 17.

# 3 James's Early Marxism

1. C.L.R. James, *Beyond a Boundary* (London: Hutchinson, 1963) p. 114.
2. Ibid., p. 122.
3. 'C.L.R. James and British Trotskyism. An Interview' (London: Socialist Platform, 1987) p. 1.
4. C.L.R. James, in *The C.L.R. James Archive: A Reader's Guide*, ed. Anne Grimshaw (New York: C.L.R. James Institute, 1990) p. 153.
5. James, *Beyond a Boundary*, p. 149.
6. Samuels Stuart, 'English Intellectuals and Politics in the 1930s', in *On Intellectuals*, ed. Phillip Rief (New York: Anchor Books, 1970) p. 213.
7. David Coates, *The Labour Party and the Struggle for Socialism* (London: Cambridge University Press, 1975) pp. 5–6.
8. Ibid.
9. V.I. Lenin, *Collected Works*, Volume 32 (Moscow: Foreign Language Publishing House 1960) p. 24.
10. Ibid.
11. For a succinct discussion on Trotskyism as a Marxist political tendency, see Duncan Hallas, *Trotsky's Marxism* (London: Pluto Press, 1979); and Alex Callinicos, *Trotskyism* (Minnesota: University of Minnesota Press, 1990).
12. John Archer, *C.L.R. James and Trotskyism in Britain 1934–1938* unpublished lecture (London, 1986).
13. Sam Bornstein and A.C. Richardson, *Against the Stream* (London: Socialist Platform, 1986) p. 263.

14. John Archer, 'C.L.R. James and Trotskyism in Britain: 1934–1938', unpublished lecture, London, 21 February 1986.
15. 'C.L.R. James and British Trotskyism', pp. 5–6.
16. Claudin Fernando, *The Communist Movement* (New York: Monthly Review Press, 1975) p. 109.
17. Paul Buhle, *C.L.R. James, the Artist as Revolutionary* (London: Verso, 1988) p. 51.
18. C.L.R. James, *World Revolution 1917–1936* (Connecticut: Hyperion Press Inc., 1973) p. 41.
19. Ibid., p. 22.
20. Ibid., p. 26.
21. Ibid.
22. Cited in E. H. Carr, *The Interregnum 1923–1924* (Harmondsworth: Penguin Books, 1965) p. 221.
23. James, *World Revolution 1917–1936*, p. 35.
24. Ibid.
25. Ibid., p. 84.
26. Ibid., p. 93.
27. Ibid., p. 85.
28. Ibid.
29. Ibid., p. 52.
30. Ibid.
31. Ibid., p. 53.
32. Ibid.
33. John Archer, *C.L.R. James and Trotskyism in Britain 1934–1938*.
34. Ibid.
35. Ibid.
36. Bornstein and Richardson, *Against the Stream*, p. 183.
37. Ibid., p. 184.
38. Ibid.
39. Ibid.
40. C.L.R. James, 'Black Intellectuals in Britain', in Bhikhu Pakekh (ed.), *Colour, Culture and Consciousness* (London: George Allen & Unwin, 1974) p. 159.
41. George Padmore, *Pan-Africanism or Communism* (New York: Doubleday, 1972) p. 159.
42. James, 'Black Intellectuals in Britain', p. 16.
43. Ibid.
44. C.L.R. James, *The Black Jacobins* (London: Allison & Busby, 1980) p. vi.
45. Ibid., p. 117.
46. Frank Birbabsingh, *Passion and Exile: Essays in Caribbean Literature* (London: Hansib Publishing Co., 1988) p. 97.
47. Archie W. Singham, 'C.L.R. James on the Black Jacobin Revolution in San Domingo'. Savacou 1. (Kingston: University of the West Indies, 1970) p. 86.
48. James, *The Black Jacobins*, p. 47.
49. Ibid., pp. 85–6.
50. Ibid.
51. Ibid., p. 248.

52. Ibid., p. 249.
53. Ibid., p. 240.
54. Ibid., p. 261.
55. Ibid., p. 279.
56. Ibid., p. 284.
57. Ibid., p. 283.
58. Ibid., p. 14.
59. Ibid., p. 120.
60. Ibid., p. 383.
61. Ibid., p. vii.
62. C.L.R. James, *A History of Negro Revolt* (London: Race Today, 1985) p. 54.
63. Ibid., p. 58.
64. Robert Hill, 'In England 1932–1938', in *C.L.R. James His Life and Work*, ed. Paul Buhle (London: Allison & Busby, 1986) p. 73.
65. Perry Anderson, *Considerations on Western Marxism* (London: New Left Books, 1976) pp. 10–11.
66. Ibid., p. 11.
67. For a discussion on global capitalism in the 1920s and 1930s, see A.S. Kenwood and A. L. Longhead, *The Growth of the International Economy 1820–1980* (London: George Allen & Unwin, 1983).

## 4 The American Years

1. *Who Built America? American History Project*, vol. 2 (New York: Pantheon Books, 1992) p. 421.
2. L.S. Stavrianos, *A Global History* (Englewood Cliffs, NJ: Prentice-Hall Inc., 1983) p. 481.
3. Daniel Guérin, *100 Years of Labour in the USA* (London: Ink Links, 1979) p. iii.
4. Ibid.
5. *Who Built America?*, p. 269.
6. *C.L.R. James and Revolutionary Marxism*, ed. Scott McLemee and Paul Le Blanc (Englewood Cliffs, NJ: Humanities Press 1994).
7. C.L.R. James, in *The C.L.R. James Archive: A Reader's Guide*, ed. Anne Grimshaw (New York: C.L.R. James Institute, 1991) p. 55.
8. Letter to Constance Webb, May 1939 (New York: Schomburg Center for Research in Black Culture).
9. Letter to Constance Webb, May 1939 (New York: Schomburg Center for Research in Black Culture).
10. Letter to Constance Webb, May 1939 (New York: Schomburg Center for Research in Black Culture).
11. Martin Glaberman, 'C.L.R. James, a Recollection', in *New Politics*, vol. 2, no. 4, 1990.
12. J.M. Buhle, Paul Buhle and Dan Georgakas, *Encyclopedia of the American Left* (Chicago: University of Illinois Press, 1992) contains an excellent essay on the origins of the SWP. The figures are taken from this essay.

13. Guérin, *100 years of Labour in the USA*. See Chapter 2 for a discussion of the comparative influence of the Marxist Left on the American labour movement at the time.
14. Letter to Constance Webb, September 1939.
15. Leon Trotsky, *The Revolution Betrayed* (New York: Pathfinder Press, 1972). See Chapter 9 for Trotsky's analysis of the nature of the Soviet Union in the 1930s.
16. J. Cannon, *The Struggle for a Proletarian Party* (New York: Pathfinder Press, 1970) p. 221.
17. Duncan Hallas, *Trotsky's Marxism* (London: Pluto Press, 1979) p. 106.
18. Ibid.
19. Cannon, *The Struggle for a Proletariatan Party*, p. 253.
20. C.L.R. James, extract from handwritten fragments of an incomplete unpublished autobiography (San Fernando: Oilfield Workers Trade Union Library).
21. J.R. Johnson and F. Forest, *Resolution on the Russian Question* (unpublished document, September 1941) p. 4.
22. Ibid.
23. Ibid.
24. Ibid.
25. Author's interview with Martin Glaberman (Detroit: December 1990). Glaberman stated that he disagreed with the use of the word 'fascist'. It was subsequently dropped by the Tendency and 'totalitarian' was substituted.
26. Johnson and Forest, *Resolution on the Russian Question*, p. 8.
27. Ibid.
28. B. Rizzi, *The Bureaucratisation of the World* (London: Tavistock, 1985).
29. Alex Callanicos, *Trotskyism* (Minneapolis: University of Minnesota Press, 1990) p. 56.
30. Ibid.
31. Ibid.
32. Trotsky, *The Revolution Betrayed*, pp. 246–8.
33. Callanicos, *Trotskyism*, p. 56.
34. C.L.R. James, 'Trotsky's Place in History', in *C.L.R. James and Revolutionary Marxism*, p. 107.
35. Ibid.
36. Ibid., p. 109.
37. Ibid., p. 110.
38. Ibid.
39. Ibid., p. 112
40. Ibid., p. 118.
41. Ibid., p. 124.
42. Ibid. pp. 125–6.
43. Ibid. p. 126.
44. Grace Lee, *Organising in USA, 1938–1953* (unpublished typescript of a lecture given in London, 1987).
45. C.L.R. James, Letter to Constance Webb, August 1943.
46. C.L.R. James, Letter to Constance Webb, August 1943.
47. C.L.R. James, 'Socialist United States of Europe', *New International* (April/May 1943) p. 3.

48. James Green, 'Fighting on Two Fronts Working-class Militancy in the 1940s', *Radical America*, vol. 9, no. 45, p. 12.
49. Ibid., p. 13.
50. C.L.R. James, *Spheres of Existence: Selected Writings* (London: Allison & Busby, 1980) pp. 49–50.
51. Ibid., p. 56.
52. C.L.R. James, *Education, Propaganda, Agitation* (unpublished document, 1943).
53. Ibid.
54. Ibid.
55. James, *Spheres of Existence: Selected Writings*, p. 60.
56. Ibid., p. 63.
57. Ibid.
58. Ibid., p. 68.
60. Resolution of the Johnson–Forest Minority, July 1947 (Detroit: unpublished manuscript, Raya Dunayevskaya Collection, Wayne State University Archive of Labor and Urban Affairs).
61. Ibid.
62. Ibid.
63. Ibid.
64. C.L.R. James, *A Balance Sheet 1940–1947* (Detroit: unpublished manuscript, Raya Dunayevskaya Collection, Wayne State University Archive of Labor and Urban Affairs, 1947) p. 14.
65. Ibid.
66. Ibid.
67. Ibid.
68. C.L.R. James, extract from fragments of an incomplete unpublished autobiography (San Fernando: Oilfield Workers Trade Union Library).
69. Grace Lee Boggs, 'C.L.R. James: Organising in the USA 1938–1953' in Selwyn Cudjoe and William Cain (eds), *C.L.R. James: His Intellectual Legacies* (Massachusetts: University of Massachusetts Press, 1995) p. 163.
70. Constance Webb written comments on C.L.R. James's letter to her 10 April 1947.
71. C.L.R. James, *At the Rendezvous of Victory* (London: Allison & Busby, 1984) p. 65.
72. Ibid., p. 66.
73. Ibid.
74. Ibid., p. 68.
75. Ibid., p. 67.
76. Ibid.
77. Ibid., p. 69.
78. Ibid., p. 70.
79. James, *Spheres of Existence: Selected Writings*, p. 80.
80. Ibid., p. 83.
81. Ibid., p. 84.
82. Ibid., p. 83.
83. Ibid., p. 94.
84. Ibid., p. 95.
85. Ibid., p. 10.

86. C.L.R. James, F. Forest, and Grace Lee, *Invading Socialist Society* (Michigan: Bewick Editions, 1972) p. 3.
87. Ibid.
88. Ibid., p. ii.
89. Ibid., p. 10.
90. Ibid., p. 12.
91. Ibid., p. 13
92. Ibid., p. 2
93. Ibid., p. 53.
94. James, *A Balance Sheet 1940–1947*.

## 5 James and the Race Question

1. C.L.R. James, *The Black Jacobins* (London: Allison & Busby, 1984) p. 283.
2. Kent Worcester, *C.L.R. James and the American Century (1938–1953)* (unpublished manuscript, 1983).
3. 'Race Riot in Knoxville: Uncle Tom is Dead', editorial veteran, 6 September 1919, in Theodore S. Vincent (ed.), *Voices of Black Nation: Political Journalism in the Harlem Renaissance* (California: Ramparts Press, 1973) pp. 138–9.
4. Phillip Foner, *Organised Labour and the Black Worker 1619–1973* (New York: International Publishers, 1976) p. 141.
5. Ibid., p. 149.
6. Ibid., p. 182.
7. Tony Martin, *Race First* (Connecticut: Greenwood Press, 1976) p. 13.
8. Wilfred D. Samuels, *Five Afro-Caribbean Voices in American Culture* (Boulder, Colorado: Belmont Books, 1977) p. 19.
9. Ibid., p. 1.
10. Ibid.
11. W.B. Turner and Joyce Moore Turner (eds), *Richard B. Moore, Caribbean Militant in Harlem* (Indiana: Indiana University Press, 1992) p. 155.
12. Foner, *Organised Labour and the Black Worker 1619–1973*, p. 219.
13. Ibid., p. 216.
14. Ibid., p. 220.
15. For a discussion on this, see Horace B. Davis, *Nationalism and Socialism* (New York: Monthly Review Press, 1973) Chapter 3.
16. Ibid., p. 62.
17. Ibid., p. 17.
18. C.L.R. James, *The Atlantic Slave Trade and Slavery* published in Amistad I (New York: Vintage Books, 1970) p. 123.
19. K. Marx and F. Engels, *Selected Correspondence* (Moscow: Progress Publishers, 1975) p. 125.
20. Ibid., p. 140.
21. Ibid., p. 79.
22. Documents of the Second Congress of the Communist International (London: New Park Publications, 1977) pp. 109–10.
23. Ibid.

24. Wilson Record, *The Negro and the Communist Party* (New York: Atheneum, 1971) p. 18.
25. Ibid., p. 19.
26. Earl Ofari, 'Marxism, Nationalism and Black Liberation', *Monthly Review*, Vol. 22, No. 10 (March 1971) p. 22.
27. Record, *The Negro and the Communist Party*, p. 22.
28. Ibid.
29. Ibid., p. 25.
30. Ibid., p. 29.
31. Ibid., p. 59.
32. Ibid., p. 63.
33. Ibid.
34. Ibid.
35. Mark Naison, 'Marxism and Black Radicalism in America', *Radical America*, vol. 15, no. 3 (May–June 1971).
36. George Padmore, 'New Leader', 9 January 1946.
37. Leon Trotsky, *Black Nationalism and Self-Determination* (New York: Pathfinders Press, 1972) p. 15.
38. Ibid.
39. Ibid., p. 21.
40. Leon Trotsky, *Black Nationalism and Self-Determination* (New York: Merit Publishers, 1967) p. 24.
41. Ibid., p. 25.
42. Ibid.
43. Ibid., p. 26.
44. Ibid.
45. Ibid.
46. Ibid., p. 29.
47. Ibid.
48. Ibid.
49. Ibid.
50. Ibid., p. 31.
51. Leon Trotsky, *Black Nationalism and Self-Determination* (New York: Pathfinders Press, 1972) p. 32.
52. Ibid., p. 40.
53. Ibid.
54. Ibid., p. 50.
55. C.L.R. James, 'Revolution and the Negro', in Scott McLemee and Paul Le Blanc (eds), *C.L.R. James and Revolutionary Marxism* (Englewood Cliffs, NJ: Humanities Press, 1994) p. 77.
56. Ibid.
57. Ibid., p. 84.
58. Ibid.
59. Ibid.
60. Ibid., p. 85.
61. Ibid. p. 87.
62. James, *Future in the Present*, pp. 126–7.
63. Ibid.
64. C.L.R. James, Letter to Constance Webb, 28 July 1944.
65. C.L.R. James, Letter to Constance Webb, 1944.

66. Ibid.
67. C.L.R. James, Letter to Constance Webb, 1944.
68. Ibid.
69. Ibid.
70. C.L.R. James, 'On the Negro Question', in Tony Bogues, Kim Gordon and C.L.R. James *Black Nationalism and Socialism* (London: Socialists Unlimited, 1979) p. 33.
71. Ibid., p. 36.
72. Ibid., p. 37.
73. Ibid., p. 46.
74. James, *Future in the Present*, pp. 119–20.
75. Tony Martin, *The Pan-African Connection* (Massachussetts: Schenkman, 1983) p. 165.

## 6 Breaking New Ground

1. Letter to Membership (Detroit: Unpublished Johnson–Forest document located in Martin Glaberman's Collection, The Archives of Labor, History and Urban Affairs, Wayne State University, 1947) p. 1.
2. Ibid., p. 2.
3. *Report on Discussion on Break with Socialist Workers' Party* (Detroit: Johnson–Forest document located in Martin Glaberman's Collection, The Archives of Labor, History and Urban Affairs, Wayne State University) p. 3.
4. *Who Built America?* Volume 2. American Social History Project (New York: Pantheon Books, 1992) p. 445.
5. Ibid., p. 446.
6. Ibid., p. 457.
7. Ibid., p. 461.
8. *Report on Discussion on Break with Socialist Workers' Party*, pp. 17–18.
9. C.L.R. James, F. Forest and Ria Stone, *Invading Socialist Society* (Detroit: Bewick Editions, 1972) p. 13.
10. Ibid., p. 14.
11. Ibid., p. 6.
12. Ria Stone, 'The American Worker'. Original unpublished document in *Internal Bulletin of The Johnson–Forest Minority*, no. 8 (4 September 1947) p. 1.
13. Ibid.
14. Ibid., p. 2.
15. Ibid., pp. 3–4.
16. Ibid., p. 23.
17. Ibid.
18. For a good review of this current, see M. Levin, *Marx, Engels and Liberal Democracy* (London: Macmillan Press, 1989) Chapter 6.
19. Johnson–Forest Conference Resolution 1947 in the Martin Glaberman collection.
20. Ibid.
21. C.L.R. James, 'We Join the SWP', in *Internal Bulletin of the Johnson–Forest Minority*, no. 12 (29 September 1947) p. 2.

22. These figures are taken from *Internal Bulletin of the Johnson–Forest Minority*, no 12 (29 September 1947) p. 5.
23. Phil Romano, letter to the organisation in *Internal Bulletin of the Johnson–Forest Minority*, no. 12 (29 September 1947) p. 16.
24. W. Gorman, 'The Civil War and the Labour Party', in *Internal Bulletin of the Johnson–Forest Minority*, no. 12 (29 September 1947) p. 10.
25. Ibid.
26. Ibid.
27. David McLellan, *Marxism after Marx* (London: Macmillan Press, 1980) p. 281.
28. Ibid., p. 287.
29. Ibid., p. 283.
30. Perry Anderson, *Considerations on Western Marxism* (London: Verso, 1976) p. 44.
31. C.L.R. James, letter to Constance Webb (1948).
32. Martin Glaberman, 'Organising in USA: 1938–1953' (London: unpublished speech, 1986).
33. C.L.R. James, *Life of Captain Cipriani* (London: Nelson, 1933) p. 10.

## 7 The New Universals

1. Karl Marx, *Selected Works*, Volume 1 (Moscow: Progress Publishers, 1973) p. 15.
2. C.L.R. James, *Spheres of Existence* (London: Allison & Busby, 1980) p. 80.
3. Martin Glaberman, 'Organising in the USA 1938–1953' (London: unpublished typescript of lecture, 1986).
4. C.L.R. James, Letter to Constance Webb (21 October 1948).
5. V.I. Lenin, *Philosophical Notebooks. Collected Works*, Volume 38 (Moscow: Progress Publishers, 1972) p. 55.
6. C.L.R. James, *Notes on Dialectics* (London: Allison & Busby, 1980) pp. 10–11.
7. Ibid., p. 13.
8. Ibid., p. 15.
9. Ibid., p. 16.
10. Ibid.
11. Ibid., p. 17.
12. Ibid., p. 20.
13. Ibid., p. 18.
14. Ibid., p. 26.
15. Ibid.
16. Ibid.
17. Ibid.
18. Ibid., p. 30.
19. Antonio Gramsci, *Selections from the Prison Notebooks* (New York: International Publishers, 1987) p. 402.
20. Ibid., pp. 412–13.
21. James, *Notes on Dialectics*, p. 34.
22. Ibid., p. 37.
23. Ibid., pp. 160–1.

24. Ibid., p. 155.
25. Ibid.
26. Ibid., p. 138.
27. Ibid., p. 39.
28. Ibid.
29. Ibid., p. 140.
30. Ibid., p. 143.
31. Ibid.
32. Ibid., p. 172.
33. Ibid.
34. Ibid., p. 174
35. Ibid.
36. Ibid., p. 175.
37. Ibid., p. 176.
38. Ibid., p. 177.
39. Ibid., p. 178.
40. Ibid., p. 179.
41. Ibid., p. 180.
42. Ibid., p. 191.
43. Ibid., p. 209.
44. Ibid., p. 218.
45. John Molyneux, *Marxism and the Party* (London: Pluto Press 1978) p. 16. My discussion on the party is influenced by both this work and my activities in left political parties.
46. Karl Marx and Friedrich Engels, *Selected Works*, Volume 1 (Moscow: Progress Publishers, 1973) p. 119.
47. Ibid., p. 120.
48. V.I. Lenin, *What is to be done?* (Moscow: Progress Publishers, 1973) p. 121.
49. Ibid., p. 196.
50. Ibid., p. 69.
51. Rosa Luxemburg, *The Russian Revolution and Leninism or Marxism* (Ann Arbor, University of Michigan Press, 1971) p. 185.
52. Rosa Luxemburg, *The Mass Strike, The Political Party and the Trade Unions* (London: Young Socialist Publications, undated) p. 32.
53. Luxemburg, *The Russian Revolution and Leninism or Marxism*, p. 108.
54. Carl Bogg, *Gramsci's Marxism* (London: Pluto Press, 1976) p. 59.
55. Joseph Femia, *Gramsci's Political Thought* (Oxford: Oxford University Press, 1987) p. 70.
56. Gramsci, *Selections from Prison Notebooks*, p. 196.
57. Ibid., p. 419.
58. Boggs, *Gramsci's Marxism*, p. 77.
59. Femia, *Gramsci's Political Thought*, p. 136.
60. C.L.R. James, *World Revolution* (Connecticut: Hyperion, 1973) p. 53.
61. C.L.R. James, *State Capitalism and World Revolution* (Michigan: Facing Reality Publishing Committee, 1969) p. 14.
62. Ibid., p. 3.
63. Ibid., p. 37.
64. Ibid., p. 40.
65. Ibid., pp. 40–1.

66. Ibid.
67. Ibid., p. 51.
68. Ibid., pp. 93–4.
69. Ibid., pp. 103–11.
70. Ibid., p. 103.
71. Ibid., p. 102.
72. C.L.R. James, *Modern Politics* (Michigan: Bewick Editions, 1973) p. 115.

## 8 *James, Marx and the Notion of Happiness*

1. Frank Füredi, *Mythical Past, Elusive Future, History and Society in an Anxious Age* (London: Pluto Press, 1992) p. 132.
2. Ibid., p. 131.
3. Ibid., pp. 127–8.
4. Hannah Arendt, *The Origins of Totalitarianism* (Florida: Harcourt Brace Jovanovich, 1973) pp. 308–11.
5. Herbert Marcuse, *Negations, Essays in Critical Theory* (Boston: Beacon Press, 1968) p. 21.
6. Füredi, *Mythical Past, Elusive Future, History and Society in an Anxious Age*, pp. 139–40.
7. S. Baumer, *Main Currents in Western Thought* (New Haven: Yale University Press, 1970) p. 789.
8. *Who Built America? American Social Project* (New York: Pantheon Books, 1992) pp. 501–5.
9. C.L.R. James, 'Letters to Constance Webb', in *The C.L.R. James Reader*, ed. Anna Grimshaw (Oxford: Blackwell, 1992) p. 127.
10. Ibid., p. 128.
11. C.L.R. James, letter to Constance Webb, 6 May 1944. (New York: Schomburg Center for the Research of Black Culture).
12. Ibid., 7 July 1944.
13. C.L.R. James, 'The Struggle for Happiness, an Essay on American Civilisation' (unpublished manuscript, 1950) p. 1.
14. The original text was called *Notes on American Civilisation*. It was being reworked before James's death, and according to Anna Grimshaw was to be called *Struggle for Happiness*. In this study I alternate between these two titles.
15. C.L.R. James, 'The Struggle for Happiness, An Essay on American Civilisation', p. 5.
16. Ibid., p. 6.
17. Ibid., p. 8.
18. Cedric Robinson, *Black Marxism* (London: Zed Books, 1983) p. 259.
19. Ibid.
20. The phrase was first used by Dr Rupert Lewis, Reader in the Department of Government, University of the West Indies, Mona Campus.
21. James, 'The Struggle for Happiness, An Essay on American Civilisation', p. 17.
22. Ibid., p. 19.
23. Ibid., p. 20.

24. Ibid., p. 21.
25. Ibid., p. 23.
26. Ibid., p. 24.
27. Ibid., p. 28.
28. Ibid., p. 30.
29. Ibid., p. 54.
31. Ibid., p. 61.
32. Ibid., p. 68.
33. Ibid., pp. 75–6.
34. Ibid., p. 77.
35. Ibid., p. 69.
36. Ibid., p. 81.
37. Ibid., p. 90.
38. Ibid., p. 109.
39. Ibid.
40. Ibid., p. 110.
41. Ibid., p. 109.
42. Ibid.
43. Karl Marx, *Economic and Philosophic Manuscripts of 1844* (New York: International Publishers, 1967) p. 108.
44. James, 'The Struggle for Happiness, An Essay on American Civilisation', p. 124.
45. Leon Trotsky, *Literature and Art* (New York: Pathfinder Press, 1972) pp. 29–30.
46. Antonio Gramsci, *Selections from Prison Notebooks* (London: Lawrence & Wishart, 1971) p. 57.
47. James, 'The Struggle for Happiness, An Essay on American Civilisation', p. 127.
48. Ibid., p. 132.
49. Ibid., p. 133.
50. Ibid., p. 135.
51. Ibid., p. 141.
52. Ibid., p. 149.
53. Ibid., p. 157.
54. Ibid., p. 158.
55. Ibid., p. 173.
56. Ibid., p. 179.
57. Ibid., p. 181.
58. Ibid., pp. 196–7.
59. C.L.R. James, *Spheres of Existence* (London: Allison & Busby, 1980) p. 81.
60. C.L.R. James, 'Dialectics and History', edited version of *Dialectical Materialism and the Fate of Humanity* (Massachusetts: Radical America, undated) p. 18.
61. Ibid., p. 21.
62. James, 'The Struggle for Happiness, An Essay on American Civilisation', p. 209.
63. Ibid., pp. 210–11.
64. Ibid., pp. 213–14.
65. Ibid., p. 250.

66. Ibid., p. 254.

67. Ibid., pp. 287–90.

68. Ibid., p. 303.

69. Ibid., 304.

70. Ibid.

71. Ibid, pp. 306–11.

72. Ibid., p. 347.

73. Ibid., p. 340.

74. Ibid., p. 344.

75. Ibid., p. 384.

76. Ibid., pp. 386–7.

77. Ibid., p. 261.

78. Norman Geras, *Marx and Human Nature* (London: Verso, 1983) p. 24.

79. W. Peter Archibald, *Marx the Missing Link: Human Nature* (New Jersey: Humanities Press, 1989) p. 84.

80. Ibid.

81. Karl Marx, 'German Ideology', in *Selected Works*, Volume 1 (Moscow: Progress Publishers, 1973) p. 27.

82. Karl Marx, *Capital*, Volume 3, p. 820.

83. Ibid.

## 9 *James, Independent Marxism and the Marxist Tradition: A Summary, 1934–53*

1. C.L.R. James, *Mariners, Renegades and Castaways* (London: Allison & Busby, 1985) p. 7.

2. Ibid., p. 97.

3. Ibid., p. 98.

4. Ibid.

5. Ibid., p. 122.

6. Ibid., p. 126.

7. Cedric Robinson, 'C.L.R. James and the World System', in Selwyn Cudjoe and William E. Cain (eds), *C.L.R. James: His Intellectual Legacies* (Massachusetts: University of Massachusetts Press, 1995) p. 256.

8. Johnson–Forest, *Balance Sheet Completed* (unpublished manuscript, 1951) p. 15.

9. Ibid., p. 24.

10. Ibid., p. 25.

11. Ibid., p. 9.

12. Martin Glaberman, 'The Marxism of C.L.R. James', in *C.L.R. James Journal*, vol. 3 no. 1 (Winter 1992) p. 59.

13. Alrick Cambridge, 'C.L.R. James: Freedom through History and Dialectics', in Alistair Henassey (ed.), *Intellectuals in the Twentieth Century Caribbean*, Volume 1 (London: Macmillan Education, 1992) pp. 163–4.

14. Aléx Callinicos, *Marxism and Philosophy* (Oxford: Oxford University Press, 1983) p. 60.

15. Karl Marx, *Economic and Philosophic Manuscripts of 1844* (New York: International Publishers, 1967) p. 114.
16. Callinicos, *Marxism and Philosophy*, p. 42.
17. C.L.R. James, *Spheres of Existence* (London: Allison & Busby, 1980) p. 56.
18. C.L.R. James, *Dialectics and History*, edited version of *Dialectical Materialism and the Fate of Humanity* (Massachusetts: Radical America, undated) p. 1.
19. C.L.R. James, *The Struggle for Happiness* (unpublished manuscript, 1950) p. 185.
20. Ibid.
21. James, *Dialectics and History*, p. 2.
22. C.L.R. James, *Notes on Dialectics* (London: Allison & Busby, 1980) p. 15.
23. James, *The Struggle for Happiness*, p. 1.
24. James, *Notes on Dialectics*, p. 15.
25. C.L.R. James, *Invading Socialist Society* (Michigan: Bewick Editions, 1972) p. 14.
26. H. Stuart Hughes, *Sea Change, The Migration of Social Thought (1930–1965)* (New York: Harper & Row, 1975) p. 151.
27. Harold Mendelsohn, *Mass Entertainment* (USA: College and University Press Services Inc., 1966) p. 44.
28. James, *The Struggle for Happiness*, p. 161.
29. James, *Invading Socialist Society*, p. 4.
30. C.L.R. James, *State Capitalism and World Revolution* (Michigan: Facing Reality Committee, 1969) p. 93.
31. C.L.R. James, an interview in *Black World* (November 1971) p. 8.
32. Alex Callinicos, *Trotskyism* (Minneapolis: University of Minnesota Press, 1990) pp. 65–6.
33. James, *Invading Socialist Society*, p. 8.
34. Aristotle, *The Politics* (London: Penguin Books, 1992) p. 59.
35. Ibid.
36. Martin Jay, *Marxism and Totality* (California: University of California Press, 1984) p. 26.
37. Karl Marx and Friedrich Engels, *The German Ideology* (London: Lawrence & Wishart, 1974) p. 58.
38. Cited in David McLellan, *Marxism after Marx* (London: Macmillan Press, 1979) p. 170.
39. James, *Invading Socialist Society*, p. 59.

# Selected Bibliography

## Primary Sources

*The Raya Dunayevskaya Collection* (Detroit: Wayne State University Archives of Labor and Urban Affairs).
The following documents were used from this collection:

*The Balance Sheet 1940–1947.*
*Education, Propaganda, Agitation: Post War America and Bolshevism* (July 1945).
*Historical Retrogression or Socialist Revolution* (September 1945).
*The Johnson–Forest Minority, the WP and the Fourth International* (1947).
*A Letter to Membership* (April 1947).
*Production for Production Sake* (December 1942).
*The Resolution of Johnson–Forest Tendency* (July 1947).
*Resolution of the Minority on the Negro Question* (January 1945).
*Resolution on the Russian Question* (September 1941).
*Resolution on the Workers' Party* (1946).
*Socialism and the National Question* (October 1943).

*The Martin Glaberman Collection* (Detroit: Wayne State University Archives of Labor and Urban Affairs).
The following documents were used from this collection:

*Balance Sheet Completed* (1948).
*Draft Memorandum on Perspectives of Johnson–Forest Tendency* (1951).
*Internal Bulletins of Johnson-Forest* (July 17 1947–September 29 1947).

## Published books and writings by C.L.R. James used

*At the Rendezvous of Victory: Selected Writings* (London: Allison & Busby, 1980).
*Beyond a Boundary* (London: Hutchinson & Co., 1963).
*The Black Jacobins* (Canada: Vintage Books, Random House, 1963).
*Fighting Racism in World War II* (New York: Monad Press, 1980).
*Future in the Present: Selected Writings* (London: Allison & Busby, 1977).
*History of Negro Revolts* (London: Race Today Collective, 1985).
*Invading Socialist Society* (Michigan: Bewick Editions, 1972).
*The Life of Captain Cipriani: An Account of British Government in the West Indies* (London: Nelson, 1932).
*Mariners, Renegades and Castaways: The Story of Herman Melville and the World We Live In* (London: Allison & Busby, 1985).
*Minty Alley* (London: New Beacon Books Ltd, 1971).
*Notes on Dialectics* (London: Allison & Busby, 1980).

*Spheres of Existence: Selected Writings* (London: Allison & Busby, 1980).

*State Capitalism and World Revolution* (Michigan: Facing Reality Publishing Committee, 1969).

*World Revolution 1917–1936: The Rise and Fall of the Communist International* (Connecticut: Hyperion, 1973).

## Books, Pamphlets and Journals with C.L.R. James's Writings or on C.L.R. James

Buhle, Paul (ed.), *C.L.R. James: His Life and Work* (London: Allison & Busby, 1986).

Buhle, Paul, *C.L.R. James: The Artist as Revolutionary* (London: Verso, 1988).

Buhle, Paul and Paget, Henry (eds), *C.L.R. James's Caribbean* (Durham, NC: Duke University Press, 1992).

Glaberman, Martin, 'Marxism of C.L.R. James', *C.L.R. James Journal*, vol. 3, no. 1.

Glaberman, Martin, 'C.L.R. James: A Recollection', *New Politics*, vol. 2, no. 4.

Gomes P.I., *The Marxian Populism of C.L.R. James* (Trinidad: Department of Sociology, University of the West Indies).

Grimshaw, Anna, *C.L.R. James Archive: A Reader's Guide* (New York: C.L.R. James Institute, 1991).

Grimshaw, Anna, *The C.L.R. James Reader* (Oxford: Blackwell, 1992)

Singham, Archie, 'C.L.R. James on the Black Jacobin Revolution in San Domingo', *Savacou 1*, 1970.

*The Beacon*, vol. 1, nos 1–6 (1931), Trinidad.

*Caribbean Quarterly*, A Tribute to C.L.R. James, vol. 35, no. 4.

*Radical America*, C.L.R. James Special Issue, vol. 4, no. 4 (May 1970).

## Interviews with C.L.R. James

'C.L.R. James and British Trotskyism' (London: Socialist Platform Ltd, 1987).

'C.L.R. James', book review in *Third World*, vol 1, no. 2 (1984).

Griffith, Patrick, 'C.L.R. James and Pan-Africanism', in *Black World* (November 1977).

## Unpublished manuscripts and letters by C.L.R. James

Letters to Constance Webb 1939–1948 (New York: Schomberg Center for the Research of Black Culture).

The Struggle for Happiness: An Essay on American Civilisation (New York: C.L.R. James Institute).

[Both these primary sources have subsequently appeared in published works edited by Anna Grimshaw.]

Fragments of an autobiography (Trinidad: Oilfield Workers Trade Union Library).

## Secondary Sources

### Unpublished theses, lectures and articles on C.L.R. James

Agyemony, Solomon Kwesi, *A Study of Radical Political Thought in Colonial Trinidad* (MPhil, University of the West Indies, Trinidad and Tobago, 1980).

Archer, John, *C.L.R. James and Trotskyism in Britain, 1938–1943* (Race Today, London).

Boggs, Grace Lee, *C.L.R. James in the USA, 1938–1953* (Race Today, London).

Glaberman, Martin, *Organizing in the USA, 1938–1953* (Race Today, London).

Gomes, P.I., *C.L.R. James: Marxism Paradigm and the Transformation of Caribbean Social Structure* (PhD Thesis, Fordham University, 1980).

La Guerre, John, *Colonial Intellectuals in Politics: A Case Study of C.L.R. James* (MSc Thesis, University of the West Indies, 1968).

Singh, Kelvin, *Economy and Polity in Trinidad 1917–1938: The Influence of Ethnic Class and Imperial Factors* (PhD Thesis, University of the West Indies, Trinidad and Tobago, 1980).

Worcester, Kent, *C.L.R. James and the American Century, 1938–1953* (unpublished paper, n.d.).

Worcester, Kent, *C.L.R. James and the American Century*. Paper presented April 1991, Wellesley College.

### Interviews

Author with: Martin Glaberman, December 1990. Original member of Johnson–Forest Tendency.

Author with: Darcus Howe, November 1990. Political activist and close relation of C.L.R. James.

### Books

Anderson, Perry, *Considerations on Western Marxism* (London: Verso, 1979).

Anderson, Perry, *In the Tracks of Historical Materialism* (London: Verso, 1983).

Arendt, Hannah, *The Origins of Totalitarianism* (New York: Hannest/HBJ, 1973).

Aristotle, *The Politics* (London: Penguin Books, 1992).

Benn, Dennis, *The Growth of Political Ideas in the Caribbean 1774–1983* (Institute of Social and Economic Research, University of the West Indies, 1987).

Beribalsingh, Frank, *Passion and Exile Essays in Caribbean Literature* (London: Hansib, 1988).

Boggs, Carl, *Gramsci's Marxism* (London: Pluto Press, 1976).

Buhle Maxi Jo, Paul Buhle and Dan Georgakas, *Encyclopedia of the American Left* (Illinois: University of Illinois, 1992).

Buhle, Paul, *Marxism in the USA* (London: Verso, 1987).

Brereton, Bridget, *A History of Modern Trinidad 1783–1962* (Kingston: Heinemann).

Bryan, Patrick, *The Jamaica People 1890–1902* (London: Macmillan, 1991).

Callinicos, Alex, *Making History* (Cambridge: Polity Press, 1989).

Callinicos, Alex, *Marxism and Philosophy* (Oxford: Oxford University Press, 1985).

Callinicos, Alex, *The Revolutionary Ideas of Marx* (London: Bookmarks, 1983).

Claudin, Fernando, *The Communist Movement from Comintern to Cominform*, Part 1 (New York: Monthly Review Press, 1975).

Davis, Horace, *Nationalism and Socialism: Marxist and Labor Theories of Nationalism to 1917* (New York: Monthly Review Press, 1973).

Eagleton, Terry, *Criticism and Ideology: A Study in Marxist Literary Theory* (London: Verso, 1978).

Foner, Phillip S., *Organized Labour and the Black Worker 1619–1973* (New York: Praeger Publishers, 1976).

Femia, Joseph, *Gramsci's Political Thought* (Oxford: Oxford University Press, 1981).

Füredi, Frank, *Mythical Past, Elusive Future: History and Society in an Anxious Age* (London: Pluto Press, 1992).

Gramsci, Antonio, *Selections from the Prison Notebooks* (London: Lawrence & Wishart, 1971).

Guérin, Daniel, *One Hundred Years of Labour in the USA* (London: Inklinks, 1979).

Hallas, Duncan, *Trotsky's Marxism* (London: Pluto Press, 1979).

Held, David, *Political Theory and the Modern State* (Stanford, CA: Stanford University Press, 1989).

Hennessy, Alister, *Intellectuals in the Twentieth Century Caribbean*, Volumes 1 & 2 (London: Macmillan Education, 1992).

Jay, Martin, *Marxism and Totality* (California: University of California Press, 1984).

Kolakowski, Lezek, *Main Currents of Marxism*, Volumes 1 to 3 (Oxford: Oxford University Press, 1978).

La Guerre, John Gaffar, *The Social and Political Thought of the Colonial Intelligentsia* (Kingston: Institute of Social and Economic Research, University of the West Indies, 1982).

Lenin, V.I., *Selected Works*, Volumes 1–3 (Moscow: Progress Publishers, 1970).

Levin, Michael, *Marx, Engels and Liberal Democracy* (London: Macmillan Press, 1989).

Lukács, Georg, *History and Class Consciousness: Studies in Marxist Dialectics* (London: Merlin Press, 1971).

Luxemburg, Rosa, *The Mass Strike, the Political Party and the Trade Unions 1906* (London: Young Socialist Publications, undated).

Luxemburg, Rosa, *The Russian Revolution: Leninism or Marxism* (Michigan: University of Michigan Press, 1961).

Martin, Tony, *The Pan-African Connection* (Massachusetts: Schenkman, 1983).

Martin, Tony, *Race First* (Connecticut: Greenwood Press, 1976).

Marx, K. and F. Engels, *Selected Works*, Volumes 1–3 (Moscow: Progress Publishers, 1969).

Marx K. and F. Engels, *German Ideology* (London: Lawrence & Wishart, 1970).

Marx, Karl, *Capital*, Volume 3 (New York: International Publishers, 1974).

McLellan, David, *Marxism after Marx* (London: Macmillan Press, 1979).

Moore, Richard, *Collected Writings 1920–1972*, eds W.B. Turner and Joyce Moore Turner (Indiana: Indiana University Press, 1992).

Molyneux, John, *Marxism and the Party* (London: Pluto Press, 1978).

Molyneux, John, *What is the Real Marxist Tradition?* (London: Bookmarks, 1985).

Padmore, George, *Pan-Africanism or Communism* (New York: Doubleday, 1972).

Rampersad, Arnold, *The Art and Imagination of W.E.B. Du Bois* (New York: Schocken Books, 1976).

Record, Wilson, *The Negro and the Communist Party* (Durham, NC: University of North Carolina Press, 1951).

Rennie, Bukka, *History of the Working Class in the Twentieth Century: Trinidad and Tobago* (Toronto: New Beginning Movement Books, 1974).

Rieff, Phillip, *On Intellectuals* (New York: Doubleday, 1970).

Robinson, Cedric, *Black Marxism* (London: Zed Books, 1983).

Ryan, Selwyn D., *Race and Nationalism in Trinidad and Tobago* (Toronto: University of Toronto Press, 1972).

Samuels, Wilfred D., *Five Afro-Caribbean Voices in American Culture* (Colorado: Belmont Books, 1977).

Sander, Reinhard W., *West Indian Literature of the 1930s* (Westview, CT: Greenwood Press, 1988).

Therborn, Goran, *The Ideology of Power and the Power of Ideology* (London: Verso, 1980).

Thompson, John B., *Studies in the Theory of Ideology* (Berkeley: University of California Press, 1984).

Trotsky, Leon, *The Revolution Betrayed* (New York: Pathfinder Press, 1974).

Trotsky, Leon, *Transitional Program and Socialist Revolution* (New York: Pathfinder Press, 1974).

Trotsky, Leon, *Literature and Revolution* (New York: Pathfinder Press, 1974).

Trotsky, Leon, *On Black Nationalism and Self-Determination* (USA: Merit Publishers, 1972).

Tully, James and Q. Skinner, *Meaning and Context* (Princeton, NJ: Princeton University Press, 1988).

*Who Built America?* Volumes 1 & 2, American Social History Project (New York: Pantheon Books, 1992).

# Index